RUMOURS OF WARS

By the same Author

RUMOURS

OF

WARS

BY

A. J. P. TAYLOR
Fellow of Magdalen College, Oxford

HAMISH HAMILTON
LONDON

PRINTED IN GREAT BRITAIN
BY WESTERN PRINTING SERVICES LTD., BRISTOL

TO
ROBERT BOOTHBY
W. J. BROWN
and
MICHAEL FOOT

CONTENTS

ACKNOWLEDGEMENT

I MUST thank the editors, publishers, and proprietors of *The Times Literary Supplement*, the *Manchester Guardian*, the *New Statesman and Nation*, *History Today*, *The New York Times Magazine*, the *New Republic*, and the *English Historical Review* for permission to reprint essays which first appeared in the pages of these periodicals.

A.J.P.T.

A*

I

HISTORY IN ENGLAND

In ENGLAND there are no schools of history; there are only individual historians. The records of historical study in England show many great historians who have tried to found schools; but the records have little to say of their followers. Acton alone was perhaps successful; and many historians regret his success—so much so that the *Cambridge Modern History*, his most ambitious project, is now being rewritten. For nearly a quarter of a century Dr. Trevelyan, in Cambridge, and Sir Maurice Powicke, in Oxford, were in their different ways titular heads of their respective schools. Their works have set an example of scholarship and fine writing; but he would be a bold man who could claim that they had shaped historical studies in their universities. Even the *Oxford History of England*, the most important co-operative venture of our time, is in essence a collection of individual volumes which happen to appear with the same binding; and the critic praises the achievement of Stenton or Ensor, while looking askance at the series as a whole. The English historian calls no man master. He works alone, following his own bent, thinking occasionally of the reader (though not often enough), but rarely of his colleagues and never of his critics.

Yet, in spite of this individualism, it is possible to detect a certain shape and tendency in recent historical writing. The historian is coming to show an increasing awareness of society —awareness both of society as a problem in the past, and awareness of the needs of society in the present. The tendency should not be exaggerated. Historians have always been aware that the characters and events with which they deal have taken place in time; and many, if not most, historians have tried to relate the past to the needs of the present. Still, with this warning, the generalization can stand. The tendency may be seen in the popular series edited by Mr. A. L. Rowse, in which the attempt is made to relate a single great figure to a wider historical theme—even though it must be added that the attempt is more praiseworthy than the achievement. The great figures remain great figures, suspended above events rather than absorbed in them. A more ambitious and more successful example is Sir Maurice Powicke's masterpiece, *King Henry III and the Lord Edward*, a work of mediaeval constitutional history, but also of much more—an exploration of the mediaeval mind in its political character, the portrait of an age drawn in its own terms rather than according to the dogmas of later generations.

A striking illustration of the same tendency is given in the most recent attempt at that most ambitious of projects, a History of England. Some twenty years ago Dr. Trevelyan produced a one-volume *History of England*, in which everything was judged according to the standards of nineteenth-century liberalism, a history avowedly political in character. Indeed, Dr. Trevelyan has confessed this limitation by producing more recently *English Social History*; and he regards social history as 'history with the politics left out'. This is a curious doctrine, a last gesture of defiance on behalf of the political historians of the past. For it implies, on the one hand, that politics is not a social activity and, on the other, that—while it is political to make speeches or to pay taxes or even to fight wars—there is no political significance in the way men till the fields, mine coal, write verses, or build houses. In other words, social history is no more than entertaining gossip about the past, without pattern or purpose. The new *History of England*, by Professor Feiling, rejects this arbitrary division: it treats politics as part of the life of the time, not as something standing above ordinary life and unaffected by it. Moreover, Feiling tries to escape from narrow geographic limits. His England embraces Scotland, Ireland, and the Empire—a curious definition perhaps to foreign eyes, but revealing of the new English awareness of the Commonwealth.

There is a more striking way in which Feiling's book is representative of the modern trend. Trevelyan's *History* may quite fairly be described as Whig, and though it would be unfair to describe Feiling's *History* as Tory it would not be entirely undeserved. Though Feiling cannot altogether escape his own tastes and prejudices, he is at heart concerned to show how the past worked, rather than how it was preparing the present. He writes of the Saxons or the Cavaliers as men, not as his ancestors; and he regards their institutions as instruments created by them for their own purposes, not as crude fumblings towards the British democracy of the twentieth century. This method of approach is not new; what is new is that it should be applied in a general history of England designed for the general reader. To interpret the past in its own terms has always been the concern of historians. But to show how the political methods of the past can be analysed in detail was the achievement of *The Structure of Politics at the Accession of George III*, by Sir Lewis Namier. Though this book was published more than twenty years ago, it can be no more ignored in a discussion of modern history than the *Origin of Species* could be ignored in a discussion of biology. Just as there was a fundamental division between pre-Darwinian and Darwinian biologists, so the writers on English history can be divided into those who have absorbed Namier's methods and conclusions, and those who have not. The essence of the 'Namier way' was the welding together of separate biographical essays to compose the political portrait of an age. He showed principles and parties as they appeared to the working politicians of the time rather than as the abstract creations of political philosophers; perhaps nothing is more symbolic of our age than this shift in emphasis from the fine phrases of the party programme to the practical questions of party finance.

To judge from the articles in learned periodicals younger historians are applying the Namier method in other fields— principally in studying the realities behind the civil wars of the fifteenth century and in analysing the actual workings of party in the nineteenth century. Meanwhile, one historian has shown himself fully able to bend the bow of Achilles. Professor J. E. Neale's *Elizabethan House of Commons* has adapted Namier's method to the politics of the sixteenth century—adapted and some ways improved on it. There is the same building up of a picture from individual biographies; the same insistence on practical questions—how did men get elected? Why did they seek election? What did the great questions of the age mean in practice? More than this, it is shown how the feeling and even the procedure of the Elizabethan House of Commons reflected the practical needs of the time. Most books fall short some- where: there is a gap between promise and performance. Neale's is a rare instance of success at every point; not the least of its success is its achievement as a work of literature—like

Namier at his best can be read for the enjoyment of fine writing as well as of great scholarship.

The political structure of the past is not, of course, the only field in which the relation of the individual with society needs to be explored. Indeed, since the beginning of the century it has been constantly foretold that the new history would be economic history. At mid-century it has to be recorded that the prophecy has not yet been fulfilled. There have been many and important studies in economic history; none has yet brought a new vision. Sir John Clapham, one of the two great economic historians of our time, was himself doubtful whether economic history would ever bring this new vision. His posthumous work, *A Concise Economic History of Britain, From Earliest Times to* 1750, might almost have been written to show that economic history had neither rhythm nor meaning; and it cannot be claimed that other economic historians have done much to challenge Clapham's doubts. One economic historian, Professor Tawney, has indeed transcended economic history and held out prospects of a universal vision; these remain prospects. There are hints that younger scholars, inspired by Tawney, may in time transform for us the Great Rebellion of the seventeenth century and bring to life the Republic that never was. As it is, Tawney's unwritten works remain, with Namier's, the lost masterpieces of the twentieth century.

If economic historians have hesitated to reduce history to a pattern, this hesitation has not been shared by the philosophical historians. This is perhaps the wrong term—historical speculators or moralists who use history as their text would be nearer the mark. In the past this moralizing from history was the speciality of Roman Catholics, such as Mr. Hilaire Belloc, Chesterton or Mr. Christopher Dawson, who today seems to combine most successfully the character of scholar and moralist. Now the habit has spread. In 1950 Professor Butterfield joined the ranks of the historical moralists, in a work which discussed the relations between history and Christianity. Butterfield has indeed outdone his colleagues in versatility. He has produced, too, a pioneer work on the history of science, —perhaps the topic crying out most strongly for historical exploration—and, almost simultaneously, accompanied this with a detailed, though pre-Namierite, study in eighteenth-century politics. For these achievements he should receive at any rate the tribute which Dr. Johnson paid to the woman preacher. Yet even this is dwarfed by Professor Toynbee's *Study of History*, the most grandiose moral effort by a historian in this generation; not surprisingly it has proved a best-seller both in its extended and in its more compact form. Though it draws its arguments from the past, it does not study the past in the sense usually understood by the historian; its method is that of the blackbird, not of the beaver. All the same it too is a sign, though maybe a distorted one, that society expects guidance from the historian and that some historians try to give it.

Though professional historians shrink from projects of world-history, they are aware of the world outside their own country. Even a historian could hardly fail to notice the impact of Europe on England during the past half-century; and European studies are taking a more important place in English historical writing. It is difficult, though not impossible, for a historian to become as deeply grounded in the history of another country as in that of his own; at present there is no one in England who has mastered some topic of foreign history as fully, say, as Elie Halévy mastered the history of nineteenth-century England. However much the historian may wish to meet the demand for foreign history, he cannot overcome the obstacles which modern society puts increasingly in his way. To understand a foreign community, past or present, requires leisure, wealth, freedom of travel; these are the casualties of our time. Foreign archives become more and more inaccessible —Moscow and Berlin vanished beyond recall, even Vienna and Paris still showing the scars of war. It seems likely then that English writing on European history will be distinguished by novelty of interpretation rather than by its detailed contribution to original scholarship; and the historians of the Middle Age, with their cult of manuscript sources, will raise shocked hands at this trend—little better in their eyes than 'journalism'. The only work in this field which might make a full claim to be a work of research is probably the Rev. J. M. Thompson's *French Revolution*; and even this is mainly a synthesis based on the exploration of others.

Nevertheless English writing on European history, however summary it may appear, shows a truly historical spirit. To take a handful of these surveys at random: Brogan on France, Sumner on Russia, Barraclough on Germany, Hugh Seton-Watson on Eastern Europe—all of these contribute

something to the history of the country concerned which might
have escaped a native historian. Even more sharply than works
on English history they illustrate, too, the habit of our time.
If they are contrasted with the work of a historian of the
previous generation, say with that of H. A. L. Fisher, they all
—in spite of their difficulties—show a consciousness of society
and of social issues. Fisher saw men as individuals; his successors see them as magnates, as bourgeois liberals, or as
peasant nationalists. Implicit in them all is the doctrine: 'Tell
me a man's class and I will tell you how he behaves.' This
doctrine is essential if the history of Russia, of Germany, or of
France is to be brought within a reasonable compass. Nevertheless, the historian has to bear in mind that these class
descriptions—like the national labels that he must also use—
are stereotypes; they are the historian's shorthand which may
be safely used in order to save space, but not in order to save
thought. No doubt Neale and Namier also use stereotypes in
their treatment of English history; Neale speaks of great
aristocrats or Namier of merchants and thinks that something
has been explained by the phrase. But the stereotypes of Neale
or Namier are built from a detailed analysis of many individual
cases. In foreign history the stereotypes have to be taken
ready made. Yet which, one may ask, was the 'typical'
bourgeois radical—Clemenceau or Caillaux? Which the
'typical' Hungarian squire—Kossuth or Deak? Which the
'typical' Russian inspired by industrialism—Witte or Lenin?
And the stereotype breaks in our hand if we seek to explain
Bismarck as the 'typical' Junker.

To make these criticisms is to complain against the inevitable; without stereotypes there could be no writing of
history, only the accumulation of biographies, and the historian
is aware of the dangers that they involve. There is another
more obscure danger with which contemporary historians are
faced. Are they aware of their own stereotype? In recognizing
society as their material in the past, do they respond too easily
to the claims of society in the present? In other words, do they
give society the history that it wants? There has always been a
tendency to complacency in writing the history of England;
and—considering the unique success of British political life
—the complacency is perhaps not unjustified. Nowadays the
historian is faced with the problem in a more acute form.
There is a growing, and justified, demand for contemporary

history, the history of our own times, Much of this history—
in foreign affairs, in the history of war, in administration—
can be written only with the favour of a Government department. Hence we have seen the growth of the 'official historian',
blessed by a Minister and uniquely free to explore the records
of some department of State. No one will question the good
will or conscious impartiality of these official historians. Nevertheless, it is difficult to write with detachment of a department
of State in which the historian has been living as a member
for some years; difficult to criticize those who have shown
personal friendship and official generosity; difficult to transcend
the conflict of loyalties. The official histories of the war, both
military and civil, have to be written; the documents from the
Foreign Office have to be officially published. But it is equally
important that these official works should be ruthlessly
scrutinized by historians free from departmental or even
national loyalties.

The writing as well as the accumulation of contemporary
history has, in fact, begun; English historians may claim to
have surpassed all others in studying the present, or immediate
past, historically. In this field, too, Namier—temporarily abandoning the eighteenth century—has been the exemplar; we
shall have to wait long before the origins of the war are better
displayed than in his *Diplomatic Prelude*. All the same, Namier,
with others, such as Mr. Wheeler-Bennett and Miss Wiske-
mann, cannot escape the limitations of their time. Historians
are usually men of liberal minds. Before the First World War
the liberally minded thought that Germany had been hardly
used; and British historians of the origins of the First World
War tended to be too sympathetic to the German case. Before
the Second World War the liberally minded thought that
Germany had not been used hardly enough; they rejected
'appeasement' as weakness and desired a Grand Alliance
against Hitler. This outlook, or prejudice, is reflected in the
writings of Namier and his associates. It is now being questioned
by some younger historians who judge the policy of the Soviet
Union more sceptically; but they, in their turn, reflect the
experiences of 1950 (instead of those of 1938), and neither is
a truly historical attitude. There is unfortunately an easy
answer: since the Soviet Union refuses to supply historical
evidence it is impossible to make any historical judgement
about its conduct.

Such are the inevitable and inescapable problems which confront the contemporary historian. There is a deeper problem which confronts all historians, whether of recent or more remote times—the problem of presentation. The classical masters of English history from Gibbon onwards were also classics of English literature; the line ended with Maitland. Professional history in England has passed through a bad half-century, in which historians have been content to write heavily and clumsily, accepting the worst German models instead of the best French. No one, for instance, could claim that the late Professor Tout—a giant in research—was a master of English prose; it would be invidious to mention other names. A historian who wrote well was dismissed as an 'amateur' who wrote 'literary history', not the gnarled, graceless prose of the professional. A race of 'amateur' historians was allowed to grow up, no scholars themselves but expert in popularizing the discoveries of scholars for a wider public. This disgraceful era is coming to an end. The professional historian is ceasing to raise disdainful eyebrows on the news that his colleague has written a book that can be read for pleasure. No historian is ever likely to depreciate the value of 'research'; but there has been something wrong with a profession which made this the sole, as well as an essential, qualification for office and promotion. What used to be called 'vulgarization' is now equally the duty of the professional scholar. Tired metaphors and flabby sentences should be as unforgivable in a historian as a faulty reference or an inaccurate quotation; and it would be no bad thing if academic promotion were open only to those who could hold listeners or win readers. For, although history may claim to be a branch of science or of politics or of sociology, it is primarily communication, a form of literature. No historian is worth his salt who has not felt some twinge of Macaulay's ambition—to replace the latest novel on the lady's dressing-table. It is to the credit of English history at the present time that some historians have felt this ambition and a few have even accomplished it. The historian has to combine truth and literary grace; he fails as a historian if he is lacking in either.

II

HISTORY WITHOUT MORALITY

HISTORY is for us what the classics were for our ancestors. It is the largest school in our universities; it ranks second only to fiction in the lists of publishers; and it is the bran-tub from which we make a lucky dip for generalizations on social behaviour or the character of individuals. It is right that most professional historians should put first the merits of research. History can no more flourish without it than the classics can keep going without accurate texts. But we also need the professional historian who can raise his head from the researcher's desk and ask what we are up to; point to our defects and make the generalizations which are dangerously left to the Toynbees and other historical speculators. The younger generation of historians is disturbingly short of these (younger means, absurdly enough, anyone under fifty); and Professor Butterfield is performing a great service both to historians and the wider public when he acts as intermediary between the two. His new book[1] is his most effective. The essay-form has disciplined him, making his thought clearer and more compact. He is not a brilliant writer, and this is all to the good. We have quite enough clever historians; and we need someone to remind us that, the more we generalize and simplify, the more we get away from the opaqueness of the historical material.

Years ago Butterfield made a discovery which established his fame. This discovery was the Whig interpretation of history, not so novel an idea as he made out, but a discovery all the same. The English history that was being taught and practised was, he claimed, a version imposed on the past for the benefit of the present; events were studied not for themselves, but always because they were supposed to be growing into something else and finally, of course, into the glorious British constitution of the Victorian age. But what is the alternative to Whig history? The obvious answer would be:

[1] Herbert Butterfield, *History and Human Relations*.

9

Tory history. Butterfield did not like this answer, and he has long been fumbling for another one. Now he has found it; and the answer is: 'technical history'. This answer serves his purpose in another way. Though Butterfield is a professed Christian, he does not care for the relentless moral fervour with which Lord Acton denounced every historical character before the bar of Christianity. Butterfield expects Christians to behave as Christians and he tells them so; but when he comes to this wicked world, he is prepared to examine it according to its own rules. The great scientists of the seventeenth century believed that they were serving the glory of God when they discovered the laws which governed the Universe; and 'in the field of history the Christian should be the first and most extreme in demanding the scientific attitude'. The historian, Butterfield says, must 'empty himself' (an infelicitous phrase) before he turns to the study of the past or even of the present. Here again is technical history, as opposed to the history of moral judgements.

Butterfield has also some good things about technical history in another sense. The great literary historians of the past, he says, were concerned with narrative. They wanted to find out what happened and set this out in a pleasing form. The present-day historian is concerned with analysis: he wants to know why things happened, to show cause and effect rather than a simple sequence of events. There can be no doubt that this is a true account of the present trend. The work of Neale and Namier, which shines pre-eminent in modern English history, gives abundant confirmation of it. It would be wrong to exaggerate the conflict between the two schools. The literary historian who understands something of deeper causes will write a better narrative than if he were confined to the clash of personalities and accumulated facts; and on the other hand the analytic historian needs to present his results with grace and art, as our two great examples do. In fact no historian attains the highest excellence whose work cannot be read for pleasure as well as with intellectual profit. Still there is a difference. The analytical historian is 'technical' in Butterfield's sense. Neale and Namier have 'emptied themselves', where Froude and Lecky did not.

There is nothing more difficult than to state the obvious in a convincing way, perhaps also nothing more dangerous. When Butterfield makes the case of 'technical history', every historian will second him and will be inclined to say that it is the only history deserving of the name. Clearly the historian must be historically minded when he approaches the past. How dreary and barren we now find those histories of the seventeenth century which explain everything by the wickedness of Charles I or of Cromwell; how unsatisfying even the modern compromise which acquits or condemns both. We need rather to understand what was in their minds and to grasp the 'tragic inevitability', in Butterfield's phrase, of the conflict between Cavaliers and Roundheads. We must judge men according to their standards, not according to ours. At this point I rebel; and I do not care whether it is rebellion against Ranke, as well as against Butterfield. It is all very fine to say that we must find out what Cromwell or Napoleon was trying to do instead of having a preconceived notion of what they ought to have done. But where is this process to stop? We can bring ourselves to understand why the Roman Church set up and operated the Inquisition; we can even understand why Hitler wanted to exterminate the Jews. Can we let it go at that? Is it enough to say: 'the Inquisition tortured and burnt thousands of heretics; Hitler sent millions of Jews to the gas-chamber. They did a fine job according to their lights'? Pursue this argument to its logical conclusion and the only wicked Nazis were the ones who tried occasionally to spare a political opponent or a Jew.

Men have to have something to admire; and the worst of technical history is that the only thing it leaves them to admire is technique. 'Statecraft' is all that matters. Napoleon was unrivalled as a general; Bismarck as a diplomat; Lenin as a revolutionary. They went wrong only when they made mistakes. It is strange indeed that the Christian Butterfield should join hands with Professor Carr and out-do Machiavelli. The explanation is not far to seek. Christianity and humanism are incompatible. Mr. Butterfield believes in God; therefore he does not believe in men. He holds, no doubt correctly, that only Christians can be judged according to the rules of Christianity; and so does not judge others at all. He does not discriminate among unregenerate mankind; or rather, the only distinction he makes is that some are cleverer than others. It is very revealing that Butterfield avows himself as a Marxist for practical purposes: 'Technical history *is* the materialist interpretation of the past.' He only complains, rightly enough,

that Marxists are not sufficiently skilful and flexible in applying their own technique.

But can any technical history produce satisfactory results
even from a technical point of view? In some of the most
provocative essays in the book Butterfield claims to approach
contemporary events with a historian's detachment. As elsewhere in the book, there are many good things well said.
Much innocent pleasure can be derived from his strictures on
the so-called 'independent historians' who are hired by the
Foreign Office and other government departments and who
yet claim to present the record with complete detachment.
Even here I doubt whether he has hit the centre of the target.
He seems to fear that vital evidence will be concealed; the real
danger is that too much material is being published, because
of an exaggerated respect for the documents and for those who
produced them. Still it is always agreeable to see an arrow
being discharged at the great and respectable even if it hits
them in the wrong place. But Butterfield makes also a judgement of events. He argues that the great issue which dominated
the first half of the twentieth century was the struggle between
Germany and Russia for the mastery of Central and Eastern
Europe; and he even inclines to underwrite the German case
that they were 'the guardian and bulwark of a thing which they
called Western Civilization'. He goes on to suggest that British
policy abandoned the Balance of Power when it backed Russia
against Germany in 1914 or 1941. He recommends instead
the Bismarckian maxim:

> Let the rascals fight it out if they like; but intervene to prevent
> whichever one it might be from destroying the other; because it is
> necessary for the safety of civilization that both should exist and
> operate as a check upon one another.

The best comment on this comes from another essay: 'Some
of the best diplomatic historians I ever met were almost the
worst diplomats in the world when it came to transacting
business in real life.' The Balance of Power is a matter of facts,
not of names; and the evidence is there in both world wars that
Germany would have knocked Russia flat if the weight of
everyone else had not been thrown in the other scale. In any
case, the question, Russia or Germany? was not the deciding
issue in 1914 or in 1939. Great Britain entered both wars in
order to preserve the independence of France as a Great

Power; and the alliance of Russia was accepted in 1914 and sought in 1939 solely for this purpose. Maybe it was an impossible aim. But the advocates of co-operation with Germany, or even of neutrality in European affairs, would be more honest if they admitted that, in their fear and hatred of Russia, they are prepared to let Germany dominate the continent from the Pyrenees to the Ukraine. Germany will do this, unless you call in the Russians to stop it. There is no third choice, and never has been since 1906.

Butterfield alleges that historians for the last thirty years have been putting all the blame on Germany, simply because we went to war with her in 1914. He has his facts wrong. The disease of British (and American) history has been an obstinate sympathy with the German case. When Butterfield criticizes hostility to Germany, he will have every 'impartial' historian with him. Max Beloff once pointed out that Communists will soon be the only people to have absolute security of tenure in their jobs; no one will dare to dismiss a Communist for fear of being accused of political prejudice. Similarly, it is impossible to tell the truth about the German record without being labelled 'anti-German' and losing one's claim to academic reputation. Yet historians, like Butterfield, can justify the Anglo-American preparations for a third world war without running any risk of being called 'anti-Russian'. If I had to choose, I'd rather be anti-German and pro-Russian than the other way round; but this seems to me true 'impartiality', not a matter of personal taste. Butterfield makes out that he is a technical historian who has shaken himself free of morality. In truth, he, too, is preaching; he, too, has a moral outlook—only it is different from mine. There is the real difficulty. The historian does not only deal with men; he is a man himself, and nothing will turn him into a technician.

III

TORY HISTORY

'GOOD PEOPLE, I am the Protestant whore!' So Nell Gwynn quietened a mob which had taken her for one of her Roman Catholic colleagues. Professor Feiling[1] is a writer with too many idiosyncrasies to be so simply docketed. Still, when a man writes a massive history of England, he challenges comparison with Trevelyan, with J. R. Green, even, his publishers think, with Macaulay. Compared with these Feiling is the Tory historian. Yet this is an elusive category. The Whig interpretation of history is easy to define; all our political thinking rests on it. It is the story of English liberty, founded by Magna Carta, consolidated by the glorious Revolution, expanded by the great Reform Bill, and reaching its highest achievement with the Labour Government. In the words of Ramsay MacDonald, 'Up and up and up and on and on and on'. It is the doctrine of history as Progress: men always getting wiser and more tolerant; houses more comfortable, food more plentiful; new laws always better than old laws; new ideas always better than old ideas; new wives, I suppose, always better than old wives (this last much practised by the Whig aristocracy).

Liberty ought to be a revolutionary doctrine, the creed of a minority; in England it has become traditional, respectable, universally accepted. This is a result of the glorious Revolution. True Toryism perished in 1688 or, at any rate, with the Hanoverian succession. What sense had 'Church and King' in the age of latitudinarian bishops and German princes? For that matter, even in the twentieth century the Tories, despite their loyal phrases, were responsible for the only real subversion of modern times, the Ulster rebellion of 1914. If Toryism means anything, it rejects the sovereignty of parliament and the doctrine of the Social Contract, which underlay the revolution of 1688. In practice, as Macaulay observed,

[1] Keith Feiling, *A History of England.*

Toryism amounts to no more than defending Whig achievements of a previous generation. In the world of ideas, the
Tories have had to make do with unprincipled adventurers,
like Bolingbroke and Disraeli, or to borrow from the other
side. Burke, whom Feiling calls 'the largest mind ever given
to politics in our island' and 'the inspiration of a second party
of Tories', was a corrupt Whig hack. A century later, the
Tories learnt their Imperialism from the renegade Radical,
Chamberlain. It would be unfair to blame Toryism for being
short of ideas. Ideas are an affair of the mind; and Toryism
distrusts the mind in politics. In essence, Toryism rests on
doubt in human nature; it distrusts improvement, clings to
traditional institutions, prefers the past to the future. It is a
sentiment rather than a principle. Feiling carries this sentiment
so far that he can even include Oliver Cromwell in it.

Though reason may be a good guide in politics, it is in-
adequate for the writing of history; and the very qualities which
make Tories detestable as politicians should make them good
historians. After all a historian should start by appreciating the
past. It is true that Gibbon, the greatest of our historians, had
nothing but contempt for his chosen subject; this merely
shows that genius can disregard all rules. In lesser men Whig
rationalism produces what has been well called 'the linotype
school of history', in which everyone behaves according to
rule, the mysteries of human behaviour vanish, and everything
moves relentlessly towards infinite improvement—or to infinite
disaster. Mr. Feiling writes with a greater understanding of
human affairs. He does not pretend to know the answer to
every problem in the universe. In his book events remain, as
they are, blurred and confused; it is like listening to a story told
entirely in echoes. When we read the narrative of a cocksure
historian, we tend to forget that the historian can never speak
with first-hand authority; he can only piece together the
accounts of others. A novelist creates his characters and therefore knows their every motive and action; Feiling never forgets
that he did not create the English people. Very often he puts
his narrative in the form of hearsay. 'We hear of Saxon
invaders on the south coast'; 'there are reports of great acts of
cruelty'. The effect is of news arriving late and contradictory
to a remote country house, where a slow-witted squire is
trying to make sense of events, in the short intervals between
hunting and fishing. It needs a writer of supreme skill, far

from slow-witted, to create this impression, so much nearer to life than our neat explanations.

Toryism starts with the squire, the lesser landowner. Everyone knows that. Feiling emphasizes again and again the permanent elements in rural society. He recognizes, as few Whig historians have done, the importance of local government; indeed even parliament bulks largest in his eyes as a gathering of country gentry. The traditional 'liberties of England' rested on law and custom, not on rational dogma; and the man who maintained them, as in Poland or Hungary, was the country squire. He maintained them no doubt for his own profit and advantage, a point which Feiling is inclined to slide over; still England would not be a free country without him. The unique feature of our history is that the conservative defender of liberty had to take other classes into partnership, and finally indeed found himself in the position of a tolerated minority. Feiling says rightly: 'in ages when everywhere in Europe public liberties were being quenched, English law defended freedom'; but he also admits that this 'venerable common law' was by the end of the eighteenth century wholly unfit to deal with a new age.

Would these changes come by violence or by agreement? This was the great question of the early nineteenth century. As we know, they came by agreement or, at any rate, by constitutional process. This is usually regarded as the greatest triumph of the Whig spirit. The new Toryism may claim almost as much credit—meaning by this an attitude of mind rather than either the practical common sense of Peel or the flashy trivialities of Disraeli. Though Tory government of the early nineteenth century needed the votes of country squires, it did not represent their outlook nor was it run by them. The squires got the Corn Laws; in return they voted for a government of administrators and soldiers, the former 'King's friends'. This is a point which Feiling does not make explicit, but it conditions all the later part of his work. If by Liberalism is meant all those who try to apply reason to politics, and who enter politics in order to improve things, then it is not only Tory landowners who are on the other side. Conservatism becomes the party also of those who are in politics simply to make things work: to promote, no doubt, their own careers, but to promote it by public service. In a splendid Tory phrase, Feiling quotes the East India Company as declaring on its extinction that the Crown had inherited 'such a body of civil and military officers as the world has never seen before'. Toryism is no longer a creed merely for the man in the country; it becomes the creed also for the man in the office. Further, when the enterprising capitalist ceases to be adventurous and becomes also a man in the office, Toryism becomes his creed too. Of course this knocks the remaining romance out of Toryism. As Feiling says regretfully of Peel, 'he was cold or deaf to some high sentiments in Tory tradition, whether religious passion or the vision of paternal government'.

Thus what may be called the Tory interpretation of history has no longer much to do with high-flown loyalty to the Crown or devotion to the Church of England: it is not even the exaltation of traditional institutions. The Tory spirit in history is shown by an emphasis on administration, by getting ideas out of history and putting humdrum personal motives and office routine in. Until reading Feiling's book I had thought that the opposite to Whig history was history as it really worked; I now see for the first time that when you take ideas out of history you put Toryism in. When Tout emphasized the administrative history of Edward II against Stubbs's search for the growth of the British constitution, he was not being a better historian than Stubbs; he was being a Tory historian. When Namier empties Hanoverian Whiggism of principle and analyses the personal or family motives which took men into politics, he is not being a better historian than Macaulay; he is being a Tory historian. When Sir Charles Webster admires Palmerston for the efficient way in which he organized the Foreign Office instead of for the great liberal principles which he tried to apply, he, too, is unwittingly opening the gates to the Tory interpretation of history. In fact, as Sir William Harcourt might so wittily have said: 'We are all Tories nowadays.'

History is no doubt best conducted, like the British constitution, on the principle that Whig plus Tory equals eternal truth. This principle works only so long as it is clear that Toryism is only half the truth, just as Conservatives are only a substantial minority of the nation despite the Union Jack on their platforms and their masquerade as the National party. Tory history becomes dangerous only when it is presented as impartial history. Feiling, for instance, appears extremely fair and detached until you look at his treatment of the Radicals. Try him on Wat Tyler, on the Levellers, on the Chartists, and

you discover a point at which his English sympathies break
down. It is revealing that the only spiteful remark in the book
is about Major Cartwright, first advocate of universal suffrage.
Characteristic also is the judgement that Tom Paine 'had not
a rudiment of English feeling, nor was he a thinker', this of the
author of *The Rights of Man*, the best statement of democratic
belief in any language. The administrator sees the reformer and
the agitator as disturbing elements, upsetting office-routine
and putting forward impractical ideas based on a Utopian faith
in human reason.

It was no doubt inevitable that Tory history should gradually take the place of a Whig interpretation which had
become traditional and formal. More than this, our whole
educational system is now directed to turning out administrators; and these administrators want history with passion left
out and with machinery put in. Above all, Whig history was
the work of an age which believed in progress. Now even
George Macaulay Trevelyan votes Conservative and appeals to
others to do so. For Feiling, British greatness ended in 1918;
the rest is 'aftermath', redeemed only by Neville Chamberlain.
This is history written in the spirit of a Roman of the late
Empire. The administrator still sits at his desk, the army
officer still drills his men; but the wall is crumbling, the
barbarians are breaking in, nostalgia has taken the place of
hope. Yet even nostalgia is a human sentiment. If we survive
at all, both Trevelyan and Feiling will be outmoded; what we
must expect is history that will be neither Whig nor Tory, but
Byzantine.

IV

Democracy in America

THERE is an æsthetic pleasure to be had from the play of ideas; another from skill of expression. The great political thinkers give us the first, but rarely the second. We read their books to discover how men have regarded the problems of society; we do not take them away to read on the continental beach or at the fireside of an English hotel. Though Marx had a certain journalistic scurrility, there are few laughs in *Capital*. Lenin wrote as a peasant ploughs, turning over the sods with boorish persistence. Aristotle is as dreary as discarded lecture-notes, which is indeed the form in which his works have survived. Even the *Social Contract* would be unimpressive if it were not the book which set up the guillotine in the Place de la Concorde and sent the French armies marching across Europe. Tocqueville is the great exception. We should read *Democracy in America* with delight, even if there were no democratic countries left in the world and America did not exist.

Tocqueville went to America in 1831, ostensibly to study their prisons. In reality, like the Webbs in Russia a hundred years later, he wished to divine the shape of things to come. The Webbs were convinced that Russia was the Fabian Utopia; he believed that America was a democracy and that the universal victory of democracy was inevitable. Neither cared much for the country that they were supposed to be describing. The Soviet Communism of the Webbs is a country that never existed nor ever will; and posterity is more likely to read Malcom Muggeridge's *Winter in Moscow* if it wishes to know what Russia was like in 1933. Similarly, Tocqueville never returned to America and did not keep up the friendships he had formed there; he preferred Nassau Senior and John Stuart Mill. His picture of the Americans pales against the pages of *Martin Chuzzlewit* in which a great genius set out once and for all the soul of a people. Sainte-Beuve said of Tocqueville: 'He began to think before he learnt anything'; and

he missed much in the United States that did not suit his
thesis. He went there when Andrew Jackson was President;
yet he failed to grasp the significance of the Jacksonian revolution. He did not trouble to study American history and therefore regarded many things as democratic or uniquely American
that were in fact part of the English heritage. Accustomed to
the class-struggle of French politics, he thought that the two-
party system would disappear where there was no aristocracy.
Schooled to accept nationalism in Europe, he imagined that the
American states would become distinct nations. Though he
made the brilliant prophecy that Russia and the United States
would be the two world powers of the future, he did not foresee the growth of industry in the United States. His description
of the United States is at best a portrait of a limited Anglo-
American community in New England, a community that was
already being dwarfed by the advance of the frontier.

These criticisms are irrelevant. Tocqueville's subject is not
America; it is democracy in America and, before he gets to the
end, democracy without geographical excuse. Royer Collard
described Tocqueville as an aristocrat who had accepted defeat;
and this is the spirit of his book. Though he dreaded democracy
he was convinced it was coming; he wanted to discover its
defects and to lay down, in good time, how they could be
minimized. By democracy he meant sometimes universal
suffrage, sometimes any form of representative government
but most of all, a society in which respect for rank had ceased
to exist. Democracy and equality were, for him, interchangeable terms; and, despite his seemingly detached air, equality
was fundamentally distasteful to him. The thing that most
shocked and alarmed him, for instance, during the revolution
of 1848 was that his house-porter spoke rudely to him when he
came home late one evening. Hence, as he described America,
he was always looking over his shoulder at the streets of Paris
and even at his own porter. Many of his remedies for the
defects of democracy were no more than that the French
should cease to be French and should become American—
coca-cola civilization in fact. He feared the rule of the majority
and foretold, rightly, that it could be the most intense and
ruthless of tyrannies. He wanted to preserve exceptions, to
avoid that uniformity which equality seemed to imply. But he
very often gave the impression that the exceptions he wanted
to preserve were the agreeable frivolities which suited the

French aristocracy of the eighteenth century. Uniformity, no doubt, is hateful; but is M. de Charlus necessary in order to prove that it does not exist?

Tocqueville believed in liberty. His concern with it captivates us and makes us accept him as a great political thinker. Liberty is essential to us; and we hope that Tocqueville knows the secret how it may be preserved. When it comes to the point, he disappoints us. His only serious advice is to base society on religion; and by religion he means not moral rules or vague ethics, but revealed Christianity. This is to dodge the problem, or even to deny it. For the problem is how to preserve the freedom of the individual, how to limit the power of the majority, when rank and traditional standards have vanished. Tocqueville merely proposes that we shall pretend that one traditional standard has not vanished. The process of reason and equality is to be arrested at the gates of Heaven; and men are still to respect God even though they have ceased to respect M. de Tocqueville. He did not need to journey to America in order to discover this remedy: it has always been the stock-in-trade of conservative writers. The remedies which he thought peculiar to America, on the other hand, are watery. The jury system, to educate jurors in legal principles; local government, to provide variety and to check the tyranny of the centre; freedom of association, by which he meant limited companies and not trade unions. Indeed it did not occur to him that men who worked for their living needed liberty: the only freedom he offered them was the freedom of the frontier, the freedom to move elsewhere. It is the same, at bottom, with the famous speech which he made just before the outbreak of revolution in 1848. Again he diagnosed, but failed to cure. He foresaw an upheaval, caused by the resentment of the poor against the rich: wealth, he declared, could not be respected when all other privileges had ceased to exist. His solution was the teaching of economics. Men should be taught that wealth, like poverty, was an inevitable outcome of economic laws; then they would accept both. In short, elementary economics plus the New Testament will keep the masses quiet.

The fatal word has slipped out. Mr. J. P. Mayer, who is editing the complete works, made his name by dubbing Tocqueville 'the prophet of the mass-age', and though Tocqueville spoke always of the majority, he would have welcomed the description—it was the masses that he feared. The pub-

lishers describe *Democracy in America* as being 'with the
Capital of Karl Marx, the most important political work of the
nineteenth century'. They are right in their judgement; right
especially in coupling the two books. What Tocqueville called
the majority, Marx called the proletariat; both were convinced
that the masses would become all-powerful and that the class-
culture of their time was doomed to perish. The only difference
between them was that, whereas Marx was delighted at the
thought that bourgeois liberty, bourgeois justice, bourgeois art,
were doomed, Tocqueville was concerned to save as much as
he could from the wreck. Hence he has become the guide of
all despairing conservatives who are too enlightened to imagine
that the world will stand still. Marx or Tocqueville—you take
your choice. Either you are glad the age of the masses is
coming; or you hope to temper the shock. No third alternative
is offered.

Yet the whole thing is a swindle, a gigantic bugaboo put
over by two writers of genius. Tocqueville set off the individual
against the masses; but what are the masses but an assembly
of individuals? Every individual is a member of some majority
occasionally—even I have found myself in this embarrassing
position. 'The masses' is no more than a term of abuse for
the majority when we disagree with it. 'The masses' is always
the man next door, never ourselves. Am I the masses if I
enter a public-house? sit on the beach at Brighton? go to a
football match? Certainly not, I am still the divine individual.
All the others who are swilling beer, paddling in the sea, shout-
ing their heads off—they are the masses, the proletariat; they
will tyrannize over me, force me into their pattern, crush all
intellectual and artistic initiative. We really ought to advertise
for some member of the masses to turn up and put himself on
show; no one would answer the advertisement. Communists,
in their leather jackets, claim to be the masses; on examination,
they always turn out to be the leaders of the masses. The
masses themselves dissolve into individuals, with all kinds of
different characters and tastes, shoved—poor chaps—into a
procession for fear of something worse. The masses looked
all alike to Tocqueville, just as we are said to look all alike to
the Chinese. No doubt all writers—Tocqueville, Marx,
Beverley Nichols, and W. H. Auden—look very much alike
to a skilled lorry driver. Everyone is a snob; what you are
snobbish about depends on what you start from. The Soviet

system is not the dictatorship of the proletariat; it is a dictatorship over the proletariat. The tyrannies under which we groan, such as the clumsy lurchings of the B.B.C., are not the tyrannies of the majority: they are the work of stuck-up bureaucrats (admirers, no doubt, of Tocqueville), who would soon mend their ways if the majority had more hold on them.

In short, most of the things that Tocqueville foresaw have not come to pass. This provides an illustration of the general principle: sociology, like most works of the human intellect, is most entertaining when it is most thumpingly wrong. It would be even more interesting if a group of Tocqueville's admirers (and Marx's, too) would turn themselves into 'the masses', in order to see whether they would then behave according to the rules.

V

THE MAN OF DECEMBER

SOME historical characters—I would say most—become simpler as you know more about them. The lines get stronger, clearer; you see a whole man, you know how he will behave, how he will face difficulties, how he will respond to success. In the end he will go into one of those two pigeon-holes that are so jeered at and yet are essential for the moral judgement that we finally have to make: he can be docketed as 'a good thing'—or a bad one. But some few escape us and baffle examination. The more we strip off their disguises, the more new disguises appear. Such was Louis Napoleon, the man of mystery. Conspirator and statesman; dreamer and realist; despot and democrat; maker of wars and man of peace; creator and muddler; you can go on indefinitely, until you begin to think that he had no character at all, that at the heart of him was a gigantic nothing. All the greatest political observers of the time tried to penetrate his secret: Tocqueville, Marx, Thiers, Victor Hugo—all failed to make sense of him. Bismarck called him a Sphinx, and added: he was a Sphinx without a riddle. Was it not rather that he had too many riddles, and riddles to which he himself did not know the answer?

Everything about him baffles inquiry. Was he the son of his father? It seems unlikely. Yet if not, then of whom? He was a master of concealment. Whatever his other failings, he left few traces. The letters of Napoleon I fill sixty-four volumes; the letters of Napoleon III, even if they could be brought together, would not fill one. He talked endlessly to a great variety of witnesses, but—like the smoke of the cigarettes that he was one of the first to favour—his talk was vague and intangible; it vanished into the air, leaving only a faint romantic odour, a thin cloud of mystery. He was a creature of the Romantic movement, a Byronic hero gone seedy and rather out-at-elbows. Bulwer Lytton and the young Disraeli had the same touch, both in their writings and in their lives: an artificial excitement, a grandeur of ideas and a triviality of performance.

24

The men who grew up in the thirty years after the battle of Waterloo played out their lives in the shadow of the great Napoleon, Napoleon I. He had done great things; they manufactured great phrases. When Napoleon I called himself Emperor of the French, this was an empire which stretched across Europe to the frontiers of Russia and Turkey. Napoleon III, as Emperor, ruled only over the old Kingdom of France, and all that he added to his empire in nearly twenty years was Savoy and a scrap of Indo-China. This was a typical gesture of the Romantic movement, and its great legacy to our own time: the name on the bottle was more important than the drink inside it; the man who writes the advertisement is more important than the man who makes the goods—as for the goods themselves, they are of no importance at all.

One writer has called Louis Napoleon 'the modern Emperor'; another 'the first mountebank dictator'. Perhaps they are the same thing. The radicals of 1848 had claimed that they were bringing the masses into politics. The response had been disappointing. It was Louis Napoleon who first got the djinn out of the bottle. He said himself: 'Other French governments have ruled with the support of perhaps one million of the educated masses; I have called in the other twenty-nine million.' This determined his policy. Napoleon I did great things and then sought to present them in a striking way; Napoleon III looked for things that would appear striking and only then dressed them up as important. He deceived everyone, including himself. He could be an idealist free trader with Richard Cobden; a respectable sovereign with Queen Victoria; an unscrupulous schemer when he was with Bismarck. But there was also the myth that he had created for himself and which took in even him. He really saw himself as the all-wise dictator, the Cæsar who would reconcile all the classes in France and would remake the map of Europe. 'When a man of my name is in power, he must do great things.' He thrashed about like a lion in a cage, convinced that it ought to be ranging the jungle; always looking for great things to do, never finding them. He was no lion; he would have made an agreeable, though untrustworthy, domestic cat.

Great men in public life love power. That is what stamps them. They fight to get it and they use it ruthlessly when it is in their hands. Louis Napoleon would not pass this test of greatness. He loved conspiracy: the process of intrigue by which he moved towards power or the endless plans for using it. But he hated the action which threatened to follow these plans. For instance, the *coup d'état* of 2 December 1851 had been planned months before and put off at least twice. When it came to the point, Louis Napoleon hesitated again and might have put it off once more, had not the politicians of the assembly forced his hands, by beginning to make plans against him. And that, he thought, was unfair as well as being dangerous: like other conspirators, he claimed a monopoly in dishonesty.

The famous meeting at Plombières was a perfect example of his methods: the secret messages through somebody else's doctor; Cavour's trip to Plombières under a false name; the long discussions which left nothing on paper. The two men re-drew the map of Italy in a few bold strokes; war and peace, and the future destinies of a nation, were settled between the puffs of a cigarette. Napoleon was roused only when they turned to discuss the trick with which they could provoke war; the conspirator's device was the thing that won his interest and held it for hour after hour. Cavour displayed all his gifts in devising schemes to lure Austria into the war that was to be her ruin; and Napoleon was delighted. It was very different when the time came to put the plans into action. Then Napoleon was all for delay, as fertile in excuses as he had once been in plans, and resentful when Cavour held him to his bargain. Six weeks before the war for the liberation of Italy broke out, he told Cavour that the war would have to be postponed for at least a year; and then no doubt he would have been for further delay. 'You should know how to wait as I do.' But his waiting had no purpose. He preferred to dream rather than to act; to make great plans, not to carry them out. He was a procrastinating adventurer; more of a scoundrel in his thoughts than in his deeds.

It was the same when Bismarck discussed the future of Germany with him at Biarritz in 1865. Napoleon supplied the keynote of the talks: 'We must not make events; we must let them happen.' Imagine a man who has lived by robbing banks saying: 'We must not blow open the safe; we must wait for it to fall open.' Bismarck is often credited with having tricked Napoleon at Biarritz: he got permission to go ahead with his plans for defeating Austria, yet promised Napoleon nothing in return. There was no trickery in this; it was what Napoleon wanted. But, again, not for the sophisticated reason so often given. He did not avoid formulating his demands for German territory for fear that Bismarck would think them too great and give up war against Austria. It was his old line of waiting. He did not know what to demand; he only knew how to wait, or so he thought. The conversations at Biarritz suited him even better than the bargain at Plombières. With Cavour he had had to commit himself to action, however grudgingly; with Bismarck he committed himself only to inaction, a course of policy which he meant to follow in any case. Bismarck was to provide the action; and Napoleon was somehow to profit from it. He was like a man who haunts the gambling-rooms in the belief that, if he encourages others to bet, he will one day draw a great prize.

The twenty years when Louis Napoleon ruled France were a period of great creative activity in every country of Europe. The steam engine and the railway spread across the Continent. In France, too, the Second Empire promised energy and creation; yet it was in these twenty years that France lost the leadership of Europe in politics, in economics, in culture. The Second Empire claimed to be Wagner and turned out to be Offenbach—a frivolous echo of the past, not an inspiration for the future. It was the bastard of the great Napoleon—in name, in policy, even in men. It was said at the time that, though Louis Napoleon was not the son of his father, everyone else at Court was the son of his mother. Morny was his illegitimate half-brother; Walewski the illegitimate son of Napoleon I. Its emotions were sham, also. This system which claimed to care for the masses was run by the most dishonest politicians who have ever governed France. All of them, even Napoleon himself, were convinced that the Empire would not last; and they plundered France while the opportunity lasted. Under the July monarchy Guizot had said to the French middle classes: 'Get rich.' The statesmen of the Second Empire applied this doctrine.

In foreign affairs there was the same contradiction between the phrases and the reality. Napoleon liked to believe that his empire had sprung from the resentment which every Frenchman felt against the settlement of Europe made at Vienna in 1815 after the defeat of his uncle. In reality, this settlement had given France a position of primacy in Europe and had made her secure: if it was changed, France was bound to suffer. Hence Napoleon was constantly driven forward; and as constantly shrank from the results. In Sorel's words: 'His name was his fortune and his undoing. His origins condemned him to success.' Any other Frenchman might have defended the settlement of 1815; a Napoleon could not. Louis Napoleon believed that nationalism was the winning cause in Europe; and he meant to associate himself with its success. Despite his inaction, he could never support conservatism when it came to the point; and he tried to satisfy German and Italian nationalism without injuring France. In the outcome, he failed on both counts. He estranged Italy by holding on to Rome; he tried to make German unity stop at the Main; and by his very inaction took the decisive steps which ended the career of France as the Great Power of Europe.

Yet, with all his cunning, there was great good will. He really cared for Italy; he sympathized with Germany, or at any rate with German romanticism. He dreamt always of a Europe in which there would be 'a peaceful redress of grievances'; and he was the first European statesman in a responsible position to put forward plans for general disarmament. But, of course, they were plans in which the preponderance of France had to be recognized and made permanent. Disarmament, as always, seemed most attractive to the power that was on the decline.

Though he ruined France as a great power, he made France what she still is—as far as looks go. The Paris which tourists admire, the Paris of the opera and the great boulevards, is the creation of Napoleon III. Like every adventurer who has arrived Napoleon wanted something solid to show, something that would assert his permanence against the facts. And the Paris of Napoleon III has not done badly—better, at any rate, than the Berlin of Hitler or the Rome of Mussolini. Yet even this was a fraud. Its real purpose was to make long, wide streets so that a revolt could be put down easily, hardly a gesture of confidence towards the twenty-nine million. And having tricked others, Napoleon here misled himself. When his empire fell, there was no whiff of grapeshot; not a shot was fired. The boulevards had failed of their purpose.

We imagine nowadays—and even take pride in the thought —that dictators, swindling their way to power and keeping power by a succession of tricks, are a disease peculiar to the twentieth century. But there is nothing new in Hitler or Mussolini: Louis Napoleon had all their cards up his sleeve, except, perhaps, their brutality. He did not need a Nietzsche to put him beyond good and evil; he had arrived at the idea for himself. Certainly he owed his success to the same historic causes. The great French revolution destroyed the history of France before going on to destroy the history of Europe. Destroy tradition; destroy the political values on which a community has been built up, and only class war remains.

Marx did not discover this class war. He observed it in France and then generalized it as a formula for the future. That is the only way of the prophet: to foretell as the future what has already happened. Marx's prophecy has come off better than most, but in one vital point he went wrong. He supposed that the class war would be fought to a finish, that one side would win. And, since the bourgeoisie could not exterminate the proletariat, the proletariat would exterminate the bourgeoisie. There has been a different outcome: someone has slipped in between, played off one class against the other and exploited both. This, not his ragbag of ideas, was the great historical innovation of Louis Napoleon. He appealed to the fears of the middle classes when he made the *coup d'état* and presented himself as 'the Guardian of Order'. But he was also, in his muddled way, a socialist; he did more for the French working classes than any other French government before or since; and when he died a trade-union representative was the only man to come from France to his funeral.

But there was also another France, the France that had been created by the great revolution after what had been destroyed: the France that cared for liberty and the Rights of Man. This made the great difference between Louis Napoleon and his twentieth-century successors. The generals and civil servants and business men of Germany no doubt thought Hitler a barbarian; but once he had gained power, they licked his boots. The writers and political leaders of France never forgave Napoleon for the trickery and violence by which he had come to power. They turned their backs on him and condemned him to rely on his fellow-gangsters. It is not surprising that many Frenchmen supported Napoleon, especially in his hour of success; what is surprising and honourable is that so many Frenchmen opposed him from beginning to end. It was easy to be against Napoleon when he turned out to be the man of Sedan. It was his doom that he was branded from the start, and branded in history, as the man of December.

VI

CRIMEA:
THE WAR THAT WOULD NOT BOIL

JOHN BRIGHT, with ponderous Victorian wit, called the Crimean War 'a crime'; most historians have presented it as a bewildering series of diplomatic and military blunders. With the experience of the last few years to enlighten us, we should do better: we know that the diplomatic tangles since 1945, which may seem bewildering to the future historian, conceal the reality of 'the cold war'. The Crimean War was the cold war in an earlier phase. Two world systems, mutually un-comprehending, lurched against each other, each convinced of its defensive good faith. The struggle between them was fought in a ragged way at the edges. Both sides shrank from the head-on collision which would have produced a war to remake the world—Russia from lack of strength, the Western Powers from lack of conviction. Though the Crimean War seemed in-decisive, great decisions followed from it. Without it neither Germany nor Italy could have been united; without it Europe would never have known 'the liberal era', that halcyon age which ended in 1914 and which, for centuries to come, men will regard as 'normal times', just as the barbarians looked back to the peace and security of Augustan Rome.

The Crimean War is often treated in England as a war over the Eastern Question, a war to secure the route to India, and thus a rehearsal for Disraeli's 'peace with honour' campaign in 1878. This is to err both in time and place. The war had little or nothing to do with the security of India. The Suez Canal was not built; the overland route catered for a few travellers in a hurry; for that matter Russia's land-route to India was still in the future. The Crimean War was fought for essentially European considerations—against Russia rather than in favour of Turkey. It was fought for the sake of the Balance of Power and for 'the liberties of Europe'; more positively, it aimed to substitute diplomacy by agreement, the Concert of Europe, for the settlement of affairs at the dictation of a single Great Power. Disraeli was a consistent disciple of Metternich when he criticized the Crimean War and yet opposed Russia in 1878: the Crimean War had general altruistic motives, the crisis of 1878 was caused solely by the defence of Imperial interests. In other words, 1878 was a Tory affair; the Crimean War, with all its muddle, sprang from Whig principles, the last fling of a dying party.

British policy in the Near East had not been consistently anti-Russian before the Crimean War, though it became so afterwards. Canning, for instance, co-operated with Russia throughout the Greek war of independence; and though Palmerston thought of working with France against Russia in the Near East in 1833, he ended up by working with Russia against France in 1839 and 1840. Throughout the eighteen-forties, and indeed until the beginning of 1853, British suspicions were turned against France both at Constantinople and in Egypt; and Great Britain and Russia often made common cause in resisting French encroachment. Nor can there be an easy dividing line in their attitude to the Ottoman Empire, as though Russia wanted to break it up and Great Britain wished to preserve it. Both Powers found it a convenience; and both Powers doubted its capacity to survive. Their difference was in timing, not in judgement of the situation.

The British attitude to Russia was very different when it came to Europe; hence the Crimean War makes sense only with a European background. Ever since 1815 British statesmen had been obsessed with the thought that, if France ceased to dominate Europe, Russia would take her place; as Napoleon had said, in fifty years all Europe would be either Republican or Cossack. Hence Castlereagh's rather absurd alliance with France and Austria in January 1815; hence Canning's calling in of a New World to redress the balance of the Old (though the New World did not respond to his invitation); hence Palmerston's welcome to the July monarchy in France and his Quadruple Alliance with Spain and Portugal as well in 1834. This was one side of British policy: to maintain France as a Great Power and yet to keep her harmless—just strong enough to check Russia's domination without reviving the same taste in herself. The other element in British policy was to develop the independence of Central Europe, so that it could hold its own against both Cossacks and Republicans

B*

without constant alarms or war. This was what was meant by
the favourite description of Prussia and Austria as Great
Britain's 'natural allies': they were serving the purposes of
British policy without any effort on the British side. Curiously
enough, Metternich and Palmerston, who were supposed to
hate each other so much, were pursuing exactly the same aims
and served each other's needs. So long as the 'Metternich
system' worked, Central Europe was independent of both
France and Russia; and the Balance of Power in Europe freed
Great Britain from European commitments.

The revolutions of 1848 ended this finely drawn policy.
The fall of Metternich was a disaster to the British position;
and it was little consolation to make out that he had fallen
because of his refusal to take British advice. The revolutions
of 1848 seemed to make France more powerful than before;
to weaken Prussia; and to threaten Austria with elimination
from the ranks of the Great Powers. Europe would become
either Republican or Cossack. Though this bitter saying was
not at once fulfilled, it seemed at most postponed. On the one
side, France emerged from the revolutionary year under the
rule of a new Bonaparte, inescapably committed to the overthrow of the treaties of 1815 and almost as much to the restora-
tion of French domination in Europe. On the other, the
revolutions in Central Europe—in Germany, in Italy and in
Hungary—were defeated only with Russian backing; so far
as Hungary went, only with Russian military aid. By 1850,
Francis Joseph of Austria and Frederick William IV of Prussia
seemed to be Russian dependants, subservient not only from
ideological similarity, but from their inability to hold their
monarchical power except with Russian support. The Holy
Alliance was the Cominform of Kings.

The defeat of the revolutions of 1848 with Russian aid had
a profound effect on British public opinion. Before 1848 fear
of Russia had been a diplomat's calculation; there had been no
'Russian bogey'. After 1848 British liberals picked up the
habit of continental radicals and began to regard Russia as the
tyrant of Europe. War against Russia was regarded as the
preliminary to any radical success elsewhere. The old diplomatic apprehension of Russia now seemed tepid and half-
hearted. In radical circles, for instance, it was common doctrine
that Palmerston was in Russian pay; the proof was found in
his reluctance to launch the great European 'war of liberation'.

This theory can be found worked out in the essays which Karl Marx wrote on *The Eastern Question*; he learnt it from the pro-Turk lunatic, Urquhart. Except among radicals and exiles, fear of France still predominated in England until the spring of 1853. Indeed, belief that the British were more apprehensive about Belgium than about Turkey was one of the factors which led Tsar Nicholas to act so carelessly and so provocatively in May 1853, when the war-crisis first began to stir.

There was, of course, another and more obvious cause of Russian confidence. A coalition ministry had been formed in England at the end of 1852 under Lord Aberdeen; and Aberdeen, though a free trader, was an old-fashioned Tory. He had no sympathy with radical hostility to Russia; great confidence in the Tsar's good faith; and great distrust of Napoleon III. If Aberdeen had had his way there would have been no Crimean War. Russia would have strengthened her position in Turkey, consolidated her reactionary hold over Europe; and Great Britain would have consoled herself by taking Egypt. This would have been a reasonable, though not an idealistic, solution; hence the later regrets of Lord Salisbury, a reasonable man without ideals, that it was not adopted. It could only have been adopted by a purely Tory cabinet; and from such a cabinet Aberdeen was barred by his free-trade doctrines. Instead, he was saddled with Whig colleagues, Palmerston and Russell, who were both in their way friendly to France and who both, without yet distrusting the Tsar, wished to draw a sharp line against any new Russian advance. Russell had been Prime Minister; Palmerston was going to be. They were both pretty clear that a firm line against Russia would be a winning card in the game for public favour which they were playing against each other. Here too, if Palmerston and Russell had had their way, there would have been no war. The Tsar would have stepped aside from the Eastern Question before his prestige was involved and waited for a more favourable opportunity. Perhaps even, as we go on dreaming nowadays, Russian despotism would have saved everyone the trouble of a war by crumbling from within. It was this mixture of conciliation always too grudging and firmness always too late which, on the British side, produced the Crimean War.

There was, however, another principal in the war, one often forgotten in British and even in Russian accounts. Neither the Tsar nor the British Government wanted war; Napoleon III

did. Not necessarily the Crimean War as it worked itself out,
but a war which would disrupt the existing structure of Europe.
Thus Great Britain became involved in war in order to preserve
the Balance of Power and to defend the liberties of Europe;
Napoleon III pushed into war in order to overthrow the
Balance of Power and to clear the way for French domination.
After all, it is a simple calculation that if the allies of a Great
War fall out the defeated party will come into his own. In 1853
the calculation was made in Paris; now it is made in every
German village. The Crimean War was not a good war from
Napoleon III's point of view; a war in Poland, in Italy, or on
the Rhine, would have been much better. But it was better
than no war at all. On the other hand, Napoleon III had learnt
from his uncle's failure—had learnt, that is, in the scrappy,
illogical way, in which men use the past to prop up their own
prejudices. Napoleon III supposed, though wrongly, that his
uncle's great mistake had been to quarrel with England; his
key to success was therefore to be the British alliance, and the
Crimean War was welcome to him in that it gave him this
alliance. In the long run, however, Napoleon III did no better
with the British alliance than his uncle had done without it—
unless it is better to die in Chislehurst than at St. Helena.

By the summer of 1853 France, Russia and Great Britain
were all tugging themselves into war in their different ways.
The Tsar, though with no deep-laid plans for encroaching on
Turkey, had grown too confident; regarding Prussia and
Austria as his satellites, he supposed that he could display his
prestige at Constantinople without risk. When this proved
mistaken, he—like the Russians generally when they are
challenged—felt genuinely threatened with aggression; and in
Russian eyes the Crimean War was a defensive war. The
British Government, though also without deep-laid plans,
would not allow the Tsar's claims and, in their anxiety to win
the alliance of France, often acted more firmly than Napoleon
III expected or desired. Napoleon, on his side, wanted to
shake Russia's prestige and to build up his own; but most of
all, he wanted to keep in step with the British, who, with the
same motive, constantly quickened the pace until the two fleets
tumbled into the Black Sea more to prove mutual good faith
and enthusiasm as allies than to oppose Russia. As a matter of
fact, when the British and French fleets entered the Black Sea
at the end of 1853, the Crimean War, not yet started, had

already been won so far as the original causes of war, or excuses for it, were concerned. That is, the Tsar was quite prepared to drop his immediate claims on Turkey, once it became clear that England and France intended to resist them. This did not satisfy the western allies. With their public opinion roused and their resources mobilized, what they wanted was a decision, not merely the withdrawal of the present Russian demands. The problem of the Crimean War, never solved, lay here. The Russians had dropped their demands because the British and French fleets had entered the Black Sea. How could the renewal of these demands be prevented when the British and French fleets went away again?

The problem had two sides, military and diplomatic. The military problem was, how to get at the Russians, in order to inflict on them the defeat which would make them accept the terms needed for Europe's security? The diplomatic problem was, what were the terms which should be imposed on the Russians when they were defeated? The two problems were mixed up throughout the war. Sometimes the allies tried to devise terms which would make a defeat of the Russians unnecessary; sometimes they dreamt of a defeat so decisive as to spare them the trouble of devising terms. At bottom the problem was insoluble. The Western Powers could not alone inflict on Russia a decisive and lasting defeat; nor, even were she defeated, could they devise terms which would ensure against a renewal of her expansion. It would have been a different matter if Austria and Prussia, the states of Central Europe, could have been drawn into the war. Hence the real decision of the Crimean War came from the two Germanic powers when they decided to stay out of it. Austria and Prussia were 'the third force'. Their persistence in this line of policy both caused the Crimean War and led to its being indecisive. Until the beginning of 1854 the Tsar had regarded them as reliable satellite states, dependent on his support. As soon, however, as he depended on their support, they ceased to be satellites. He could no longer keep France out of the Near East by a threat from Prussia on the Rhine and from Austria in Italy.

The Western Powers imagined that 'the third force' had come over to their side and that a full-scale defeat of Russia was in sight. Certainly a coalition of all the Great Powers of Europe against Russia would have excluded her from Europe, might even have destroyed her as a Great Power. Poland would have been restored, Turkey secured; Louis Napoleon would have become master of Europe. This was an outcome more unwelcome to Prussia and Austria even than Russian domination of Turkey. Whereas the Western Powers wanted a decision, the Central Powers wanted no decision; and they got their way. Prussia had the great advantage that she was indifferent to the affairs of the Near East, though concerned with the general European balance. Hence her neutrality was genuinely impartial. Her only aim, which seemed craven enough, was to ensure that no fighting took place on Prussian soil. This no doubt benefited Russia and won her gratitude; but since Prussia did not promise anything to the Western Powers, she did not disappoint them either. When the war ended, Prussia was not at first invited to the Peace Congress at Paris. This seemed a humiliation; later events showed the enormous gains to be won from keeping out of other people's quarrels. Any contemporary statesman who wishes to reap the advantages of the third course should study the policy of Prussia during the Crimean War.

Austrian policy is equally instructive: it shows the disadvantages of a neutrality which offends both sides. Whereas Prussia was neutral from indifference, Austria was neutral from being too deeply committed. She had her own grounds for opposing Russia. Russia's control of the mouth of the Danube, where her troops had established themselves in 1853, cut one of Austria's main economic arteries with the outer world. Thus the practical aim of Austrian policy was to get Russia out of Rumania and to get herself in. But there were complicating factors. If Austria entered the war on the side of the Western Powers, she would bear the brunt of the fighting; worse, an allied victory, expelling Russia from Europe, would make Napoleon III supreme and thus clear the way for the national principle. Austria would win Rumania at too high a price if she lost her Italian lands, the symbol of her Imperial greatness. Yet, apart from her anxiety about Rumania, Austria dared not favour Russia nor even keep a resolute neutrality, for fear that Napoleon III would explode Italy against her. As a result Austria followed the worst of all policies. She offended the Tsar by refusing to promise a secure neutrality; she offended the Western Powers by refusing to go to war. She pressed her alliance on England and France in order to conciliate them; she failed to operate it and left them more estranged then before. Neutrality, like virtue, has its merits if maintained inviolate; it can also be sold for a high price. The one impossible thing is to be up for auction and to remain virtuous at the same time.

The first stage of the Crimean War was the stage when the Western Powers imagined that 'the third force' could be drawn into the war and a real decision thus produced. This stage lasted until the summer of 1854, by which time Prussian neutrality was certain and Austrian belligerence uncertain. The Crimean War, in the strict sense of the term, followed— the war with all its blunders and muddles which perplexed contemporaries and baffled posterity. Yet the confusion had a simple cause—how could the allies get at Russia when the great neutral buffer of Central Europe was interposed between them? The allies had hoped that the Russians would obligingly remain in Rumania in order that they might be defeated there; instead the Russians withdrew from Rumania in July 1854. In their perplexity the allies decided on Sebastopol, the Russian naval base in the Crimea, which was supposed to be vulnerable to an amphibious operation. As a matter of fact, it took nearly a year's fighting and the mobilization of armies on a continental scale for this amphibious operation to succeed.

It takes two to make a war. Russian strength in the Near East lay in her proximity; her strength in the European balance lay in her army. Her naval power in the Black Sea was a secondary affair; and it could always be checked if the British and French fleets, or even the British fleet alone, passed the Straits. If the Russians had abandoned Sebastopol and sealed off the Crimea, the western allies would have scored a success of prestige; but Russia would have been no weaker than before. The allies would have cruised undisturbed in the Black Sea until their position became ridiculous; they would then have retired, and Russia's pressure on Turkey could have been resumed. But autocratic monarchies also have their prestige. The Tsar did not grasp that if the allies failed to defeat him, he had won; whereas, whatever efforts he made at Sebastopol, he could not defeat the allies. Russia's military strength lies in withdrawal; but this has always to be imposed upon her by her enemies, instead of being a conscious choice. Alexander I fought Napoleon at Austerlitz and even wanted to fight on the frontier in 1812; Stalin was only saved from catastrophe on the frontier in 1941 by being caught unprepared. In the Crimean War, the Tsar obligingly provided the maritime powers with the battlefield which they could never have found for themselves. Instead of being withdrawn, the Russian armies in Sebastopol were reinforced; and Russia exhausted herself for the sake of the maritime powers. The allies lamented that they had not taken Sebastopol by a *coup de main* when they landed in 1854; if they had, there would have been no Crimean War and nothing would have been achieved at all. For the essence of war is not to take this point or that, but to destroy, or at least to weaken, the military strength of the enemy. This was accomplished by the year's fighting in front of Sebastopol. The Russian armies were greatly weakened; Russia's military prestige lessened; most of all, Russia's economic resources were intolerably strained. It took Russia a generation to recover from the effort of the Crimean War; and in this generation Europe was remade without Russian interference.

The defeat of the Russian armies, and the weakening of Russian power, were the real result of the Crimean War; but this was a result too vague to satisfy the victorious allies. Their victory had to be translated into a treaty of peace; yet they had no clear idea what this treaty should contain. As on other occasions, the Western Powers knew what they were fighting against, not what they were fighting for. They were fighting against Russia; and their real wish was that Russia should cease to exist or—what amounts to the same thing—become a modest and satisfied member of an Anglo-French world. Napoleon III was prepared to accept the logic of this wish. When Sebastopol fell, he proposed to the British Government a programme which would sweep Russia from Europe and destroy her as a Great Power—the programme of full national reconstruction, especially of Poland, which would incidentally make France supreme in Europe. The British Government had the exactly opposite aim: they had wished to destroy Russian supremacy in Europe without putting French supremacy in its place. Yet on the other hand they were the more eager of the two to continue the war until a 'decision' had been reached. A characteristic compromise followed. Each accepted the other's negative: the war was brought to an end, without any positive war-aims being drawn up.

This is not to say that the Crimean War accomplished nothing, nor even that the Treaty of Paris contained nothing of moment. Apart from the weakening of Russian power, which could not be put into a treaty, the Crimean War had two achievements, one which lasted for nearly eighty years, the other for fifteen years. The more permanent outcome, as things go in international affairs, was the independence of Rumania, freeing the mouths of the Danube from either Russian or Austrian control. The Russian army had withdrawn in July 1854; the Austrian army had taken its place, and the Austrians had hoped to annex Rumania. But they would not pay the French price, which was to give up Italy; therefore they had to withdraw in their turn, and Rumania became a genuinely independent state, a buffer between Russian interests and those of Central Europe, until the time of Stalin and Hitler.

The more prized achievement of the treaty of Paris was the 'neutralization' of the Black Sea. Russia was forbidden to maintain a fleet in the Black Sea, or to rebuild her naval arsenals; it is true that the same restrictions were imposed on Turkey, but since the Turks could maintain a fleet in the Sea of Marmora they could always dominate the Black Sea in time of war. The neutralization clauses of the Treaty of Paris were a rehearsal for the demilitarization of the Rhineland in the Treaty of Versailles, and equally futile. Either Russia accepted them because she feared England and France; in that case she would repudiate them when she ceased to fear England or France. Alternatively Russia accepted them because she had changed her ways and given up aggression against Turkey; in that case they were unnecessary. The British and French would not keep their fleets in the Black Sea indefinitely; they were not even sure that they would remain indefinitely on good terms. Hence they tried to make the Russians promise that they would continue to behave as though the allied fleets were still in the Black Sea when in fact they had been long withdrawn. A treaty of peace can only define the conditions of the present; it cannot bind the future. This the Russians demonstrated fifteen years later, when they repudiated the Black Sea clauses of the Treaty of Paris. The British doctrine of the sanctity of treaties was upheld only by the pious pretence of a conference in London, at which the Powers, to no one's surprise, confirmed what Russia had already done. The neutralization clauses taught a lesson which was ignored in 1919: if you wish to perpetuate a military victory, you must perpetuate the balance of forces which produced that victory.

The Crimean War was, in short, a war that did not come off, a war without a decision. But that was itself the decision. Though Russian strength was not broken, Russian influence in Europe was lessened. Though French prestige was increased, France did not become dominant in Europe. Napoleon III thought he had freed his hands in order to remodel Italy and Germany to his own taste; it turned out that Italy and Germany had freed their own hands to remodel themselves against him. Cavour and Bismarck, not Napoleon III, were the real victors of the Crimean War. If there were a moral to be drawn from the Crimean War which might apply to the present, it would be this: in a war between Russia and the west, it is the Powers which keep out who will be the real gainers. Last time it gave Prussia mastery of Germany.

For the British, the Crimean War, though superficially inconclusive, was less of a disappointment than it was to Napoleon III. They had set out to lessen Russian power; and they had succeeded. Later on, they imagined that they had intended to give Turkey the chance of reforming herself; and were correspondingly embittered when no reform followed. Nevertheless, the Crimean War brought real gains to the British. The Balance of Power in Europe was strengthened, not overthrown; and Great Britain did not need to intervene in a continental war for sixty years thereafter. Two generations of peace are something to be thankful for; it is more than we have had in our lifetime.

VII

BISMARCK'S MORALITY

HISTORICAL reputations are a sort of political barometer; every generation gets the heroes it deserves. Professor Geyl recently gave a brilliant demonstration of this in the case of Napoleon. In English history, Henry VIII, hero of the late Professor Pollard, is going down; and Elizabeth, courted by Professor Neale and Mr. Rouse, is coming up. No doubt, in our era of decline, we prefer subtlety to animal vigour. Bismarck is the German barometer, the test of what German historians think of themselves and of the world. Of course, there are other significant German figures—Luther and Goethe, for example. Luther has gone down with the general decline of religion; unless you take his faith seriously, he was a repellent boor. Goethe is always produced when the Germans are feeling sorry for themselves. He has to act as excuse for the concentration camps and the gas-chambers; after all, a nation which produced Goethe cannot be wholly bad. Goethe was certainly a poet of the highest genius; apart from this, he was a complacent prig, servile and self-satisfied. He won't really do if the Germans are to escape the fate of Sodom and Gomorrah. Bismarck, with all his faults, is a better card for the Germans to play. He has that essential quality of the significant figure: he can be made to sparkle whichever way you look at him.

It is all the more surprising that hitherto there has been no good life of Bismarck. The standard German life by Max Lenx is no more than an enlarged obituary. Grant Robertson's splendid sketch, written during the first German war, gives out in 1871 when Bismarck had nineteen years of high office still ahead of him. During the second German war Erich Eyck, a German living in England, wrote a three-volume life which was published in Switzerland. He has now produced a reduced version in one volume[1] for the English reader. It would be a poor compliment to say that this is the best life of Bismarck;

[1] Erich Eyck, *Bismarck and the German Empire.*

it is the only life of Bismarck and will hold its own for years to come. For one thing, it covers the whole story from beginning to end. Or rather, to be precise, it gives out when Bismarck left office and omits the last eight years when Bismarck conducted a malicious and unscrupulous campaign against William II who had dismissed him. Still, it is more important that Dr. Eyck has read and digested the enormous mass of Bismarck literature. Even more than Napoleon, Bismarck has been the victim of too much scholarship. For the first eight years of Bismarck's time in office alone, there are forty-four volumes of published documents from the Austrian, Prussian, and French archives. No one has really sorted them out till Dr. Eyck faced them. Then there have been endless works of meticulous research, conducted as solemnly as the study of Holy Writ; every scrap of Bismarck's writing, every fragment of his conversation, have been assembled in the fifteen volumes of his Collected Works; and Bismarck added to the confusion in probably the most misleading work of autobiography ever written. Dr. Eyck is the master of his subject. Even though the bibliographical apparatus has been omitted in the English edition, the reader can have confidence that Dr. Eyck has examined all the evidence before passing judgement.

This last sentence suggests one of Dr. Eyck's defects. He is by training a lawyer, by profession a liberal journalist; and he took up history to relieve the tedium of exile. It is not so easy to become a historian as is sometimes supposed. Dr. Eyck gives the impression that he is always out for a verdict; and so far as Bismarck is concerned it is usually a verdict of guilty. Bismarck himself claimed that he kept five balls in the air; Dr. Eyck tends to insist that one ball must have been the decisive one and the others just kept spinning to deceive the audience. Bismarck had political genius of the highest order; certainly therefore he knew what he was doing. Dr. Eyck interprets this as meaning that Bismarck knew where he was going, a very different matter. The nineteenth century was an age of political optimism, and therefore most politicians thought in terms of objective—even though what they accomplished often turned out very differently from what they intended. Dr. Eyck's attitude is all right for them. But Bismarck was not a political optimist. He did not want to go anywhere; quite the reverse, he wished to slow things down. Most of the things that Bismarck accomplished—the war with

Austria, the war with France, the so-called unification of Germany—would have been accomplished anyway. What Bismarck really achieved was to make them less decisive than they would have been otherwise. He propped up the Habsburg monarchy for fifty years after its collapse; he preserved France as a Great Power; he retarded German unification until the days of Hitler; within his own limited Germany he staved off the triumph of plebiscitarian democracy.

This criticism leads to the deeper defect in Dr. Eyck's approach. His judgements are those of a contemporary, not of a historian. Dr. Eyck grew up dreaming of a liberal constitutional monarchy in Germany, associated with the Western Powers and with a liberal German Austria, and pushing Russia far to the east. Bismarck did not share this dream; and therefore Dr. Eyck condemns him. For instance, he condemns Bismarck for not making an alliance with England against Russia in 1879; yet such an alliance would certainly have led to war in the Near East. In fact, Dr. Eyck is not far removed from the conviction now widespread in the Western world—when is war not wicked, not a crime against humanity, not destructive, in fact when is war not war? When it is against Russia. Yet Dr. Eyck expresses a judgement on Austrian politics which is to me much more shocking than anything Bismarck ever did. He condemns Francis Joseph for dismissing his German ministers in 1879 and writes: 'We now know that in fact Francis Joseph brought about the collapse of his dynasty by banishing his faithful German subjects to the wilderness.' In other words Francis Joseph ought to have left power in the hands of the German minority—simply because they were middle-class liberals—and not attempted to conciliate his Slav subjects.

Dr. Eyck's verdict on Bismarck is that, though he was a wicked man, he accomplished a glorious work. He describes his enormous achievement—'the fulfilment of the dream of the German nations, their unification in a powerful and glorious Empire'. Again, 'the critics of his methods and his personality never can, nor will, doubt his singular greatness and his everlasting glory'. Bismarck's reputation for wickedness is a very curious affair. He has become the Old Nick of modern times; yet what did he do that others did not? He treated Austria much more considerately than Lincoln treated the southern states; he used his victory over France with much more moderation than Napoleon III would have used a victory over

Prussia. He bullied Denmark in 1864. Was this worse than
the way Palmerston bullied Greece in 1850 or China in 1860?
Though he was jealous of political rivals, he was no more
jealous than Gladstone was of Chamberlain. It is difficult to
discover noble idealists among the European statesmen with
whom Bismarck had to deal—Gorchakov? Thiers? Andrássy?
Disraeli? Bismarck did not lack morality; what he lacked was
uplift. He could not make his voice quaver with unselfish zeal,
as Gladstone's voice quavered when he occupied Egypt. Bismarck fought 'necessary' wars and killed thousands; the
idealists of the twentieth century fight 'just' wars and kill
millions. Bismarck defended national sovereignty, or rather
accepted it as a fact; this was no more wicked than to reject
the Schuman plan on the same grounds.

Though Bismarck lacked humbug, he did not lack principles.
Only they were not liberal principles. They were principles
founded in distrust of human nature, principles of doubt and
restraint. When men dislike Bismarck for his realism, what
they really dislike is reality. Take his most famous sentence:
'The great questions of our time will not be settled by resolutions and majority votes—that was the mistake of the men of
1848 and 1849—but by blood and iron.' Who can deny that
this is true as a statement of fact? What settled the question of
Nazi domination of Europe—resolutions or the allied armies?
What will settle the question of Korea—majority votes at Lake
Success or American strength? This is a very different matter
from saying that principles and beliefs are ineffective. They
can be extremely effective if translated into blood and iron and
not simply into resolutions and majority votes. As a matter of
fact Bismarck never underrated the importance of principles;
rather he erred in taking the principles of others too seriously.
He conducted political war first against the Roman Catholics,
then against the Social Democrats, because he thought that
they meant what they said—the Catholics that they were loyal
only to the Pope, the Socialists that they were revolutionaries.
The basis of our modern liberal democracies is that men do
not mean what they say. This was indeed the justification for
our first liberal act—the emancipation of the Roman Catholics
from the penal laws. Nowadays, Mr. Attlee does not really
believe that Mr. Churchill wishes to exploit the poor; and Mr.
Churchill does not really believe that Mr. Attlee would lead
the country to ruin. Most of our present troubles with the

Russians spring from the conviction of Roosevelt and his advisers that the Communist leaders did not mean what they had been saying for thirty years—at least no more than Roosevelt meant what he said at election time. Unfortunately the Communists are old-fashioned—like Bismarck.

Bismarck was old-fashioned in a more fundamental sense. He came from a peaceful, stable society; and he valued stability above movement. First inside Germany and then in Europe he achieved a balance of opposing forces, and so created a generation of stability. Men fall easily into the habit of taking security for granted; and the generation which flourished after 1878 soon regarded internal order and European peace as normal. In fact the years between 1878 and 1914—years with no revolutions outside Russia and no wars outside the Balkans—were the most abnormal years in modern history; and whatever the future has in store for us it is pretty certain that we shall never see the like of them again. Instead of dismissing Bismarck as a nasty man, it would be wiser to bear in mind that these years were his doing; that without him the great war of all against all—of class against class, of nation against nation—would have got under way sooner.

Finally, when judging Bismarck as a politician, one has to remember one other thing, which is not obvious to a German writer: Bismarck was dealing with Germans. The personal spite; the raucous evocation of Power; the irritation at opposition—these were qualities which he shared with other German politicians. The restraint; the ability to see into the minds of others; the readiness to risk his own prestige for the sake of peace and moderation; these were the things that Bismarck added. No doubt Germany and German policy in Bismarck's day had many faults; but no German since has done any better. I suspect that Bismarck would have preferred this cool praise to the eternal glory and moral disapproval which Dr. Eyck offers him.

VIII

NIETZSCHE AND THE GERMANS

EVERY artist wants to live for ever. Though he creates primarily because he must, still he expects his creation to win immortality for him. There are many paths to this heaven, all of them difficult; the most certain of them is when men can say—'this is the phrase that launched a thousand ships'. It does not matter if the phrase is misinterpreted, torn from its context, made to do work for which it was never intended. The great thing is to crystallize the beliefs and delusions of a generation in a single sentence. Rousseau would have been appalled by the terror which was conducted in the name of the Social Contract; Darwin was bewildered by the political doctrines which were built round the survival of the fittest; Marx would have railed against the dictatorship of the proletariat as it is practised in Russia. For that matter, Jesus Christ would have been dismayed by the doctrines and, still more, the practice of the Christian churches. Every great movement crucifies its founder; and in so doing gives him immortality.

Nietzsche has had the same fate, or achieved the same destiny. He was captured by the dictators of our time. Hitler kept a bust of him on show and consoled Mussolini for the disasters of 1943 with a set of his complete works. Nietzsche's great phrases seemed made for Fascism; it was inconceivable without them. The Will to Power, the Master Race, the Superman—Fascism did not need to look farther for its philosophy. Plenty of others lived by picking up the sweepings of Nietzsche's study. Freud declared that he had avoided reading Nietzsche in order to preserve his open mind—a sure confession that he looted from him. Bernard Shaw, always tawdry when it came to systematic thinking, could never have got along without the ideas he took over from Nietzsche and from his English contemporary, Samuel Butler. Nietzsche would certainly have repudiated his disciples. For one thing, he detested the Germans; he tried to make out that he was of Polish descent, and wished that he could write his books in French. He called himself '

46

good European' and perhaps he was right to lecture in Switzerland. Dr. Oscar Levy, his English translator, used to write protestingly to the newspapers whenever Nietzsche was blamed for the behaviour of the Germans or of the Nazis; and now an American, Professor Kaufmann, has carried out a mission of rescue on a larger scale.[1] This is the most sensible exposition of Nietzsche's philosophy ever made; if it fails to reveal the full secret it is because it forgets that Nietzsche, as well as being a philosopher, was something more important— a writer of the highest genius.

Nietzsche knew it himself. He said with perfect truth: 'One day it will be recognized that Heine and I have been by far the first artists of the German language—at an incalculable distance from everything that mere Germans have done with it.' Nietzsche invented a style so personal and so powerful that it can be recognized in a single sentence or even in a single phrase. Carlyle did the same; and Nietzsche admitted the likeness, though he dismissed, rightly, the triviality of Carlyle's ideas. It is, after all, very rare for a great writer to be a great thinker; and anyone who has ever tried to read any philosophy must know that the other way round it is rarer still. Nietzsche liked to think that he was a philosopher first of all. He wrote of *The Will to Power*: 'a book for *thinking*, nothing else; it belongs to those to whom thinking is a *delight*, nothing else'. Yet even this phrase gives him away. Whoever the reader may be, the writer is obviously getting a *delight* in expressing his thoughts, as well as thinking them. In fact Nietzsche's genius was his curse: if he had written less well, he would have never won the admiration of those solitary souls, the dictators.

It was Nietzsche who made the great discovery: 'God is dead.' This was not a declaration of atheism. In that case Nietzsche, always accurate, would have said: 'God does not exist.' He was announcing the end of faith in the supernatural and, still more, the end of the spirit-body dualism on which all Western morality had been based. How were things to be kept going when the sanctions of tradition and the supernatural were removed? Nietzsche was the first to answer: 'Become who you are.' Develop according to your own rules and not according to rules made up outside by others. Nietzsche also thought that he had discovered this rule of development; in formulating it, he made the great mistake which opened the

[1] Walter A. Kaufmann, *Nietzsche: Philosopher, Psychologist, Antichrist*.

door to every misunderstanding. The motive of human action, he supposed, was the Will to Power. The phrase, as Nietzsche designed it, was a provocation, almost a joke; it was a jeering reference to the contemporary German craze for the power of the state. Though a reference, it was also a repudiation. Far from wanting power over others, Nietzsche's man should want power over himself; or, to put it another way, should want to develop his powers. Nietzsche spoke constantly of 'over-coming'; but the most important sort of overcoming was to overcome yourself. Even the 'overman' has the same signifi-cance: though a conqueror, he is primarily a self-conqueror. This is, too, the only sense in which the superman is 'bred': he breeds himself. Nietzsche was as knocked over as all his contemporaries by Darwin's supposed discovery that man was an animal. He was not, however, so silly as to try to escape from this by turning man into a superior animal. Nietzsche's superman is not a biological type at all: he is the individual who has lifted himself out of the animal ruck by heaving at his own shoestrings. How do you tell the superman? Nietzsche's answer at last gives him away and shows that he was a great writer more than a great philosopher. For the answer is a joke on a cosmic scale. It is the doctrine of 'eternal recurrence': everything has happened before and will go on happening over and over again. Only a superman could stand such a doctrine; therefore you present it to him like a piece of litmus paper. If he is not a superman, he will go off his head. And this is exactly what Nietzsche did: as a last and colossal joke, the litmus-test produced a result of a most surprising kind. Or was Nietzsche's madness the effect of the disease with which he is alleged to have deliberately infected himself in his only sexual encounter? This too would be a joke of a Nietzschean charac-ter: '*boshaft*', meaning malicious and sarcastic at once, was his favourite word for such pranks.

Nietzsche's doctrines had a logical form and can be pre-sented in a logical way. Since he was the first modern thinker to face a non-theological universe, he anticipated most of the ideas that have come after. He anticipated psychoanalysis; he anticipated existentialism; even eternal recurrence is now a commonplace in the scientific world. He prided himself most on his methods, not on his results; and his method was that of ceaseless inquiry. He imagined himself as a latter-day Socrates; and what he hated in Christianity was its dogmatism, its eleva-

tion of faith over reason. 'Convictions are prisons.' His ideal
was Goethe: 'the man of *totality*: he fought the mutual ex-
traneousness of reason, sensuality, feeling, and will . . . the
man of tolerance, not from weakness, but from strength'.
Indeed he chose the title of his last work, *Ecce Homo*, as an
echo of Napoleon's remark when he met Goethe: *voilà l'homme*.
Yet when every effort has been made to turn Nietzsche into a
man of balance and reason or the great Stoic of our times,
doubt raises its head; the Socratic questioning starts again,
this time at Nietzsche's expense. Certainly Nietzsche disliked
the Germans, hated anti-Semitism, despised those who lived
for public success. All the same, he gave them plenty of
openings. As he exposes himself to perversions, he has the air
of the elderly woman anxiously demanding of the enemy
officer: 'When does the raping begin?' Carlyle preached
silence in forty volumes; Nietzsche preached sanity and
tolerance in works that were raving mad and savagely in-
tolerant from the beginning.

It will not do to blame all the misunderstanding on his
sister, as Professor Kaufmann and others have done. Certainly
Frau Förster-Nietzsche set out to capture Nietzsche for
German nationalism at its most nonsensical; and she spent
forty years editing his works in such a way that his subversive
thoughts were obscured. But he had given her the excuse and
the opportunity. From Luther to Hitler the Germans have
always wanted an iron framework of discipline to keep them
in reasonable order; when they lose this, they go mad, as
Nietzsche did, and it was only to be expected that the Germans
would follow his example rather than his teaching. Nietzsche
himself felt detached from the community; he was an individual in the void, and he supposed that he was preaching to a
few individuals equally detached. His success came when a
whole society lost its bearings and threatened to disintegrate.
It is all very well to call for the superman so long as you can
by sure that the right kind of superman will respond to the
call. If Mussolini and Hitler turn up instead, who is Nietzsche
to say they do not conform to the terms of the advertisement?
Nietzsche himself said of Napoleon: 'the revolution made
Napoleon possible; that is its justification. For such a prize the
anarchical crash of our entire civilization is welcome.' The
words could be written up over the bunker, if it still exists, of
the Chancellery in Berlin. If the Fascists and Nazis, with their

will to power and their freedom from slave-morality, beyond good and evil, were not the supermen of Nietzsche's imagination, they were too near it to be comfortable.

The truth is that the individual judgement, with all its enterprise and courage, needs to operate in a settled community. The pioneer must be ahead of his fellows, but not out of sight; otherwise he goes mad or they do—probably both. Blake wrote in much the same style as Nietzsche and with much the same drift; but this never provoked Gladstone, nor even Neville Chamberlain, to set himself alight in the cellars of 10 Downing Street. Everyone who has escaped from religious dogma must have been captivated by Nietzsche at some time or other; but most escape the thraldom and discover that it is individualism run mad. It is the philosophy of the *rentier* who imagines that he owes nothing to society, though society owes much to him. Perhaps this is only another way of saying that the job of court-jester is attractive only so long as there is a court to laugh at the jests. Anyone who sets out to be a heretic had better postulate first a society tolerant yet respectable; in fact he had better be an Englishman.

IX

BISMARCK AND EUROPE

LEGENDS of Bismarck sprawl over the history of the later nine-teenth century. First, the contemporary legend—the Bismarck who produced calculated effects on diplomats and politicians, wore military uniform and revealed only late in life that he had done it in order to save the wear-and-tear on his more expensive civilian clothes. Then the legend of German historians who saw in Bismarck the maker of German unity and for whom he could do nothing wrong or even mistaken. And, the reverse of this, the legend primarily of French historians, though often accepted in England too, for whom Bismarck could do nothing right—the man who planned the downfall of France as a Great Power and was responsible for three invasions of 'the national territory'. More recently there has grown up a version, to which I myself have contributed a little, of Bismarck as the thwarted conservative, exponent of the doctrine of 'the lesser evil', of whom one might say that everything he did he did un-willingly and only because anyone else could have done more of it. Though his political offspring were illegitimate, they were 'only little ones'. The study of Bismarck has become a modern scholasticism, each act and each saying combed over and elaborated on as though it were Holy Writ or one of those few documents which, surviving by chance, give mediaeval his-torians the illusion that they are engaged in a more scientific discipline than ours.

I have recently been fortunate enough to start examining Bismarck's diplomacy all over again. It would be foolish to pretend that it is possible to shut out of mind the versions of those who have gone before—Sybel and Ollivier, Friedjung and Matter, Grant Robertson and Marcks, Eyck and Srbik. But all of them had some political axe to grind; they were all concerned to show that he had failed or, more rarely, succeeded. I have clean hands. I really do not care—though this may sound untrue—I do not care about the Germans any more one way or the other. I am prepared to believe that Europe is

finished; and I am only curious to know what happened to
Europe in the second half of the nineteenth century without
worrying any more about the outcome. So much of the diplomatic record has now been published that it is possible to
write the story virtually from the archives, at any rate so far as
Austria, France, and Prussia are concerned. Some details of
British diplomacy could, no doubt, be added from further
study of the archives, though I do not think they would be
details of much moment. Russian policy is admittedly still
obscure; and a documentary study of this between 1863 and
1871 would be one of the most welcome tasks which a Soviet
scholar might perform. But even here the broad outline is
clearer than it was a few years ago. I would add two points of
caution or of apology. First, I am only concerned to look again
at Bismarck's diplomacy, not at his work in Germany. I am
convinced that his decisive achievement was in domestic
politics and that the Bismarckian compromise or contradiction
within Germany—it comes to much the same thing—is what
mattered most in European history. Second, there can be no
doubt that Bismarck was a great man. He ran down his
predecessors and exaggerated his own achievement; he made
more mistakes than he or his admirers would admit; he
knocked sometimes at the wrong door and more often at doors
that were already open. All the same, it is impossible to read his
most casual utterance without feeling that here was someone
outsize. It would be a waste of time to try to prove anything else;
and equally unnecessary to be reiterating how great he was.

It is a great mistake to begin the story of German unification
with Bismarck's accession to power in 1862, or even to treat
the events of 1848 as a preliminary without relevance. Everything, including Bismarck's own work, springs from the
revolutionary year. It is now widely held that France or Russia
or both of them would have forbidden national unification in
1848. There seems little evidence of this. The French radicals
supposed that national Germany would be their ally in liberating Poland; and though Bastide, Foreign Minister from May
until December 1848, saw no reason to encourage a national
Germany, his only approach to Russia was made to deter the
Tsar from reviving the policy of the Holy Alliance. The Tsar's
policy in 1848 was simple: he was determined not to move his
armies beyond Russia's frontiers. Hence, he refused to intervene even in Slesvig-Holstein, though an important Russian

interest—free passage of the Sound —was at stake there. In fact the only Power who threatened action over the Elbe duchies was England, the Power which otherwise favoured German unification. This is what Palmerston meant by his complaint against 'the parcel of children' at Frankfurt. The German liberals, he thought, ought to be creating 'a natural ally' for Great Britain on the continent instead of threatening the security of the Baltic. In any case, whatever the attitude of France and Russia to a hypothetical liberal Germany, neither of them made any objection to the consolidation of north Germany under Prussia. The Erfurt union, which made Prussia supreme north of the Main, was carried through without objection from either Russia or France. It is true that the Tsar's object in intervening in Hungary was, in part, to restore a balance in central Europe between Prussia and Austria; but he held, as the French did, that this balance was improved rather than the reverse by the strengthening of Prussia in northern Germany.

Russia followed the same policy in the crisis of 1850 which ended with the agreement of Olomouc. Certainly the Tsar wished to prevent a war between Prussia and Austria; but he wanted a settlement without either victors or vanquished. His real aim was to consolidate both Prussia and Austria as a neutral conservative buffer between Russia and western Europe. Hence he declared that he would support whichever was attacked; though, in fact, at the crisis Russia promised Austria only moral support. It was not danger from Russia which led the Prussians to give way; nor, for that matter, was it military weakness. Prince William was confident that Prussia could win; and this opinion was shared by the Russian generals who had seen Austrian troops in action in Hungary. Paskievich, the Russian commander-in-chief, even believed that Prussia would be a match for Russia and Austria combined. Prussia's real weakness was that both Frederick William IV and his conservative ministers regarded war with Austria as 'wicked'. They gave way more from conviction than from fear; and after 1850, as before it, Prussia was committed to the policy of reconciling hegemony north of the Main and partnership with Austria. This was also Russia's policy, as was shown in the spring of 1851, when the Tsar forbade Schwarzenberg's programme of uniting Germany under Austria—the Empire of seventy millions.

Though Bismarck welcomed the settlement of Olomouc, no one has contributed more to the version that Prussia thereafter became subservient to Austria. This version cannot be sustained. There was perhaps subservience when Manteuffel, the Prussian foreign minister, made a defensive alliance with Austria for three years in 1851. This certainly implied a Prussian guarantee for Austria's possessions in Italy, which she steadily refused thereafter; but it also barred the way against what seemed more likely in 1851—an Austrian alliance with Napoleonic imperialism. At any rate, there was no subservience in the alliance, when it was renewed on 20 April, 1854. Though it, too, seemed to serve an Austrian purpose— by guaranteeing the Danubian principalities (later called Rumania) against Russia—this was in reality only the bait by which Austria was held from making an alliance with England and France. If Austria had joined the Western Powers in war against Russia, Prussia could not have stayed out. Whichever side she joined, she would have had to bear the main brunt of a war fought probably on her own soil—a war from which she could not possibly have gained and in which she might well have lost her Polish lands. As it was, Prussia performed the great service to Russia of keeping Austria neutral at no cost to herself; and, by advocating neutrality at the Diet, won the leadership of the German states as well. Yet this was the time when Bismarck denounced the incompetence of his official superiors. He opposed the alliance with Austria. At the beginning of the war he would seem to have favoured supporting Russia; at the end of it he preached, in one of his most famous compositions, that Prussia should make a third in the coming partnership between Russia and France. His own action in 1879 is the best comment on this policy. As Imperial Chancellor, Bismarck judged Manteuffel to have been right and himself wrong; but he took care not to say so.

Bismarck overrated all along the dynamism of the Franco-Russian entente. He thought that Napoleon III and Alexander II were set on remaking the map of Europe, both east and west, in the immediate future and that Prussia must hasten to play the jackal with them if she were not to be left out of things. Official Prussian policy, whether under Frederick William IV and Manteuffel or under the Prince Regent and the despised Schleinitz, stuck to its old line: support for Austria once she had recognized Prussian hegemony north of the Main. This policy came within sight of success in the Italian war of 1859. If Napoleon had insisted on his original aim of liberating Venetia as well as Lombardy, even more if Alexander II had taken the opportunity to reopen the Eastern Question—in fact, if France and Russia had been as dynamic as Bismarck supposed—Austria would have had to pay Prussia's price. As it was, she lost Lombardy and thus ended the war without Prussia's help. The real turning point came in the following year, 1860. In July Schleinitz and Rechberg, the Austrian foreign minister, met at Teplitz and agreed on a defensive alliance between their two countries—an alliance which Bismarck himself quoted as a precedent in 1879. The awkward question of Prussian hegemony north of the Main was postponed to a military convention that was to be negotiated subsequently. All this was a preliminary to a meeting of the two German rulers with the Tsar at Warsaw in September. They believed that Alexander II had taken fright at Napoleon's revolutionary policy and would now urge joint resistance in Italy. When it came to the point Alexander II could not give up his hopes for revising the settlement of 1856 in the Near East with French help and therefore would do nothing against Italy, Napoleon's satellite. The Holy Alliance turned out to be a mirage; and the Prussians were quick to draw the lesson. They screwed up their terms in the military discussions with Austria; and when these broke down, the alliance vanished with them. If there was a decisive moment in the relations between Prussia and Austria, it was in April 1861, and not after Bismarck became Prime Minister.

Bismarck's predecessors perhaps had different allies in mind. Schleinitz counted on the 'liberal' alliance with England, so far as he counted on anything at all. This policy was ruined by the American civil war, which locked up British military resources in Canada. Moreover, the British were increasingly aware that their navy was out of date. These factors, rather than any ideological swing towards isolationism, made Great Britain ineffective during Europe's years of destiny. Bernstorff who followed Schleinitz looked instead to France; his object was to replace Russia as France's continental ally. When Bismarck arrived in October 1862, he certainly meant to play the role of a Prussian Cavour; but with this difference from Cavour (as from Bernstorff) that he intended to co-operate with Russia as well as with France—a partnership therefore

c

that would be anti-British as well as anti-Austrian. In fact he
missed the bus (if there was ever one to catch). He assumed
that the Franco-Russian entente was solid; instead it collapsed
before he had been in office six months. Almost his first act
was to ask in Paris what the French attitude would be 'if things
hot up in Germany'. He was too late. Drouyn de Lhuys,
enemy of Russia and advocate of alliance with Austria, had just
returned to the Quai d'Orsay. Bismarck's query was brushed
aside. Three months later the Polish revolt blew the Franco-
Russian entente sky-high. Years afterwards Bismarck built up
the story that he had pulled off a great stroke of policy by
supporting the Russians in Poland and therefore winning their
gratitude. This is untrue. The Russians thought they could
deal with the Poles alone and much resented Prussian patronage. Moreover Bismarck's step ensured that, if it came to war
over Poland, Prussia would have to fight for the sake of
Russia's Polish lands; and he had to beg to be excused from
the alliance with Russia within six weeks of making it. Even
as it was, the quarrel over Poland was disastrous for Prussia.
The great hope of Prussian policy had been that the French
threat to Venetia and Russian threats in the Near East would
so embarrass Austria as to make her surrender the hegemony
of northern Germany to Prussia without a war. This hope was
now ruined. The Franco-Russian entente had never been a
threat to Prussia; rather it gave her security. The entente was
directed against Austria; and France would not endanger it by
seeking gains on the Rhine. The French threat there, if it ever
existed, was created by the estrangement between France and
Russia, not by their entente. No doubt Russia was now prepared to tolerate a Prussian war against France; but so she
always had been, and this was a very different thing from
active support—that the Russians never offered.

The truth is that, once the Franco-Russian entente broke
down, Prussia was forced back to friendship with Austria as
her only means of security. Here again Bismarck later created
a myth—the story that the Slesvig-Holstein affair was a trap
for Austria from the beginning. I think rather that, as so often,
Bismarck, always impulsive and always exaggeratedly nervous
of the aggressive designs of others, rushed himself into a
commitment and then had to exercise all his great genius in
order to get out of a tangle of his own making. For there is
the fact. In January 1864 he made an alliance with Austria

which did not include that recognition of Prussian hegemony north of the Main on which his predecessors had always insisted. His motive was fear, not gain; fear that, as in 1848, Prussia would be pushed forward in Slesvig by German feeling and then have to face a coalition of the Powers, reinforced this time by Austria. The Conference of London which tried to settle the Slesvig question showed that these fears were exaggerated. The Russian government was estranged from the Western Powers both by the Crimean War and, more recently, by the Polish affair. Besides, the Russians did not object to Prussia's gaining control of the Sound as long as she did not do it on a basis of nationalist enthusiasm. They objected much more to Austria's getting a foothold there and would have preferred an isolated Prussian action. Thus, curiously enough, the partnership with Austria—which Bismarck had insisted on as essential—was the one thing that worried the Russians and made them hostile. Still they did not mean to act in 1864—as, for that matter, they had refused anything but moral reproofs in regard to Slesvig both in 1848 and 1850. The real opposition in the previous crises had come from England; and the British —estranged from Russia by the Crimean War, suspicious of Napoleon III as a result of his annexation of Savoy, and with their forces tied in Canada—had no means of action. It is inconceivable that there could ever have been an Anglo-Austrian alliance to check Prussia in Slesvig; and, short of this, there was nothing the British could do. They twice took soundings for French support, in February and again in June. Both met with the same response. Napoleon would not act against the 'national' principle; Drouyn, who hated nationalism in general and Prussia in particular, demanded concrete gains on the Rhine—a prospect more unwelcome to the British than the Danish loss of the Duchies.

The three non-German Powers were in fact far more suspicious of each other than concerned about what might happen in Germany. The only thing that alarmed them was Prussia's alliance with Austria—Bismarck's own doing. Had he acted alone against Denmark, he would have had the approval of all the Powers except Austria; but he would have had to act on a liberal basis. Prussia's foreign danger, in short, was increased, if not created, by Bismarck's conflict with the liberals. He made the Austrian alliance, not to trick Austria, but to save himself. This is, I think, the answer to the disputed question

whether Bismarck was ever sincere in his conservative partnership with Austria. He was a man of extremes. He could conceive a full return to the system of Metternich; hence in
August 1864 he pressed on Austria not only a Prussian
guarantee of Venetia, but a campaign for the recovery of
Lombardy. He could also conceive of a 'revolutionary' alliance
with France, by which Prussia expelled Austria from Germany
north of the Main while France gained land on the Rhine.
What he never foresaw was the moderate outcome—neither
reactionary nor revolutionary—for which he has been so much
praised. Moderation is said to be the most difficult of policies;
it was certainly difficult for Bismarck.

I make no doubt that the offer of an alliance which he made
to Austria in August 1864 was genuine. It seemed to him 'in
the logic of the situation'. If Prussia was not to follow a revolutionary course, she must follow a reactionary one. Once more
he asked less than his predecessors. In his exaggerated fear of
French aggression, he offered Austria alliance against France
without demanding Prussian hegemony north of the Main.
William I, not Bismarck, insisted on this condition; and the
Austrians thought Prussia so dependent on their support that
they named Silesia as their price. The deadlock drove Bismarck off on the alternative 'revolutionary' course. He screwed
up tension against Austria; and in May 1865 spoke openly of
his policy as 'war against Austria in alliance with France'. A
new compromise followed in August 1865, the Treaty of
Gastein. This compromise came mainly from the side of the
Austrians; and Bismarck accepted it merely because it was
offered. But he was also bewildered by the failure of his
'revolutionary' policy to explode. When he approached the
French for an alliance, they refused to display territorial
ambitions. Napoleon went ostentatiously into the country; and
left policy to be defined by Drouyn the conservative.

In October 1865 Bismarck visited Napoleon at Biarritz in
order to clear up the mystery of French policy. It is often said
that he tricked Napoleon by vague talk of future French gains
in Germany. This is not so. It is true that the two rogues
discussed 'advantages which might offer themselves un-
sought', advantages, of course, in Germany; but this was a
casual theme. Napoleon's overriding interest was Venetia; he
was determined to complete the work of 1859 and not leave to
his son 'a volcano for a throne'. His price was Venetia; and

Bismarck paid it. He promised that he would not guarantee Venetia to Austria; and in return Napoleon promised that he would not make an alliance with Austria against Prussia—'he would not go and stand beside a target'. This was the essential bargain of Biarritz: Venetia for Italy, and French neutrality in a war between Prussia and Austria. Bismarck gave the bargain a positive shape when he concluded his alliance with Italy in April 1866; this ensured Napoleon that he would get what he wanted, and Bismarck was able to wage a limited war against Austria. Napoleon, not Bismarck, made the moderate programme possible and enabled Prussia to win hegemony north of the Main without a general European upheaval. To the very last Bismarck could not believe in his own success. In May 1866 he offered the Austrians peace if they would share the military headship of Germany. The Austrians would have agreed if they could have had in exchange a Prussian guarantee of Venetia; this, owing to his bargain with Napoleon, was the one thing that Bismarck could not give. Venetia compelled Bismarck to go to war. It also compelled Napoleon to favour war—it was the factor which wrecked his proposal for a European Congress. Most paradoxically of all, it even led the Austrians to want war. By May 1866 they had come to believe that the only way out of their difficulties was to surrender Venetia and gain Silesia in exchange. This would win Napoleon as an ally against both Prussia and Russia; it would free their southern frontier; and it would restore their prestige in Germany. But it was only possible by means of war against Prussia. Therefore, in the last resort, it was the Austrians who were eager to bring the war on. It is a curious fact that every European war between 1815 and 1914 was exploded by the Power standing on the defensive: England and France insisted on the Crimean War; Austria on the wars of 1859, 1866, and 1914; and France on the war of 1870. It is also a curiosity how little military considerations weighed in the decision to provoke war or to avoid it. Thus, the Prussians accepted the compromise of August 1865, although they were confident of victory. There is little foundation for the later story that they put off war until they could clinch their military superiority by making an alliance with Italy. And this alliance, when it was made in April 1866, was concluded for its political effect on Napoleon, rather than to divide the Austrian armies—this again was an advantage which the Prussians only discovered after it happened. On the other side, the Austrians did not provoke war in June 1866 because their military position had improved, but because it had got worse; they could bear the tension no longer. Finally, the French decision not to intervene after the Prussian victory at Sadova sprang purely from considerations of policy; the question whether the French army was capable of intervention was hardly raised. I am not sure whether any conclusion can be drawn from this odd ignoring of the basic facts.

There is another oddity. The war between Austria and Prussia had been on the horizon for sixteen years. Yet it had great difficulty in getting itself declared. Austria tried to provoke Bismarck by placing the question of the Duchies before the Diet on 1 June. Bismarck retaliated by occupying Holstein. He hoped that the Austrian troops there would resist, but they got away before he could catch them. On 14 June the Austrian motion for federal mobilization against Prussia was carried in the Diet. Prussia declared the confederation at an end; and on 15 June invaded Saxony. On 21 June, when Prussian troops reached the Austrian frontier, the Crown Prince, who was in command, merely notified the nearest Austrian officer that 'a state of war' existed. That was all. The Italians did a little better. La Marmora sent a declaration of war to Albrecht, the Austrian commander-in-chief, before taking the offensive. Both Italy and Prussia were committed to programmes which could not be justified in international law, and were bound to appear as aggressors if they put their claims on paper. They would, in fact, have been hard put to it to start the war if Austria had not done the job for them.

The war of 1866 was not the revolutionary war which had been preached by Bismarck until his visit to Biarritz; it was the moderate war as always envisaged by the Prussian statesmen whom Bismarck had despised. It is often regarded as something of a miracle that Bismarck carried it through without intervention from either France or Russia; but in truth neither of them had any objection to a Prussian hegemony in northern Germany which is all that was accomplished. The Russians, in any case, were in no state to intervene. For fifteen years after the Crimean War they almost ceased to be a military power so far as Europe was concerned. Between 1856 and 1863 the annual call-up for the army was not enforced; and the Polish revolt in 1863, itself caused by an attempted call-up, further delayed their recovery. They owed their security during this period of neglect to the Prussian buffer; and were therefore glad to see it strengthened. No doubt they would have expostulated if Bismarck had annexed the states of southern Germany or dismembered the Austrian Empire, but this was never on the programme. His moderation against Austria in 1866 has been much vaunted. Yet even he put up his terms. He excluded Austria from Germany, instead of dividing it with her at the Main. The King and the generals, who grumbled at his moderation, merely wanted some satisfactions of prestige—annexation of some Austrian territory in Silesia or a victory-march through Vienna. They certainly had no thought of destroying the Habsburg Empire. Nor is it true that Austria was reconciled by Bismarck's moderation. The Austrians had burnt their fingers in 1866 and meant to take less risks next time; but they still hoped for a next time. The war of 1866 was a milestone, not a turning-point, in Austro-Prussian relations.

The real turning-point, for all Europe, was, no doubt, that France did not intervene; but even the dramatic nature of this has been exaggerated owing to the fact that history has been written by those who opposed or regretted the decision, while Napoleon, the man who made it, remained silent. He had made up his mind all along; he was on the side of 'the revolution', on the side, that is, of Prussia in Germany, as he had been on the side of Sardinia in Italy. There was no real crisis of decision in Paris between 4 July and 10 July. It was simply that Napoleon, having deceived his ministers from the first, had now to override them. He thought—and perhaps rightly —that the European situation had changed in his favour; Prussia stronger than before and therefore less dependent on Russia; Austria excluded from Germany and therefore freer to balance Russia in the Near East; Italy contented with the acquisition of Venetia; and southern Germany 'internationally independent'. Even if he had known of the Prussian treaties of alliance with the southern States, he would have regarded this as an improvement on the German confederation. Then southern Germany had been guaranteed by both Prussia and Austria; now by Prussia alone, and with her Napoleon had no quarrel. Indeed he took Bismarck's breath away by insisting on Prussia's annexing the whole of north Germany—a victory for the revolution over moderation.

In the summer of 1866 Napoleon supposed that he had at last achieved the revolutionary coalition with Prussia and Italy; and he meant to complete it by resurrecting his entente with Russia. He was of course misled by the analogy with Italy. He supposed that, since the Italians continued to need protection against Austria, Prussia needed it also; and his half-hearted demands for compensation, which culminated in the attempted annexation of Luxembourg in March 1867, were all designed to make an alliance with Prussia acceptable to French public opinion. It is common to speak of these negotiations and especially the Luxembourg affair, as a trap which Bismarck laid for the French. If it was a trap, why did he not spring it? The truth is simpler. The affair was not of Bismarck's seeking; it was thrust on him by the French and, though no doubt he had to consider German feeling, he would have welcomed an alliance with France, if Russia had been included in it. There, it seems to me, is the real explanation. The key to European diplomacy between 1866 and 1870 is to be found in the Near East, and not on the Rhine or even in Poland. So long as Russia and France were at loggerheads in the Near East, Bismarck could not let Luxembourg go to France without implicitly taking her side against Russia. But equally he refused a Russian offer to keep Austria neutral, because this also involved paying a price in the Near East. In April 1867 at the height of the Luxembourg crisis, he first suggested the solution that was his ultimate favourite: the revival of the Holy Alliance. It was contemptuously refused by both the other parties. Austria would not join without concessions in Germany; Russia would not guarantee the integrity of Austria nor allow her gains in the Balkans. The Eastern Question dictated a peaceful outcome of the Luxembourg affair. France would not allow Russia a free hand against Turkey; Prussia would not allow her a free hand against Austria. Therefore both botched up the Luxembourg question as best they could. The great turning-point had been reached without design and before anyone noticed it. Both French and German public opinion had taken a hand in diplomacy; and henceforth they were not to be reconciled—perhaps not even to the present day.

There is not much to be said of Bismarck's diplomacy between 1867 and 1870. As always when the Near East took the centre of the stage, he had none except to keep out of the way; or, at most, to act as honest broker when the conflicts of

the other Powers threatened to involve Prussia. When the
Franco-Russian entente seemed to be working in the Near
East during the autumn of 1867, he played in with it; and,
with Italy joining in too, this was the last display of the
'revolutionary coalition'. Bismarck backed out of the Near
East as soon as the entente broke down, so as not to be left
alone on the Russian side. In March 1868 he refused a direct
Russian demand for an alliance against Austria-Hungary,
though 'of course neither Power could afford to allow the
destruction of the other'. In the autumn of 1868 he used the
Hohenzollern family influence to damp down irredentist
agitation in Rumania, so as to avoid having to choose between
Russia and Austria-Hungary; and in 1869 he helped Russia
and France to wind up the Cretan affair. He never took
seriously the talk of an alliance between Austria-Hungary
and France; it was, he said, 'conjectural rubbish', as indeed
it turned out to be. He calculated quite rightly that the Habsburg government would never dare to offend Hungarian and
Austrian-German feeling by supporting French interference
in southern Germany; and equally that Napoleon would not
break with Russia for the sake of Austria-Hungary. This
disposes of the defence put up for Bismarck by some of his
admirers that he had to provoke war against France in order
to anticipate either an Austro-French or a Franco-Russian
agreement. There was never any serious chance of the first;
and the second offered Prussia advantages, not dangers.

There is a simpler defence of Bismarck's policy in 1870,
that is, if he needs one: he did not provoke the war at all,
except in the narrowest sense of exploding it at the last
moment. Later on, when the war had become a national
legend, Bismarck tried to take the credit for it; but it was un-
earned. Of course the Hohenzollern candidature for the throne
of Spain was of his making. Its object was to act as a check on
France, not to provoke her into war. His encouragement of or
indifference towards the Spanish affair varied inversely with
the Franco-Russian entente. When France and Russia were
on good terms, this gave Prussia security, both against Austria-
Hungary and against being involved in an eastern war; whenever they quarrelled, he looked round for other means of
distracting French attention from the Rhine. He first took up
the Hohenzollern candidature in February 1869, when Russia
and France were in dispute over Crete. He dropped it as soon

c*

as they settled the question; and left it alone so long as their entente seemed within sight of renewal. He revived it once more, in the spring of 1870, when the Franco-Russian approach broke down. But the Hohenzollern candidature was primarily not a move in foreign policy at all. Bismarck's overriding concern was with southern Germany; and a Hohenzollern on the Spanish throne—like the project of declaring William I German Emperor which he aired at the same time—was designed to raise Prussian prestige south of the Main. In June 1870 Alexander II met Bismarck and William I at Ems —one of the many legendary meetings at which a war was supposed to have been plotted. In fact war against France was never mentioned. Bismarck expressed disapproval of Habsburg policy in the Near East; and he tried to persuade the Tsar that the south German princes would make a better bargain with William I than if they waited to be swept away by a more democratic wave in favour of his liberal successor. There could hardly be clearer evidence that Bismarck was not expecting the Franco-Prussian war at that time.

Of the actual war-crisis in July 1870 two things seem to me clear beyond all doubt, if one can escape from the layers of myth and prejudice. First, no one could have expected it to explode in the way that it did. According to all rational calculation, Leopold of Hohenzollern ought to have been on the throne of Spain before the French, or anyone else, knew what was happening. The actual leakage was due to the blunder of a cipher-clerk in the German legation at Madrid—an unpredictable event. Second, no one could have expected the French to turn the crisis into a war. Bismarck thought the affair would end in a humiliation for Prussia. That is why he stayed in the country and left William I to do the negotiating. The course of events was a setback for Bismarck, though he quickly made the best of things. So far as he had a settled policy, it was to incorporate southern Germany with Russian and even French approval—a decisive stroke against Austria and back to the dynamic coalition with France and Russia that he had always favoured. After all, he believed, rightly, that the Empire was the form of French government most favourable to Prussian interests; and he went on trying to restore Napoleon III even at the beginning of 1871. He had sometimes thought that a French revolution would lead to war; it was quite against his intentions that war led to a French revolution.

It is a further myth that Bismarck's diplomacy secured the neutrality of Russia and Austria-Hungary. Neither Power ever had any intention or inclination to go to war. Bismarck made no promises to the Russians of support in the Near East; and they made no promises to him. The Russians did not mobilize any troops in Galicia—they had, in fact, none to mobilize. They did not threaten Austria-Hungary. They promised the Austrians to stay neutral, if Austria-Hungary did the same; but in view of their military weakness, they would have stayed neutral in any case. For that matter, they did not believe that their interests would be injured by a French victory over Prussia—nor by a Prussian victory over France. The Austrians remained neutral solely from consideration of their own interests also. Beust wished to mobilize in order to intervene after the decisive battles had been fought; and, since he expected France to win that battle, his intention was to protect southern Germany against her. Andrássy, too, favoured mobilization; only he insisted on a declaration of neutrality so that, after the French victory which he also expected, both France and Prussia could be persuaded to join a crusade against Russia. This was as crazy as most of Andrássy's schemes. Gorchakov, the Russian chancellor, passed the correct verdict on the French dreams for an Austrian alliance when he said: 'Russia did not paralyse a support which had no chance of being realized.' Neither Russia or Austria-Hungary cared which way the war went in western Europe. So far as there was any element of calculation in their policy, it was simply that, once France was out of the way, Germany would no longer be able to follow a neutral line in the Near East—the only topic that interested them.

From Bismarck's point of view, the war of 1870 was a senseless affair; and he admitted as much in his many later apologies to the French. So far as he had any responsibility for it (and he did not have much), this sprang from his desire to weaken German liberalism by making France the national enemy instead of Russia. Whatever the responsibilities, the consequences of dividing Germany with Austria and of quarrelling with France were all that Bismarck had foreseen in his days at Frankfurt. Vienna took Berlin prisoner. In the Crimean War Prussian statesmen had worked to prevent Austria's going to the assistance of the western Powers; in the Bulgarian crisis of 1887 Bismarck had to implore the British to go to the assistance of Austria-Hungary; and a generation later his successors had to go to her assistance themselves. In 1879 Bismarck, and none other, tied 'the trim Prussian frigate to the worm-eaten Austrian galleon'—tied them together for good, although the galleon was now more worm-eaten by a generation. Was this really a triumph for his diplomacy?

To my mind, the younger Bismarck was the greater one— the Bismarck who modelled himself on Cavour rather than the Bismarck who modelled himself on Metternich, the 'mad Junker' rather than the sane one. He saw clearly that a national reconstruction of central Europe in co-operation with Russia and France was the wisest course for Prussia. But, when it came to the point, he himself prevented this. He overrated, no doubt, Russian and French dynamism; and when this failed swung away on the opposite tack. But his rejection of his own earlier policy had a deeper cause. The national principle in Europe only made sense on a liberal basis, as Cavour appreciated. Both Bismarck and Napoleon III hated the liberalism which was essential to the success of their foreign policy. Napoleon pretended to accept it; Bismarck hardly troubled to make the pretence. Germany and France could not work together except on a liberal basis; hence Napoleon III and Bismarck between them ensured that they would not work together at all. Everything sprang from this failure. Without French co-operation, Germany could not risk a national remaking of eastern Europe by Russia; therefore she had to prop up Austria-Hungary. The diplomacy of Bismarck's later years was simply an elaborate jugglery to conceal the fact that he had abandoned his earlier visions and had been forced to repeat, or even to outdo, the mistakes of his predecessors. It is curious, and more than a coincidence, that in the very weeks when Bismarck was founding his so-called 'league of peace' by means of the Austro-German alliance, Gladstone was formulating his principles of international co-operation in the Midlothian campaign. Nor is it, I think, an accident that in every subsequent world-conflict, Bismarck's heirs, the boasted real-politikers, have always been defeated by the heirs of Gladstone, those who hope to make the world anew. Once Bismarck had been one of these. He set out to remake central Europe. Instead he tied himself to the Habsburgs, and, like everyone who follows this path, ended up by believing that peace could be kept by tricks.

X

THE FAILURE OF
THE HABSBURG MONARCHY

THE HABSBURG MONARCHY was the toughest organization in the history of modern Europe; no other has stood up so long to such battering from so many sides. The Habsburgs rode out the storm of the Reformation; withstood the impact of the Turks; challenged Louis XIV; and survived the French revolution. The age of nationalism was their doom. This reason alone would justify a new analysis of the national problem in the Habsburg Empire. And there are others. In 1919, after the First World War, the national State seemed to be the pattern for the future. Now we are not so sure. Even the old-established national States of western Europe are drawing together in terms of incipient federalism; how much less likely is it that the national States of eastern Europe will survive in undiminished sovereignty. Thirty years ago writers tended to regard the great Habsburg Empire as the 'normal' civilized order from which the national States were an unfortunate decline; then, for a short time, men regarded the national States as something equally 'normal' and yet more final. Now we are coming to recognize that both were transitory like all else in history; Francis Joseph could not live for ever nor could the world stand still in 1919. The present system in eastern Europe has elements of federalism, mixed up in its communist dictatorship; and it is almost certain that no future swing of events will bring back either the Habsburgs or the national States with unrestricted sovereignty. Thus it is rewarding, at any rate as a preliminary exercise, to analyse not only the national problem in the Habsburg Monarchy, but also the attempts to reconcile nationalism with a supranational structure.[1]

This is what Professor Kann has attempted to do in his two

[1] Robert A. Kann, *The Multinational Empire*. Nationalism and National Reform in the Habsburg Monarchy, 1848–1918. Vol. i, Empire and Nationalities. Vol. ii, Empire Reform.

formidable volumes. They provide more material for a study
of the problem than has hitherto existed in any single book in
English. His work, it must be admitted, is rather uncritical. It is
an anatomy in Burton's sense, not an analysis. Material is
accumulated; quotations are piled one on top of another without discrimination. Altogether his book illustrates the modern
delusion that if only we know enough facts we shall arrive at
the answer. This is particularly true of his first volume, which
sets out to present the national problem. Kann recognizes, of
course, that nationalism is tangled up with history; and he
elaborates two principles that are common to all discussions of
the Habsburg Monarchy. One is the division between the
nations with a history—the Germans, the Magyars, and even
the Czechs—and the nations whose cultural tradition had been
completely broken, such as the Slovaks or the Ruthenes. The
other is the doctrine of 'historico-political individualities',
by which historical units, such as Hungary or Bohemia, were
identified with national claims (Magyar or Czech) which did
not in fact correspond with them. Thus history bedevilled the
national problem in a twofold way. The nations with a history
despised the nations without a history; moreover, they tried to
enforce against them, or even against other nations with a
history, claims based on history, not on national right. The
Magyars insisted on the unity of Hungary against the subject
races; the Czechs insisted on the unity of Bohemia against the
Germans; the Germans, for that matter, tried to maintain the
unity of a German-controlled empire against all comers.

Kann further recognizes that there were in the Habsburg
Monarchy two sorts of nationalism; the nationalism of landowners and the nationalism of professors—the one traditional,
the other academic. But he does not push this analysis far
enough. Like most liberal writers, he dismisses Magyar
nationalism as 'feudal' and never makes the vital point that its
real standard-bearers were the petty gentry, not the great
aristocrats. If Hungary had had to depend solely on the
Andrássys and Apponyis, its nationalism would have been as
artificial as was the Czech movement in the days when it looked
to the Thuns and Clam-Martinics. When we come to academic
or cultural nationalism, the distinctions are more complicated
and more essential. The first age of national awakening is
strictly academic. It is led by university professors and is concerned with such things as the study of mediaeval manuscripts,

the evolution of a national language from a peasant dialect, and the rewriting of history on national lines. The second stage comes when the pupils of the professors get out into the world. Then it is a question of the language used first in secondary, finally in elementary schools; the battle is fought over popular newspapers, not over learned works of research. Finally, the elementary school-teachers themselves have pupils: men of some education, who remain peasants or factory workers. We have arrived at mass-nationalism; what Kann calls, without analysing it, the integral nationalism of the twentieth century.

Each of these nationalisms is different in character, in its demands, in the weight of its support. Incredible as it may seem, Kann does not attempt these distinctions; he does not even attempt to estimate the numbers of supporters that any national movement had at any particular moment. Yet there can never be a time at which, say, the equation 'German equals German nationalist' is true. Kann accepts the consequences of this without understanding the reasons for it. He discusses the two non-national movements of the Social Democrats and the Christian Socials; but the point is lost. Yet it is a simple one. Only when nationalism becomes a mass movement do the mass movements become important. On the other hand, at this very time, they begin to lose their non-national character. In the last decade of the Habsburg Monarchy both international socialism and international clericalism were beginning to disintegrate under the impact of nationalism; and the process was carried further in the inter-war years. Nowadays even communism is shaken by the nationalist heresy.

The second volume of Kann's book deals with the attempts at reform. But, since there has been no real diagnosis, the reader is constantly puzzled by the question: 'What is it they were trying to solve?' Of course, the men of the time were equally puzzled by this question; hence perhaps their failure. It was commonly believed that the national question was a question of administration. If men could have officials, teachers, and judges using the national language, they would be satisfied. The example of Hungary was decisive and misleading. There can be no dispute that autonomous local administration in the *comitats* was the secret of Hungary's success both in surviving as a nation and then in defeating Habsburg encroachments. But it did not follow from this that, if other nationalities got autonomous local government, they too would automatically repeat Hungary's success. In fact, under dualism, Hungary became a centralized modern State and the *comitats* an empty form, at the very time when centralization was being weakened in the rest of the Empire for the sake of local autonomy. The explanation was simple. Local autonomy was a vital weapon so long as it was a question of resisting the central government; as soon as this battle had been won, it became useless and even an embarrassment. If the *comitats* had remained genuinely autonomous they would have been captured by the nationalities; and Hungary would have ceased to be a Magyar State.

In the last resort the national question is not a question of schools or of government officials—these are mere preliminaries. It is a question of power. Men wish to decide their own destinies. In a national State this leads them to resist kings and emperors and to demand democracy. In a multinational State they resist the rule of other nationalities as well. The Czechs or Rumanians or Ruthenians did not wish merely to use their own languages in school or in the courts; they were determined not to be involved in wars for the sake of German supremacy or for Magyar and Polish causes. The most extraordinary thing in all the discussions about the 'Austrian problem' is the question always left out: who was to rule? Or rather, the omission was deliberate. Every so-called solution assumed that the Habsburgs would remain in supreme control in Vienna; hence the only problem to be solved was that of local administration. Anybody can think of satisfactory schemes for chopping up the Empire into national units or historical units or a mixture of both, which would have done quite well if they had settled the essential problem; in reality they were remote from it. The more perfectly the central parliament represented the different nationalities of the Empire the more futile it became; for the more it was divided. The basic misunderstanding can be seen in the very title of Kann's book. The Habsburg Monarchy was not a multinational empire; it was a supranational empire. Nations can perhaps co-operate if they have a common loyalty to bind them together; they cannot co-operate, at any rate within a single State, merely for the sake of co-operating. The Habsburgs had once provided the common loyalty; in the nineteenth century they failed to do so any longer, and it was this Habsburg failure, not the rise of the nationalities, which doomed their Empire.

The Habsburgs are missing from Kann's book—missing that is as a principle and a cause. Francis Joseph appears merely as ruler, playing the same role as, say, a President of the United States. But Americans are not loyal to President Truman as such; they are loyal to the constitution, to the American 'idea'. The Habsburgs failed to find 'an idea'. How could they be expected to find one? For them, as much as for the nationalities, politics was a question of power; and, so far as they were concerned, it was a question of foreign power. One of the great blunders of modern political thinking is to invent an abstract entity called the State. Many States can be organizations for welfare or internal order, or whatever else suits the theorist. But some half-dozen States, called the Great Powers, are organizations primarily for power—that is, for fighting wars or for preventing them. Hence all analogies between the Habsburg Monarchy and, say, Switzerland break down. The Habsburg Monarchy was a Great Power or it was nothing. If it could have survived in war against other Great Powers it would not have undergone national disintegration.

The practical historian is thus driven back to analysing the failures of Habsburg power—failure in its armaments, failure in its system of communications, failure in its food supplies, above all failure in its foreign policy. The Habsburgs were fond of finding their doom in a 'Piedmont'; first in the original Piedmont, which nearly brought disaster to them in 1859; then in Serbia, which was the 'Piedmont of the South Slavs'. This analysis, correct enough in its way, has been much misunderstood. The essence of a 'Piedmont' was not that it represented a national challenge; the Habsburgs could deal with such. A 'Piedmont' rejected any need for the Habsburgs at all; it was a rival Power. Both Italy and the South Slav State wished to destroy the Habsburg Monarchy, not to reform it; both would have turned with a smile from the elegant plans of reform catalogued by Kann. It is ironical that they should now be the two States which feel most acutely the consequences of the Monarchy's disappearance: both have Russia on their borders. In the last resort the Habsburg Monarchy was not a device for enabling a number of nationalities to live together. It was an attempt to find a 'third way' in central Europe which should be neither German nor Russian. Once the Habsburgs became Germany's satellites in war they had failed in their mission. Their doom was of their own making.

XI

THOMAS GARRIGUE MASARYK

T. G. MASARYK, the Founder-President of Czechoslovakia, was born on 7 March 1850. Though the centenary of his birth will now pass unnoticed in the country he created, nothing can weaken his position as one of the great men of our century; even if his work prove barren, he demonstrated the nobility of the human race. His political career began in earnest when he had already been superannuated as a university professor. If he had died at the age of sixty-five, he would have been remembered only as a sociological writer who exposed some judicial scandals in Austria-Hungary.

His extra years turned him into a maker of history. Between 1915 and 1918 Masaryk brought nations into being and drew the lines for a new map of Europe. Yet Masaryk was not an extreme nationalist. He incurred the hostility of the Czechs by exposing their most famous mediaeval manuscripts as forgeries; and before 1914 he was one of the few Czechs who strove sincerely to transform the Habsburg Monarchy into a democratic federation of peoples.

Unlike most nationalist leaders, Masaryk understood power. He called himself a realist and practised 'Realpolitik' in the Bismarckian manner. Indeed he was more of a realist than Bismarck, for he knew how to use the force of ideals. He said late in life: 'Democracy is the rule of the people, but there can be no government without obedience and discipline.' His predecessors had demanded obedience from hereditary right; he claimed it from force of character. For Masaryk was a man born to rule.

Fear of Pan-Germanism, and the determination to be rid of it, was the motive of his political actions. Certainly he desired freedom for his people; but he would have been less uncompromising in his resistance to Pan-Germanism if he had not believed that it rejected the values of European civilization. He did not hate Germany; he wished 'to force Germany to be human' by preventing her rule over others. The events of 1914 convinced him that the Habsburg Monarchy had lost all independent existence; it had become merely an instrument by which Slav peoples were forced to fight for the German domination of Europe. Thus he sought an alternative to Austria-Hungary, something which would perform the Habsburg 'mission' more successfully. He found this more effective barrier to German mastery in the small nations of Central and Eastern Europe; and claimed that national freedom was the only way of organizing this great middle zone.

Masaryk tuned his arguments to his audience when he set out to convince the statesmen of the Western Powers: spoke of the rights of nationalities, of the cause of democratic freedom, and of great moral principles. These, though genuine convictions, represented only part of his realistic approach. He was well aware that the small nations of East-Central Europe could not hold their own unaided against German power; and his aim was to combine national freedom with security, not to let nationalism run riot.

Masaryk sought to overcome the weakness of German's neighbours by national amalgamation. He did not merely voice national claims; he invented nations. Arguing from the case of partitioned Poland, he represented the Czechs and Slovaks as a single people who would come together as Czechoslovaks when partition was ended; and he had the same programme for the Serbs and the Croats. Himself a Slovak, though born in Moravia, he genuinely believed that the Slovaks would gladly accept Czech history as a substitute for that which they lacked themselves and would regard Hus and Comenius as Slovak heroes. Similarly, he expected the Serbs and Croats to overlook the religious and historical differences which had lasted for a thousand years. It is curious that a professor even of sociology should have been so contemptuous of history; but for Masaryk culture was humanistic, not historical. He admired Hus and Comenius because of what they stood for, not because they were figures in Czech history; and he expected others to do the same.

He thought that nations could be remade at will, if the will were sufficiently noble; and his will was so noble that he partly succeeded. Though Yugoslavia could never be more than a federation of nations, Czechoslovakia became in some sort a genuine national State bound together by common loyalties. But this ideal of a humanistic nationalism was confined to the 'humane' classes; it lost its hold when the agrarian and urban masses came to determine the shape of politics.

Masaryk never supposed that the national amalgams could face out the German threat without assistance. Czechoslovakia and the other succession States were to give the middle zone internal peace; but their existence was to be underwritten by the support of the victorious Allies. In 1914 opinion in Western Europe had only a vague sentiment in favour of national freedom; Masaryk turned this sentiment towards concrete reality. With some justice, though with less than was supposed, he represented the Czechoslovaks as 'peoples struggling to be free'. But his plans were not based solely on support from France and the Anglo-Saxon Powers. He wrote in March 1917:

> Will Great Britain join forces with Russia, or does she consider Germany to be less dangerous to her world empire than Russia? This is the question which Great Britain has to decide, and on her decision will depend the future of the Old and the New World.

It was a disaster for Masaryk when West and East were estranged by the Bolshevik revolution; and he never gave up trying to bring Russia back into European affairs—sometimes by seeking to be reconciled with the Bolsheviks, sometimes by preparing their overthrow. For though always a man of Western culture and never sympathetic to Pan-Slavism, Masaryk was realist enough to know that Germany and Russia would partition Eastern Europe unless Russia was on good terms with the Western Powers.

Except for the name of Czechoslovakia little now seems to remain of Masaryk's work. The national amalgams have not held: Czechs and Slovaks, Croats and Serbs are separate peoples; federalism in Yugoslavia, not national union in Czechoslovakia, has been successful; and all Eastern Europe, except for Yugoslavia, has escaped from German tyranny only to fall under Russian control. For this Russia is not alone to blame. If Western countries saw the peril of Pan-Germanism as clearly as Masaryk did we should not be in our present position. The essential condition which Masaryk laid down, though perhaps now unattainable, remains true: only co-operation between Russia and the Anglo-Saxon Powers can give Europe peace and security. And in spite of the failures of the present there is in Masaryk's life a deeper lesson: nationalism without humanism is harsh and destructive; humanism without nationalism is academic and barren. If there ever is a federation of Europe or of the world it can be based only on free national States, not on the domination of a single Great Power.

XII

THE TRADITIONS OF BRITISH
FOREIGN POLICY

THE great thing about foreign policy is that it is a matter of talk, of general principles. In most public affairs, there comes a point when you proceed from talk to action. When you have talked about public health, you go on to build schools—though not to paying school-teachers enough: and when you talk about Socialism, you end up by nationalizing steel. But foreign policy is essentially a matter of saying what you are going to do. When you do it, it becomes something else. If you go to war, it becomes a matter for the War Office and the Admiralty; if you co-operate economically, the Treasury or the Board of Trade see to it. The only *action* that a Foreign Secretary ever takes is to sign treaties; and treaties (though people often forget this) are not action—they are only promises to act like this or that in a given set of circumstances. Foreign policy is displayed in discussion—either in Parliament or with foreigners—and therefore it is a good topic for an anthology in a series on the British political tradition. It is much easier to show in this way than, say, housing policy, which would have to be shown in a collection of plans and photographs—very boring for those of us who would still rather read books than look at pictures, whether still or moving.

James Joll has put together a collection of extracts—speeches, pamphlets, newspaper-articles—to illustrate the theme Britain and Europe, from Pitt to Churchill.[1] It starts with Pitt explaining in 1793 why England was going to war with revolutionary France; it ends with Winston Churchill in 1940 looking forward to an ever closer co-operation with the United States. In between are some of the best-known episodes in British foreign policy, and some not so well-known; Castlereagh refusing to join the continental Powers in a reactionary policing of Europe; Canning keeping out of interven-

[1] *Britain and Europe: Pitt to Churchill*, 1793–1940. Edited by James Joll.

tion in Spain; Palmerston defending his intervention in Greece
and Lord John Russell blessing the revolutionary unification
of Italy. You can guess what it ends up with just befor
Churchill: Munich and the argument over appeasement
which still supplies superficial parallels and superficial term
of abuse for the present day.

Throughout the nineteenth century—and indeed ever since
the wars with Spain in the sixteenth century—British foreign
policy rested on the assumption that it had a choice, even i
only a choice of evils. You could co-operate with the Holy
Alliance to maintain the existing settlement of Europe or you
could work with France to revise it; you could help Turkey
to resist Russia or you could work with Russia to impose
reforms on Turkey, or even to partition her; you could reconcile
Germany, even Hitler, by appeasement, or you could build
up a system of collective security to resist Hitler. These were
not always good choices; but they were respectable choices
honestly advocated by intelligent and well-informed men
There was a choice, because we had, or thought we had, free
dom to choose. I do not say it did not matter which policy
was chosen; all I say is that it was a balance of advantages
There's a remarkable passage in Sir Edward Grey's speech
at the time of the outbreak of war with Germany in 1914. Tha
might seem a matter of life and death. But Grey says, 'if we
are engaged in war, we shall suffer but little more than we
shall suffer even if we stand aside'. And he goes on to say that
in any case, we shall only suffer by the loss of our trade with the
continent.

We have been so used to this freedom of choice over a long
period that we perhaps fail to see how unusual it is. Most
countries have their foreign policy dictated to them by their
situation and by the behaviour of their neighbours. Very often
they have only the choice between resisting or being overrun
without a fight. For instance, this country chose deliberately
to go to war with Germany in September 1939: we declared
war and we could have kept out of it if we had wanted to—no
doubt only for the time being. Russia had no such choice in
June 1941: war was imposed upon her by Hitler and would
have been imposed whatever policy Stalin had tried to follow
It is worth while trying to understand why we had this freedom of
choice in the past: it casts a good deal of light on our policy
and still more American policy, in the present. Primarily it

came from our being a bit further off: the straits which divide us from Europe gave us that extra time for deliberation. But it is a mistake to think that British security rested only on sea-power or ever has. The fiercest and most prolonged debate over British foreign policy has always gone on between those, usually a minority, who regard sea-power as enough in itself; and those, usually in control of policy, who have insisted that sea-power was only the beginning, the foundation of British security. Curiously enough, it has usually been the Left in British history, who have been isolationists, wanting to rely solely on the strength of the British Navy—from Charles James Fox opposing the war against Napoleon to John Bright opposing any active foreign policy at all, and finally to the radicals before 1914 who opposed the ententes with France and Russia. In fact, if you pushed the question a little nearer our times, you would find the opponents of collective security and advocates of a straight deal with Germany at the time of Munich were mostly radicals gone sour from Neville Chamberlain downwards. Nevertheless isolationism, based on sea-power, has been by and large the voice of a minority in British history.

The classical basis of British security— as established at the Glorious Revolution and practised throughout the eighteenth and early nineteenth centuries—was the Balance of Power. In those days English people prized control of the seas simply because it enabled them to play their part in maintaining this Balance. Observe the phrase 'maintaining the Balance of Power'. The old school of English statesmen, from Somers and Montague in William III's reign to Palmerston in Queen Victoria's, did not think that there was an automatic Balance of Power on the continent of Europe, by which the Great Powers cancelled each other out and so left us alone. They thought that the Balance had to be constantly adjusted by changes in British policy; in fact they recognized that it demanded a more active foreign policy, even involved Great Britain more in wars, than if they had done without it. Mr. Joll remarks, quite rightly, that the Balance of Power in Europe has broken down. The old-fashioned British statesmen would have answered, 'then put it back again; make it the object of British policy to restore the Balance'. It is worth while considering why this answer does not appeal to us; the answer will tell us a lot about the change in British political thinking.

The first part of the answer is that in the second half of the nineteenth century English people got the Balance of Power theory wrong. They came to think that it worked automatically, like the law of supply and demand or any other of the famous economic 'laws' that the Victorians imagined they had discovered. In international affairs, as in economic affairs, you only had to look after your own interests and everything would be perfect; when this did not happen and the Balance broke down, at the time of the first German war, people thought that the policy of the Balance of Power was no good. People also came to think that it was wicked, cynical. This is a very old radical attitude. But not all radicals were satisfied with isolationism. They wanted to substitute something for the Balance of Power; and they thought—the idea was invented by Gladstone—that they had discovered this substitute in the 'Concert of Europe'. The League of Nations and the United Nations are later versions of the same outlook. Not rivalry, but harmony; not conflict of interests, but co-operation in improvement were to be the determining motives in international affairs. Most of all, disputes between nations were to be settled by judging rights and wrongs, not by weighing the strength of the opposing sides. This theory sounds morally superior to the Balance of Power; and so it is, so long as the same international morality is accepted by all the Great Powers. Gladstone would never have preached the Concert of Europe unless he had held—rightly or wrongly—that Russia was 'a great Christian power'—that is, had the same moral outlook as himself. It is a very different matter when you set up institutions based on international harmony, not because this harmony exists, but because you hope that these institutions will create it. This was done both with the League of Nations and with the United Nations. It is as though a man and woman who did not care for each other got married in the hope that they would then fall in love. This sometimes happens between individuals, not, I think, in the world of international relations.

To go back to the point of Great Britains' having freedom of choice; consider the consequence. That consequence is simple: it is a sensation of being morally superior. If you do things because you have to, as most continental nations have done, you cannot waste time thinking about right and wrong: you act. When you have time to weigh advantages, you also weigh moral claims. Ever since Great Britain had an independent foreign policy, this has always had a moral element. First it was the defence of the Protestant religion: then it was the defence of the kings and princes of Europe against the encroachments of the French revolution; and in the nineteenth century it became the encouraging of national liberty, and not merely of the independence of states. It would have been very difficult for English people to conduct either the first or the second war against Germany—or for that matter the present cold war against Russia—unless they had felt, and now feel, morally superior to their opponents. But in the old days British statesmen knew how to keep their moral sentiments within practical bounds. Canning defended Spanish independence against Napoleon; he did not think it worth while defending Spanish liberalism against the intervention of conservative France. Palmerston welcomed the liberation of Italy and helped to promote it; he would do nothing for Poland or for Hungary—the one was beyond his reach, the liberation of the other he supposed would have been against British interests. I do not commend this attitude; I record it. C. P. Scott, a great British liberal, once said, 'Truth like everything else should be economized'. This sensible attitude looks very different when seen through foreign eyes. And those who believe in the moral superiority of British, or now of Anglo-American, foreign policy, should ask themselves why this country has always been known abroad as perfidious Albion. Is it merely the jealousy of rival and less successful Powers? I doubt it. It is rather the price you have to pay for having freedom of choice. Compared to continental countries, England has been a bad ally. She has always assumed, rightly in the past, that her allies needed her more than she needed them —that is what the phrase 'natural allies' really means. This was expressed in Salisbury's proud sentence, 'England does not solicit alliances; she grants them'. And Palmerston meant much the same when he said that alliances were impossible between equals: one Power has to be dependent on the other and to need protection.

It may be that these considerations are now all out-of-date and that there is very little to be learnt from the study of past foreign policy. I would not easily dismiss that view. Indeed I have long thought that we learn too much from history rather than the reverse. For instance the appeasement of Germany would not have been tried so obstinately in the nineteen-

thirties, if it had not been for the recollection or myth or legend
that the appeasement of France had worked in the eighteen
thirties. And similarly a conciliatory policy towards Russia
would not be rejected so firmly now if it were not for the recollection of the appeasement towards Germany that failed a
decade ago. Both historical analogies were profoundly misleading and did nothing but harm. All the same you cannot
escape so simply from the factors that have shaped British foreign
policy in the past. At the present time we seem committed
to the doctrine that we have no longer a freedom of choice
and that policy is determined for us by the actions of others
—by the actions of either the Russians or the Americans—at
any rate not by our initiative. If this were true then indeed
every tradition in British policy would have to go overboard.
But is it really true? Or do we perversely want it to be true in
order to escape our responsibilities? Have the Straits of Dover
ceased to exist as a military factor? Has sea-power ceased to
count in the world? Even the Balance of Power is not so hopelessly destroyed, if anyone had the courage to juggle the weights
round. And even the Concert of Great Powers, or harmony of
interests, might occasionally sound a note in unison, if British
diplomatists were more concerned to act as piano-tuners.
Certainly the theory of British policy nowadays is that we have
lost freedom of choice. The practice of British policy—from
our attitude towards the Council of Europe to our attempt
to follow a more reasonable line towards China—asserts that
we are still an independent Power. Here again I do not commend; I record. Almost the last words in James Joll's book are
from the speech by Churchill in which he said that the organizations of the British Empire and the United States will have
to be somewhat mixed up . . . for mutual and general advantage. 'Let it roll on full flood, inexorable, irresistible, benig-
nant.' I wonder whether history will show that Churchill was
right.

XIII

PRELUDE TO FASHODA: THE QUESTION OF THE UPPER NILE, 1894–5

(1)

THE Anglo-Congolese treaty of 12 May 1894 and its after-math have often been discussed by historians;[1] its origins have not been made clear, and the negotiations that followed have remained obscure—the accounts of them have been based on casual (and inaccurate) references by Hanotaux and Harcourt. These obscurities can be removed with the aid of the French documents recently published[2] and of the Foreign Office archives, until the end of 1902, which are now open to public inspection.

In the eighteen-nineties Africa dwarfed all other questions in British diplomacy. Previously it had been rare to separate a topic from the general 'diplomatic' correspondence; and these independent files had been short-lived. Egypt, as a subdivision of Turkey, was the first to acquire a permanent separation for obvious reasons. In 1893 the old 'Slave Trade' file (F.O. 84) was closed and 'Africa' became a separate heading in the correspondence with France, Germany, and Belgium; these 'Africa' files bulked larger than the general 'diplomatic' files in size and importance.[3] For instance, the French 'diplomatic' files for the period when Kimberley was foreign secretary (March 1894 to June 1895) contain trivialities except for a few conversations on Armenian affairs in the autumn of 1894 and on Far Eastern affairs early in 1895. The only memorable remark is a minute by Kimberley which reads: 'It will be a misfortune if M. Delcassé becomes colonial minister.'[4]

[1] W. L. Langer, *The Diplomacy of Imperialism* (New York, 1935), i, chs. iv and ix.

[2] *Documents Diplomatiques Français* (1871–1914). Ier série, tome xi (1947). Cited henceforth as *D.D.F.*

[3] These files were closed at the end of 1898 for interesting reasons which are irrelevant here. As well there was a special 'Africa' class (F.O. 2) which contained the correspondence with the various commissioners and consuls-general.

[4] Minute by Kimberley on Phipps to Kimberley, no. 117, 18 March 1894, F.O. 27/3171.

Moreover, Africa was important to the Foreign Office i[n] another way. Starting with Egypt, and then proceeding to [a] bewildering accumulation of protectorates and chartered com[-] panies, the Foreign Office was acquiring an empire of its ow[n] which it conducted without reference to the Colonial Offic[e.] The Foreign Office staffed and administered this unofficia[l] empire, drew its boundaries, and devised its legal codes, a[l-] though the British had no previous experience of imperia[l] affairs, and negotiated with the Colonial Office as with [a] foreign power. The lord of this African empire was Sir Perc[y] Anderson, the African expert at the Foreign Office.

After the death of Gordon in 1885, the British postpone[d] though they did not renounce, the recovery of the Sudan; an[d] their diplomacy aimed at excluding others. This had bee[n] achieved in the case of Germany by the agreement of 1 Jul[y] 1890; and in the case of Italy in 1891. The Anglo-Germa[n] agreement contained a recognition of 'the British sphere o[f] influence', specifically defined on east and west and extending northward 'to the confines of Egypt'. Since this agreement wa[s] public, and was not at the time disputed by any Power, th[e] British later claimed it as 'an international instrument', giving authority to their 'sphere'. In 1890 the British were thinking solely of the danger to the Sudan from the east; and suppose[d] that, by means of the agreement with Germany and Italy, the[y] had done the trick. Early in 1894 it became obvious that bot[h] France and Leopold II, as sovereign of the Congo Free State[,] were threatening to break into the Nile from the west. Th[e] British had tried to bar the way against a French advance by a[n] agreement with Germany in November 1893, which woul[d] have allowed the Germans to advance up to the Nile water[-] shed; but the Germans dodged this dubious attraction by a[n] agreement with the French, initialled on 4 February 1894[,] and confirmed on 15 March. Leopold II was in an even[,] stronger position. He had an agreement of 1890, made with Sir William Mackinnon, chairman of the British East Afric[a] Company, which permitted him to enter the valley of the uppe[r] Nile and he claimed (though without justification) that this agree[-] ment had been approved by Lord Salisbury. However, Leopol[d] was not happy about this title, and had already thrown out a sug[-] gestion in 1892 that he might renounce it if the British govern[-] ment would instead give him a lease of the same territories.[1]

---

[1] Monson to Salisbury, no. 63, 7 July 1892, F.O. 10/577.

In 1892 no reply had been made. In 1894, through the thick African haze, the British saw both Belgian and French expeditions on the Nile. The Belgian expedition was a fact: it was supposed to be at Lado, though Eetvelde, the king's Congo agent, revealed, when the negotiations had been successfully concluded, that it had only reached Wadelai.[1] The French expedition was a vaguer, and more alarming, affair. The British did not, of course, know of the grandiose decision made by President Carnot on 3 May 1893: 'We must *occupy* Fashoda';[2] but the purport of the Franco-German negotiation was clear,[3] and the Belgians did their best to make the British flesh creep with stories of French preparations.[4] Lugard, home on leave to advise on these questions, was sent over to Paris to have a friendly chat with Monteil, the leading French advocate of advance to the Nile, and returned on 10 March 1894 with the news, 'Monteil means to march on Lado or Fashoda with an exceptionally well-organized expedition'.[5]

The final impulse to negotiations with Leopold was the impending declaration of a protectorate over Uganda, which was made on 12 April: the main purpose of this was to secure the route to the upper Nile, and therefore it was urgent both to avoid a conflict with the Congolese forces, and to bar the way against the French. Leopold, on his side, recognized that he could not afford to quarrel with both the French and the British. He was already in dispute with the French over the Franco-Congolese frontier on the Ubanghi, and hoped to get British backing here, if he met British wishes on the Nile. Moreover, he had—or so he supposed—the advantage over the French in a 'standstill' agreement on the Ubanghi, made on 20 March

---

[1] Anderson, Note on the Belgian negotiations, 13 April 1894, F.O. 10/625.

[2] Monteil to Lebon (under-secretary for Colonies), 7 March 1894, *D.D.F.*, o. 65. Unlike the Foreign Office, the French department of foreign affairs never developed an independent 'empire'; indeed, it was often in the dark as to French colonial plans.

[3] Anderson minuted on 13 February 1894 (on Plunkett to Rosebery, no. 18, 1 February 1894, F.O. 10/614): 'It is certainly probable that when the negotiations with Germany are concluded Captain Monteil will push towards the Nile.'

[4] They succeeded. Anderson minuted Plunkett to Kimberley, no. 35, 31 March 1894, F.O. 10/614: 'The presence of the French in force seems to be beyond doubt.' At this time Monteil was still in Paris.

[5] Lugard memorandum, 10 March 1894, F.O. 83/1310.

to allow of negotiations; this made it impossible for the French
to move towards the Nile, while the Congolese forces could
reach it without passing through the territory covered by the
standstill agreement.

On 5 March 1894 Rennell Rodd, one of the 'Africans' in
the Foreign Office, was instructed to go to Brussels. He was to
demand, as a preliminary, 'an unreserved abandonment' of the
Mackinnon agreement. This, it was pointed out, should not be
difficult,

> as the retirement of the East African Company from the interior
> precludes for ever the possibility of its being able to occupy and the
> to cede the Nile watershed, and as Lord Salisbury has distinctly denied
> that he gave the sanction attributed to him by misunderstanding, the
> the abandonment by Great Britain of any portion of her sphere.

Rodd was then to ask for a recognition by the Congo Free
State of the British sphere of influence (as defined in the Anglo-
German agreement of 1890) and for the transfer to Great
Britain of all treaties made or to be made in this territory by
officers of the Free State. In return Leopold was to be offered
a lease (terminable on his death) of the left bank of the Nile as
far north as Fashoda; this territory was to include the Bahr el
Ghazal, which lay between the Nile valley and the nearest
French post.[1] Both lessor and lessee would declare that they
did not ignore the contingent claim of Turkey. Finally, as an
afterthought, Anderson added the condition of 'a concession
to powers of telegraphic communication in the State territories
between the British spheres'.[2]

Rodd was unable to see Leopold II, who had developed a
convenient illness. He submitted his proposals through
Eetvelde, Congo Minister of the Interior, and the king's
factotum for Congo affairs.[3] On 17 March Leopold trans-

[1] The territory was that subsequently defined in the treaty, except that its
northern limit was fixed at the 8th parallel. This was supposed to include
Fashoda; the Intelligence Department of the War Office subsequently pointed
out that Fashoda was to the north of this line, which was then advanced to
parallel 10. (Note on the Belgian negotiations by Anderson, 13 April 1894, F.O.
10/625.)

[2] Rosebery to Rodd, 5 March 1894, secret, F.O. 10/625.

[3] Leopold conducted these negotiations with great secrecy. He told his Belgian
ministers nothing; and even de Grelle Rogier, who was in charge of the foreign
affairs of the Congo State, was unaware on 20 April that the agreement with
Great Britain had been signed on 12 April. He said to Plunkett: 'One of the

mitted counter-proposals, demanding a lease which should terminate 'only if Belgium became a republic or if the Congo passed to other hands'. Eetvelde hinted that these demands were 'trying it on'; at the same time he made it clear that, if the British did not settle, it would be easy for Leopold to agree with the French. Rodd reported:

M. de Eetvelde was constant in his assurances that it was the King's desire to anticipate this [French] movement by an occupation effected under agreement with us, that the Congo State had nothing but enemies in France &c., but the fact must not be lost sight of that if France, having become 'plus aimable', should suddenly recognize the claims of the King on the Nile, the way would be open for an agreement for mutual support in the Nile basin as against us.[1]

Anderson rejected Leopold's proposal. It was the ultimate intention of British policy to turn the Belgians out of the valley of the Nile when British forces arrived there; besides, Leopold's scheme would involve Great Britain in the internal affairs of Belgium, if ever there was a movement against the monarchy. Anderson therefore suggested 'a lease for a fixed term, renewable by consent, to be made personally to the King and his descendants, terminable by notice'; Rodd, who had gone on to Paris, should return to Brussels, and negotiate a compromise.[2] Rosebery, who had just become prime minister, thought it 'essential' to proceed without delay. The question of Uganda and, from it, of the upper Nile had dominated his tenure of the Foreign Office; it had led to endless disputes in the cabinet, and it is reasonable to suppose that he was anxious to see both questions settled while still in close touch with the Foreign Office. He therefore directed that 'the King's man' should be invited to London to settle the final details.[3] On 28 March, Kimberley, Rosebery's successor as foreign secretary, broke the news of the negotiations to Harcourt,

---

greatest difficulties arose from the jealousy of England shown by the French delegates, who seemed to imagine that the Congolese government is somehow in league with the English, or has some arrangement with them. You know very well that is not the case.' Plunkett shrugged his shoulders and, saying 'I wish it were the case', left the room. (Plunkett to Kimberley, no. 49, 21 April 1894, F.O. 10/614.)

[1] Rodd to Anderson, 17 March 1894, private; Report by Rodd, 19 March 1894, secret, F.O. 10/625.

[2] Minute by Anderson, 25 March 1894, F.O. 10/625.

[3] Minute by Rosebery, 27 March 1894, F.O. 10/625.

chancellor of the exchequer,[1] in terms which clearly implied that agreement was in sight; indeed, since Harcourt had always been the principal opponent of the Foreign Office in these questions, it would have been pointless to inform him before the matter was ripe for the cabinet.

Eetvelde therefore came to London on 9 April without any further negotiations through Rodd. He proposed an acceptable compromise. The left bank of the Nile as far north as Fashoda and as far west as longitude 30° east should be leased to Leopold for his lifetime only; the larger area of the Bahr el Ghazal outside the Nile valley (i.e. between 25° and 30° east), should be leased to the king and his successors. This suited both parties. Leopold got what he regarded as the most valuable territory more or less for good; the British got security that the Nile valley would revert to them within a few years and yet established a permanent buffer against the French. Further, in exchange for the permanent lease of a corridor from Congo territory to the Nile, Eetvelde agreed to lease to the British a similar corridor across Congolese territory from north to south (this was a last-minute addition by Anderson to his earlier request for a telegraph concession).[2] The agreement was signed by Eetvelde and Kimberley on 12 April;[3] it was to be kept secret for three months. Leopold thought that he had secured British backing against the French. The British thought that they had put Leopold as a barrier between France and the upper Nile—and an effective barrier, since there was talk of six, or sometimes eight, 'Krupp guns'. Besides, by accumulating recognitions of the British 'sphere of influence' from everyone except the French, the British hoped to argue that in some curious implicit way the French, too, had been committed to it.[4]

[1] Kimberley to Harcourt, 28 March 1894, A. G. Gardiner, *Life of Sir William Harcourt* (1923), ii, 313.

[2] These geographical details will be made clear by reference to the map in Langer, *Diplomacy of Imperialism*, i, 133.

[3] Kimberley to Plunkett, no. 23, 9 April; no. 24D, 12 April 1894, F.O. 10/613. Though Harcourt makes an obscure reference to agreement having been reached on 12 April the signature of a valid agreement then was unknown until the opening of the archives. Both British and Belgians had later good grounds for concealment.

[4] Note on the Belgian negotiations by Anderson, 13 April 1894, F.O. 10/629. At the conclusion Eetvelde said: 'the French have always referred to the Anglo German agreement as an instrument with which they have no concern. The

The French also were anxious to settle with Leopold II in order to prevent an agreement with the British such as had already been secretly made. A French delegation led by Hanotaux, then African expert at the French foreign ministry, came to Brussels on 16 April. Hanotaux offered a favourable settlement of the Ubanghi frontier, on condition that France secured 'son chemin libre' to the valley of the Nile. Leopold could not make this bargain, and negotiations were broken off on 23 April.[1] Leopold now became alarmed. The French would have 'a plausible cause of complaint', when they discovered that he had made an agreement with Great Britain shutting France out from the valley of the Upper Nile', four days before Hanotaux arrived in Brussels.[2] The British refused to delay publication; indeed they were anxious to accelerate it, for the same reason which made Leopold anxious to put it off. Nor would they cancel the agreement which had been duly signed.[3] They offered to substitute a more general agreement by which Leopold would recognize the British sphere and would admit that he must withdraw from it when given notice to do so. By this he would have had all the disadvantages of the original agreement and less security.[4] The British finally consented to alter the date of the agreement so that it should

---

may contrive to neglect it, but it will be difficult, even for French Chauvinists, after the publication of its recognition by the Congo State, to send an armed expedition to the Nile. . . . We have two weapons to oppose to them, our garrisons, and prioroccupation.' Anderson added: 'Whatever may be the efficiency of the former, there is no doubt that, unless the Mahdists bar the way, we, or they, should have start enough to secure the latter.'

[1] Plunkett to Kimberley, no. 52, 24 April; no. 55, 27 April 1894, F.O. 10/614. There is no record of these negotiations in *D.D.F.*

[2] Plunkett to Kimberley, no. 51, 24 April 1894, F.O. 10/614.

[3] According to Harcourt (Gardiner, *Harcourt*, ii, 315), Anderson was sent to Brussels on 23 April, after a row in the British cabinet, 'to see if the king of the Belgians will give it [the treaty] up'. There is no trace of this in the F.O. correspondence; indeed the Foreign Office was holding Leopold to the treaty against his will. Probably it is one of the many instances of keeping Harcourt at bay. Moreover, there is fairly decisive proof that Anderson never went to Brussels. Eetvelde, when signing the revised treaty on 12 May, deleted a reference to a conversation with Anderson, 'since he could only have seen him in London between 9 and 12 April) and the attention of France must not be called to this visit'. (Plunkett to Kimberley, no. 68, 12 May 1894, F.O. 10/615).

[4] Rosebery to Queen Victoria, 4 May 1894. *Letters of Queen Victoria*, 3rd series, ii, 396. Kimberley to Plunkett, telegram, no. 2, 5 May 1894, F.O. 10/618.

D

seem to have been made after Hanotaux's visit to Brussels; and a new agreement, virtually in the same terms as that of 12 April, was signed in Brussels by Eetvelde and Plunkett, the British minister, on 12 May. Leopold had to pay for this concession by consenting to the publication of the agreement when the British parliament met on 21 May.[1]

It is convenient to summarize here the principal provisions of the Anglo-Congolese agreement, and especially the clauses which gave rise to subsequent dispute. In the preamble Leopold, as sovereign of the Congo Free State, recognized the British 'sphere of influence' in the Nile valley, as defined in the Anglo-German agreement of 1890. In exchange for this the Free State received, by Article I, a 'rectification' of frontier towards the Nile valley (though not actually reaching it) which, in fact, amounted to a considerable concession of territory. Article II then leased to Leopold all the sphere on the left bank of the Nile which he had just recognized. The lease was in two parts: the Bahr el Ghazal and also a corridor to the Nile 25 kilometres wide to Leopold and his successors; the left bank of the Nile as far west as longitude 30° east to Leopold during his life. This article, by fixing the northern limit to the lease at latitude 10° north, obliquely gave to the British 'sphere' the northern definition which had been lacking in the Anglo-German agreement. Article III gave the British the lease of a similar corridor 25 kilometres wide across the Congo Free State from north to south. Article IV laid down that Leopold could not acquire sovereign rights in the leased territory.[2]

[1] Plunkett to Kimberley, no. 68, 12 May 1894, F.O. 10/615. The date of publication was determined solely by the meeting of parliament. There is therefore no foundation for the surmise (Langer, *Diplomacy of Imperialism*, i, 134, that publication was designed to coincide with the ministerial crisis in France. This could not have been foreseen on 12 May.

[2] This article was the only one substantially amended from the agreement of 12 April. The amendment was designed to conceal the fact that, before the signing of the agreement, Leopold had already acquired (dubious) sovereign rights by treaty with native chiefs; since it could be argued that these had been acquired by him as ruler of the Congo Free State and therefore could not be renounced without allowing the French to exercise the right of pre-emption to Free State titles, which they had been granted in 1884. The original Article II had provided that the leased territories should use the British flag with a white star in the middle. The agreement of 12 May substituted 'a special flag'; and one of equivocal significance was designed though never used. Plunkett to Kimberley, telegram, no. 2, 9 May 1894, F.O. 10/618.

By an exchange of letters both parties declared that they did not ignore 'the claims of Egypt and Turkey'. It is difficult to imagine a stranger transaction. A, in return for recognizing B's disputed title, at once receives from B the grant of part, and the lease of the rest, of the property. Yet, at the same time as B (by Article I) is making a final cession to A, both declare that they do not ignore the rights of third parties—and indeed subsequently assert these rights as against others.

(II)

The French government do not seem to have had any suspicion of the agreement between Great Britain and the Congo Free State.[1] They realized that the British and the Belgians would attempt to race them to the upper Nile; and they were confident that they would win this race—rightly, as it turned out, for Marchand was first at Fashoda. They were therefore anxious to keep the question of the upper Nile on the practical basis of a race in Africa and away from the field of diplomacy. The Anglo-Congolese treaty threatened this plan; and Casimir-Périer, who was just leaving office, at once protested against it in Brussels and London[2] as soon as it was published. Hanotaux, his successor, though an African specialist in the foreign ministry, was less of a colonial enthusiast than Delcassé; he glady accepted the description that 'he had always acted as a drag-chain on M. Delcassé'.[3] In later years, when Hanotaux's policy seemed to have led to Fashoda and Delcassé's to the *Entente Cordiale*, reputations were reversed; and even Hanotaux presented himself as a colonial enthusiast whose legacy had been squandered by Delcassé. The contrast between them, in either period, was overdrawn. Both desired a settlement with England; both desired it on colonial terms profitable to France. At all times, the colonial minister thought primarily of colonial

[1] There is no hint of pre-publication knowledge in *D.D.F.* On 30 August (Plunkett to Kimberley, no. 225, F.O. 10/617) Lambermont, of the Belgian Foreign Office, alleged that Hanotaux was aware that the agreement of 12 May was not the original one, and that he had treated the Congolese delegates harshly because of this. Again, there is no hint of this in *D.D.F.*, and Lambermont was probably cadging for British sympathy.

[2] Casimir-Périer to Bourée, 26 May 1894, *D.D.F.*, no. 109; Decrais to Kimberley, 28 May 1894, *D.D.F.*, no. 113.

[3] Phipps to Dufferin, enclosed in Dufferin to Kimberley, no. 148, 6 June 1894, F.O. 27/3185.

details; and the foreign minister (whether Hanotaux or Delcassé) primarily of the *entente*. Both men, as foreign ministers, knew that the *entente* would not be accepted by French public opinion, unless the colonial terms were tolerable; hence they sometimes seemed to the British to be driving a hard bargain. Their ultimate objective, a general settlement, did not alter.

Hanotaux understood both the broad issues and the points of detail raised by the Anglo-Congolese Treaty.[1] He was alone in this. Lord Dufferin, the British ambassador, was a former Viceroy of India, a *grand seigneur*, who knew nothing of African trivialities; besides, he was annoyed that his arrival in Paris had not led to an immediate improvement in French feeling towards England, and was hostile to the French as a result.[2] Phipps, the British minister under Dufferin, was well-grounded in African frontier questions, which he had often discussed earlier with Hanotaux; his frank reporting of the French case made the Foreign Office write him off as too French in sympathy. In England, Kimberley had only just entered the Foreign Office. He was garrulous, elderly, and had had no experience of foreign affairs for twenty-five years. Though always running over with conciliation and good-will towards France in conversation, he was dominated by Rosebery, and followed Rosebery's violent promptings without demur.[3]

[1] Hanotaux, a future Academician, kept full and well-written accounts of his conversations; this was rare for a French foreign minister. As a witness, however, he had the faults of a good writer: he would put things too sharply and exaggerated his own successes. On the other hand, when challenged, he would modify his original version without complaint—again the quality of a good writer. Thus in his Note to the British government of 6 August 1894 (*D.D.F.*, no. 209) he claimed: 'Lord Dufferin had admitted that most of the observations made to him are well-founded.' When Dufferin objected to this, Hanotaux withdrew and claimed only that Dufferin had described the French thesis as 'debatable'. Again, he fathered on to Phipps the 'self-denying' arrangement which was the high-water mark of negotiations in October; when challenged by Phipps, he admitted that they had devised it together, and that Phipps had merely given it precise form so as to submit it to London. (Phipps to Kimberley, no. 266, 9 October 1894, F.O. 27/3187.)

[2] Dufferin, too, was a distinguished writer, and therefore, like Hanotaux, an unreliable witness.

[3] Rosebery recommended Kimberley as foreign secretary to the queen thus: 'Lord Rosebery thought it would do quite well, as he spoke French, and had been the under-secretary under Lord Clarendon.' (The Queen's Journal, 5 March 1894. *Letters of Queen Victoria*, 3rd series, ii, 376.)

Anderson, who determined African policy, worked directly with Rosebery, and often informed Kimberley only when a decision had been made. Anderson had no interest in general policy or in French good-will. For him the friendship of France was of no account in comparison with any scrap of African territory; and he thwarted Phipps's efforts at conciliation with an equipment of even greater knowledge of detail. It is, of course, the duty of the permanent officials to be stiff on every detail; both English and French diplomats tried to drive as hard a bargain as possible during the successful negotiations ten years later. But there was then also the will to agree in the last resort. The disputes between England and France could never be ended merely by contesting every issue as it arose. New disputes would arise endlessly unless there was the desire for a general settlement. The British at this earlier period had no such desire. The French could never lose sight of Europe as the British had done. This held them back all along from war; it did not yet lead them to make concessions for the sake of British friendship

Hanotaux lost no time. He called on Dufferin on 1 June and warned him that the Anglo-Congolese treaty would ruin relations with France. Dufferin knew nothing about it: Hanotaux, he said, 'had surprised him in a complete ignorance of African affairs',[1] and he asked Hanotaux: 'What are we to do now? The convention is made. . . . How are we to get out of the difficulty without putting the British government in a most false position?' Hanotaux could only suggest that the convention should be withdrawn, or at any rate 'held in suspense'.[2] Dufferin appealed to Kimberley in a private letter. On 5 June Kimberley, with the authorization of the cabinet, agreed to discuss the French objections to the treaty and offered to enter 'into a general review of all African questions pending between the two governments for the purpose of such an adjustment as would place the relations of the two countries in that continent on a more satisfactory footing'; Egypt was to be excluded from the discussion as 'un trop gros morceau'.[3] Dufferin was able to

[1] So he told Revoil on 3 June, D.D.F., no. 126.

[2] Note by Hanotaux, 2 June 1894, D.D.F., no. 123. Dufferin made no official report of this interview, though he wrote privately to Kimberley. This private correspondence is not available (if it exists).

[3] Kimberley to Dufferin, no. 187A, 5 June 1894, F.O. 27/3171. Decrais to Hanotaux, telegram, 5 June 1894, D.D.F., no. 129.

pass this offer on to Hanotaux on 6 June;[1] as a result Hanotaux
speaking in the Chamber on 7 June, adopted a conciliatory
though firm, attitude, and met Dufferin for a friendly discussion two or three days later.[2] At this meeting Dufferin tried to
make out that the treaty had been made to avoid a conflict with
the Belgians, 'without thinking of the effect it would have in
France'. He added, 'It is not likely that there was much
chance of the arrangements consigned to the Anglo-German
agreement being cancelled or essentially modified'. Hanotaux
answered, 'That treaty does not exist in our eyes. . . . We
cannot admit this new diplomatic system, which consists in
claiming territories, either by arrangements between Powers
who have no right, or by simple declarations in parliament. . . .
Our rights in this part of the basin of the Nile are as serious as
those of England.' Dufferin went away with the impression,
'The real desire of the French is to prevent us from establishing
ourselves . . . in the Bahr el Ghazal and in the valley of the
Nile, and perhaps to anticipate us in the occupation of these
districts'.

The issue had been clearly stated. The British had, as they
thought, a satisfactory treaty with the Congo Free State and
did not mean to retreat from it. They therefore did not take
up Hanotaux's offer of friendly discussion and waited for him
to formulate detailed objections, the discussion of which could
be dragged out indefinitely. Besides, the British government
had their hands full with the German objections to Article III,
by which Congolese territory adjacent to German East Africa
had been leased to the British. Here the new material does not
essentially modify the existing account. The German move
was principally an attempt to blackmail the British into renew-
ing their support of Austria-Hungary and Italy in the Mediterranean; it had perhaps a secondary motive of improving
German relations with France. It did not achieve either of these
aims. It put Rosebery in a bad temper with the Germans, and
with the Triple Alliance generally.[3] The French (contrary to

[1] Dufferin to Hanotaux, 6 June 1894, *D.D.F.*, no. 133.

[2] Hanotaux in his account (*D.D.F.*, no. 139, 11 June 1894) makes Dufferin
speak of 'your speech of yesterday', i.e. 7 June. This is impossible, since Hanotaux
replied to Dufferin's letter of 6 June only on 9 June (*D.D.F.*, no. 136). Dufferin
reported only on 13 June (to Kimberley, nos. 162 and 163, F.O. 27/3185)
without mentioning the date of the meeting. 10 June seems the most likely date.

[3] Kimberley, in his muddled way, went on treating the Germans as allies; and

German belief) were not taken in, and never counted on German backing in their dispute with England; moreover, they took care to document the German failure to support them after first promising to do so. The French made sceptical inquiries whether, in view of this newly displayed friendship, the Germans would support them in the Egyptian question;[1] this is the only price at which a Franco-German *entente* could have been established. The Germans did not respond to this suggestion; and the French went on their way alone. The Franco-German co-operation is, in fact, a myth, based only on a tendentious selection of documents in the *Grosse Politik*.

The French foresaw that the British would meet the German objections and that the Germans would then profess themselves satisfied. The British, alarmed enough in any case, were urged on by Leopold II to give in to Germany. On 22 June Leopold and the British signed an agreement abrogating Article III of the agreement of 12 May. The British thus renounced their lease of a corridor across the Free State without demanding from Leopold any lessening of the advantages which he had gained and of which the corridor was supposed to be part of the price. The British surrender to the Germans strengthened the French position. The withdrawal of Article III provided a precedent for the withdrawal of other articles. Moreover, the alarm of Leopold II at German pressure showed his weakness. His Belgian ministers were furious at the dangers in which his greed for African territory threatened to involve Belgium;[2] the British government refused to promise him support.[3] In fact the British, far from acquiring in Leopold a buffer against France, had undertaken a liability; now they would not accept this liability. The object of the Anglo-Congolese treaty was to avoid an Anglo-French dispute; if this dispute was to take place, the British might as well defend their own claims rather than those of Leopold. Hanotaux, at any rate, recognized

immediately after giving way to them over Article III, consulted Hatzfeldt, the German ambassador, as to how he should deal with the French. Kimberley to Malet, telegram, no. 93, 18 June 1894, F.O. 64/1335.

[1] Herbette to Hanotaux, 17 June 1894, *D.D.F.* no. 154; 20 August 1894, *D.D.F.*, no. 223.

[2] Plunkett to Kimberley, nos. 142 and 143, 23 June 1894, F.O. 10/616.

[3] Plunkett to Kimberley, no. 114, 10 June 1894, F.O. 10/616; Kimberley to Plunkett, no. 61, 13 June 1894, F.O. 10/613; Harcourt to Kimberley, 12 June 1894, Gardiner, *Harcourt*, ii, 317.

that the weakest link was in Brussels; and on 22 June he proposed, or rather demanded, negotiations with Leopold II.[1]

Nevertheless, Hanotaux would have preferred to follow the way of conciliation with Great Britain,[2] and made repeated attempts to do so. On 18 June he asked Dufferin if he had received any reply from London; Dufferin had received nothing. Hanotaux then decided to appeal to the supposedly friendly disposition of Kimberley. On 19 June he instructed Decrais, ambassador in London, to raise in detail the question of Article II (the clause leasing territory to the Free State).[3] However, on 20 June Dufferin, though still without instructions, came to discuss Article II, and Decrais was therefore told not to raise the question with Kimberley.[4] Dufferin was probably playing at diplomacy on his own; since the dispute with Germany was not yet technically settled, he wanted to keep Hanotaux in a good temper. He listened, without objection, to Hanotaux's proposal that Leopold II should renounce Article II, as he had already renounced Article III; and himself suggested that Article II might be 'suspended'. What they wanted, he said, was some plan 'under which the principle for which he [Hanotaux] contended might be maintained, at the same time that the practical object which we had in view . . . might be arrived at'. Since Dufferin had repeatedly assured Hanotaux that this practical object was to avoid a conflict with the Belgians, a solution seemed possible—unfortunately Dufferin was being disingenuous.[5]

Hanotaux also threw out the suggestion, during the conversation of 20 June, of a Conference of the Powers who had created the Congo Free State. This sounded imposing; in

[1] Hanotaux to Bourée, telegram, 22 June 1894, D.D.F., no. 170.

[2] On 14 June Hanotaux told Phipps (to Anderson, private, F.O. 27/3185) that he was unwilling to put his objections on paper 'as he could not be so "large" in writing or show such elasticity as he had shown in conversation with "un ambassadeur courtois" '. This was an excuse with some sincerity in it.

[3] Hanotaux to Decrais, telegram, 19 June 1894, D.D.F., no. 160.

[4] Hanotaux to Decrais, telegram, 20 June 1894, D.D.F., no. 165. Decrais, in fact, saw Kimberley, though he did not report the interview. All he got from Kimberley was that there must be 'an exchange of views, in order that we might understand exactly the French objections, and what means there were of meeting and satisfying them'. Kimberley to Dufferin, no. 216, 21 June 1894, F.O. 27/3182.

[5] Note by Hanotaux, 20 June 1894, D.D.F., no. 163; Dufferin to Kimberley, no. 169, 21 June 1894, F.O. 27/3185.

eality it was an empty threat. Though France had a good legal ase, she could not count on the backing of any Great Power in he Egyptian question, let alone in the question of the upper Nile. This was so obvious in the case of Austria-Hungary and taly that France had not even asked their opinion. Germany had been appeased by the British; and on 25 June Marschall, he secretary of state, went on holiday so as to avoid further reminders of the approach he had made to France.[1] Russia was no better. On 1 June Hanotaux had invoked the Franco-Russian alliance in an appeal for Russian encouragement and support.[2] After three weeks of evasion a single sentence was extracted from Giers: 'the Emperor entirely approves the point of view of the Government of the Republic';[3] no action, not even an expression of opinion in London, followed, and the question of the upper Nile continued to revolve between Hanotaux and Dufferin.

They met again on 29 June for an acrimonious discussion. The British surrender to Germany on 22 June had increased the tension between England and France. The British government were unwilling to discredit themselves further by concessions to France; and Dufferin must have known of Rosebery's mounting irritation. Hanotaux, on his side, was being urged by the Colonial ministry to abandon conciliation and to launch Monteil on the race for the upper Nile. Moreover, he knew that Leopold was beginning to yield to French pressure; England would lose the trick in any case, and it was hardly worth while for France to make great concessions. Thus both men were on edge, embarrassed by the combativeness of those behind them, vaguely desirous of agreement, yet with no clear idea what they were discussing. The words 'ultimatum' and 'menace' were exchanged.[4] Hanotaux demanded the uncondi-

---

[1] Herbette to Hanotaux, telegram, 26 June 1894, *D.D.F.*, no. 175.

[2] Hanotaux to Montebello, telegram, 1 June 1894, *D.D.F.*, no. 122.

[3] Montebello to Hanotaux, telegram, 21 June 1894, *D.D.F.*, no. 169.

[4] The 'ultimatum' made such an impression on Hanotaux that he referred to it years later in his book, *Fachoda*, p. 76. It is true that he ascribes it to the first meeting after his speech; this is a pardonable error, and his memory was never reliable (he later ascribed the Phipps-Hanotaux agreement of 9 October to January 1895). He goes on to allege that Dufferin spoke of an ultimatum which he had in the pocket of his frockcoat. This is nonsense. Dufferin had no instructions of any kind, let alone an ultimatum. Hanotaux does not mention a British ultimatum in his note made at the time; according to this, though Dufferin used

tional withdrawal of Article II; Dufferin refused and denied th
right of France to a voice in the upper Nile. Deadlock wa
reached. Dufferin took his stick and walked towards the door
Hanotaux saved the situation. France, he said, was demanding
only the withdrawal of Article II of the Anglo-Congoles

the word, it was to describe the French demand for the withdrawal of Article II
'It is an *ultimatum* which you are presenting to us. That cannot be calle
negotiating.' Dufferin does not mention this exchange: no doubt he knew that a.
account of it would have infuriated Rosebery and made him unyielding. On th
other hand, Dufferin, at a later stage of the conversation, described Hanotaux
threat to launch Monteil on the upper Nile as 'a menace'. Hanotaux replied
'Oh! for heaven's sake do not let it have that character.' Hanotaux, in his turn
does not record this exchange, and for equally obvious reasons: the challenge
would have strengthened the impatience of the Colonial ministry. In fact, each
saw the possibility of a conflict and tried to avoid it.

There is a further curious point. In warning Monteil off the upper Nile
Dufferin used strong language (even invoking his Indian associations). He said
'It was better that I should at once inform him [Hanotaux] that if M. Monteil
attempted to act the part of a second Mizon [a French explorer who had caused
a conflict in West Africa] in the Nile valley it would simply mean war between
the two countries; and that it would be a terrible thing if we were going to revive
in Africa the miserable combats which had deluged India with French and
English blood in the middle of the last century.' At some time after the arrival
of this dispatch in London, this passage was deleted and a less offensive passage
substituted: 'On this I thought it as well to refer to the great risks which might
ensue if an energetic officer, reflecting perhaps the strong views of that Colonial
party whose extravagance M. Hanotaux admitted it was necessary to curb, were
to start on a strong military expedition unfettered by definite instructions. In the
middle of the last century India had been the scene of disastrous conflicts between
British and French troops during a period when their respective mother countries
were at peace. Were anything of a similar kind to occur in Africa . . . the consequences might be very serious, for the deliberate and unprovoked irruption of
French troops into a territory over which our jurisdiction had been proclaimed
in an international instrument such as the Anglo-German Convention would
naturally exasperate public opinion at home and produce a situation fraught with
danger to the peaceable relations of the two countries.' The original passage is
scored at the side with three large exclamation marks in red pencil. Kimberley
used red ink, Rosebery (after he became prime minister) ordinary pencil.
Harcourt, to whom this dispatch is marked as having been sent, sometimes ticked
dispatches with red pencil, but this marking does not appear to be his. The revised
version, in two copies, is on paper and in typescript similar to the original; this
proves nothing, as the same paper was used by the F.O. and the embassies, and
typescript at this period (when few typewriters were in use) is uniform—at least
I am unable to distinguish one from another. One of these copies is headed in

reaty; she was not at present discussing the Anglo-German
greement of 1890, which recognized the upper Nile as a British
phere of influence. The implication of this involved statement
vas clear: if the claims of Leopold II were dropped, France
would be prepared to negotiate about the upper Nile and to leave
t to the British—at a price. Both men saw an opening; though
he frequent mention of Monteil's name was a reminder that the
way of conciliation would not remain open indefinitely.[1]

Still, the opening was not very great. Dufferin, no doubt,
hought the agreement with Leopold II a great blunder; for
hat very reason, he did not want to be the person responsible
or withdrawing it—and no one in London would take this
responsibility. Besides the Foreign Office wanted to know what
sort of price the French would claim for recognizing the British
sphere. This was the object of a further meeting between
Hanotaux and Dufferin on 4 July. Dufferin said, 'If France
objected, was it not for France, in view of the friendly spirit in
which we had entered upon the discussion, to suggest some way
out of the difficulty?' Hanotaux replied that he must first
have some evidence that Great Britain really wished for a settlement;[2] this evidence would be the withdrawal of Article II.

Kimberley now took a hand. On 11 July he had a rambling
discussion with Decrais, in which he touched on every disputed
topic except the Anglo-Congolese treaty;[3] he was no doubt
hinting that Great Britain would be reasonably conciliatory
elsewhere if France would give up all interest in the upper Nile.
Hanotaux was not moved. He at once instructed Decrais that
a general African settlement could not be discussed until the

---

Anderson's writing: 'Substitute for passage "On this I said it was better &c.".'
The original passage had then been deleted and the new passage written in (on the
margins, the foot and the reverse) in the handwriting of one of the F.O. clerks.

It is impossible to disentangle what occurred. Presumably Kimberley (or
perhaps Harcourt) took alarm at the original passage—no doubt with a Blue
book in mind. Then, either Dufferin was asked to provide an alternative version
or Anderson drafted one, and subsequently obtained Dufferin's approval. It is
strange that no minute, recording the transaction—or hinting at it—was bound
up with the correspondence.

[1] Dufferin to Kimberley, no. 173A, 30 June 1894, F.O. 27/3185; note by
Hanotaux, 29 June 1894, D.D.F., no. 178.
[2] Dufferin to Kimberley, no. 178, 5 July 1894, F.O. 27/3186; note by
Hanotaux, 4 July 1894, D.D.F., no. 184.
[3] Decrais to Hanotaux, 12 July 1894, D.D.F., no. 190.

treaty of 12 May was out of the way.[1] In a private letter he revealed more of his thought: France could get rid of the objectionable treaty in other ways than by agreement with England (and did so shortly afterwards); the only advantage of doing it by agreement was the general improvement of relations that would follow.[2] In other words, Hanotaux was groping towards the *Entente Cordiale*; the British were thinking solely of the upper Nile. At this time, neither side made any serious move towards the other. The British would have been quite willing to be on good terms with the French, if they could have all they asked in Africa; the French thought that the British ought to sacrifice some of their African ambitions for the sake of good relations. Of the British observers, Phipps believed that Hanotaux was genuine in his desire for a general settlement; Dufferin had little hope of a concrete outcome. Phipps knew more of feeling inside France; and he grasped what appears to be the key to Hanotaux's policy—though he genuinely desired a reconciliation with England, he had first to achieve a striking success over her for the sake of French public opinion. Hanotaux never extricated himself, or the negotiations, from this dilemma; he posed the problem of the *entente*, but found no solution.

On 17 July Kimberley weakened a little. He agreed that the Anglo-Congolese treaty should be discussed before any general discussion of African questions; only he insisted that the French objections should be formulated in writing and he 'reserved full liberty of action when he saw the French objections'.[3] This was a defeat for Hanotaux: once he formulated objections in writing, he would have to insist on them instead of leaving the way open for some impossible demonstration of goodwill. At this moment, he made his only concrete gesture of conciliation. On 13 July Monteil, on the point of departing for Africa, received strict instructions from both Delcassé and Hanotaux that he was never to send 'a force or even a man into the basin of the Nile'.[4] This short-lived restriction was the only effort ever made by either side to avoid a conflict.

[1] Hanotaux to Decrais, 15 July 1894, *D.D.F.*, no. 194.

[2] Hanotaux to Decrais, private, 15 July 1894, *D.D.F.*, no. 194.

[3] Decrais to Hanotaux, telegram, 17 July 1894, *D.D.F.*, no. 196; Kimberley to Dufferin, no. 260, 17 July 1894, F.O. 27/3183.

[4] Delcassé to Monteil (with minute by Hanotaux), 13 July 1894, *D.D.F.*, no. 191.

Hanotaux now despaired of persuading the British to give up Article II. The alternative was to bring pressure to bear on Leopold II, and he, though independent as sovereign of the Free State, was already giving way before the indignation of his Belgian ministers; they regarded the Free State as embarrassment enough, and had no wish to add to its territories, let alone to quarrel with France. On 16 July Leopold agreed to send negotiators to Paris.[1] He still hoped to get British backing. Dufferin, however, was recalled to London, ostensibly to advise on the pending discussions between England and France (which were, in fact, not pending), actually to be beyond the reach of the Free State representatives.[2] On 8 August Leopold appealed directly for British support.[3] Rosebery wished to show fight—or rather wished to compel Leopold to show fight. He therefore replied, 'the King must adhere to his position that no alteration can be made in the provisions of the Anglo-Congolese African agreement without the privity and consent of Great Britain'.[4] A few days later, however, he was overruled by the cabinet,[5] and Leopold was told:

> Her Majesty's Government do not feel called upon to oppose the King's desire to sign the Arrangement with the French Government as they have not taken part in the negotiations which have been pending between France and the Independent Sovereign of the Congo and cannot insist on the Congo Government occupying territory leased to them under the Agreement of the 12th of May.[6]

On 14 August Hanotaux signed an arrangement with the

[1] Leopold to Hanotaux, private, 16 July 1894, *D.D.F.*, no. 195.

[2] Leopold complained much of Dufferin's absence. Plunkett to Kimberley, no. 201, 11 August 1894, F.O. 10/617.

[3] Plunkett to Kimberley, telegram, no. 33, 8 August 1894, F.O. 10/618.

[4] Sanderson to Plunkett, telegram, secret, 8 August 1894, F.O. 10/618. The telegram was sent on Rosebery's instructions, during Kimberley's absence at Windsor. It was made official (no. 41) the following day.

[5] Harcourt (Gardiner, *Life*, ii, 320) speaks of a cabinet on 11 August. He also speaks of the king's being given 'leave to accept'; this is, for a lawyer, a curiously slipshod way of describing the British response which, as Rosebery insisted, was negative—they did not oppose the king's desire, which is a weaker matter than giving him leave. Rosebery (*Letters of Queen Victoria*, 3rd series, ii, 419) dates the cabinet as 13 August; he also gives a correct report of its proceedings.

[6] Kimberley to Plunkett, telegram, no. 45, 13 August 1894, F.O. 10/618; Plunkett to Kimberley, no. 201, 13 August 1894, F.O. 10/617.

Congolese representatives.[1] The Free State received a favourable settlement of the Ubanghi frontier; in return it promised
'to renounce all occupation and not to exercise in future any
political action of any sort' west of longitude 30° or north of
latitude 5° 30'. This effectively removed the barrier between
France and the upper Nile. On the other hand, the French
allowed the Free State to take up that part of the lease which
did not interfere with French plans (the left bank of the Nile as
far north as Lado). They thus deserted their objection of
principle that, since the Egyptian title to these territories was
still valid, the British had no right to lease them. Their practical
aim was, however, achieved: the main purpose of the Anglo-
Congolese treaty had been defeated. Yet in the end this French
success turned to the advantage of England: Leopold at Fashoda would have been much more difficult to dislodge than
Marchand, since he would have possessed a title which the
British, at least, could not dispute. As it was, Leopold held on
to the left bank of the Nile as far north as Lado, which the
French had allowed him to retain, until his death in 1908.
Still, as the result of French diplomacy, Leopold (who remained
bound by the rest of the treaty of 12 May) had recognized the
British sphere of influence, but received only a fraction of the
price on which he had always insisted.

(iii)

The affair of the Anglo-Congolese treaty was over; the
question of the upper Nile remained. The abortive Article II
had made it acute for the first time. Before the discussions of
June the British could pretend to be ignorant of the French
objections and could claim that their 'sphere of influence' had
received international recognition. Now they knew that there
must be either negotiation or conflict; and the divided Liberal
cabinet was not a reliable body with which to start a conflict.
On the other hand, the British government had no urgent need
for French friendship, and negotiated suspiciously, in a grudging spirit. The topics discussed in September and October
resembled those settled in the agreement of 8 April 1904; what
was lacking was the cordiality.

On 8 August Hanotaux had lodged with the British government a statement of the French objection to Article II of the

[1] *D.D.F.*, no. 217.

reaty;[1] this was no more than a precaution against a possible
Blue book. On 11 August he made a more conciliatory approach to Phipps. He said, 'there is no question of the French
advancing to the Bahr el Ghazal', and added: 'Do you imagine
that two such nations as England and France contemplate for
one moment going to war on account of Sierra Leone, or any
other corner of Africa?' This was indeed the weakness of the
French position; the statement was, and remained, true of
France—it did not remain true of England. Hanotaux repeated
the offer at which he had hinted before: he might recognize the
British sphere of influence as 'part of a comprehensive settlement'.[2] The British government, having been defeated over
the Anglo-Congolese treaty, decided to explore this offer, and
Dufferin returned to Paris on 14 August with the British terms.
The British asked for the recognition of their sphere of influence; in return they would promise that 'the rights of Eygpt
shall only be in suspense, until the Egyptian government shall
be in a position to reoccupy the territories in question'.
Further, the British government would then settle all other
African questions 'in a spirit of conciliation'.[3] This proposal
was made to Hanotaux on 16 August. It seemed to him un-
equal: France was presented with a *demand* to recognize the
British sphere and would receive, in return, only a vague
promise of conciliation. However, he agreed to put the offer
before the French Council of Ministers, when it met on 30
August;[4] and the Council evidently authorized him to proceed.
Dufferin meanwhile had gone on holiday; and the negotiations
were conducted with Phipps, the British minister. Phipps was
no doubt better qualified in African detail; at the same time,
this arrangement left the British government freer to repudiate
any concession that he might make.

[1] *D.D.F.*, no. 209. The Foreign Office prepared, but did not use, an answer to
the French arguments. Kimberley to Dufferin, no. 300, 14 August 1894, F.O.
27/3183.

[2] Phipps to Kimberley, nos. 202 and 203, 11 August 1894, F.O. 27/3186.

[3] The instructions were put in the unofficial form of a private memorandum by
Dufferin, 'confirming a conversation with Lord Kimberley', 14 August 1894,
F.O. 27/3183. The instruction also contained the suggestion that Great Britain
might ask for recognition of her 'sphere' in exchange for recognizing the Franco-
Congolese treaty of 14 August. This idea seemed preposterous even to Dufferin,
and he did not put it to Hanotaux.

[4] Dufferin to Kimberley, no. 209, 16 August 1894, F.O. 27/3186. Note by
Hanotaux, 17 August 1894, *D.D.F.*, no. 218.

Phipps and Hanotaux negotiated throughout September. On the various points in West Africa agreement was reached without difficulty. A separate bargain was struck on each point; and Phipps observed honestly to Anderson that in none of them was there the special 'concession' which France had been promised;[2] no doubt Anderson thought it 'concession' enough to agree with the French at all. Hanotaux complained 'he could not see . . . any concession, any bait, offered to France at all in proportion with what had been granted to the other Powers'.[3] Still, he declared repeatedly that he would recognize the Anglo-German convention of 1890 (which defined the British sphere) when the British 'bid high enough'. Here a more serious objection arose. They had agreed not to raise the Egyptian question; and the Anglo-German convention itself defined the British sphere as extending 'to the confines of Egypt'. Hanotaux, too, would recognize the British sphere, so long as it did not involve recognizing British authority over Egyptian territory. What, then, were the 'confines of Egypt'? It was impossible for the British to answer this question, though the answer was simple. Where territory formerly Egyptian was accessible to the British, Egyptian rights had lapsed; where it was accessible to others (whether France or Italy) Egyptian rights were still valid. Phipps had never been told what was the British sphere, for which he was supposed to be contending; he made a guess and, assuming that it was defined in the Anglo-Congolese treaty, replied that the British sphere extended to latitude 10° north, that is, to Fashoda. It was held in London that a sphere extending as far north as Fashoda would effectively bar the way against France; Phipps was therefore told that he had guessed correctly.[4]

[1] Hanotaux only records a meeting on 5 September 1894, *D.D.F.*, no. 234. Phipps records this (telegram, no. 38, F.O. 27/3188, and to Kimberley, no. 223, F.O. 27/3186), and also further meetings on 12 September (telegram, no. 42, F.O. 27/3188, and to Kimberley, no. 223, 13 September, F.O. 27/3186), and on 22 September (telegram, no. 44, F.O. 27/3188, and to Kimberley, no. 247, F.O. 27/3186).

[2] Phipps to Anderson, private, 14 September 1894, F.O. 27/3186.

[3] The Foreign Office devised an answer (Kimberley to Phipps, no. 330, 14 September 1894, F.O. 27/3183), seeking to prove that Germany and Italy had been paid nothing. This was so much in contradiction with the facts that Kimberley cancelled most of the draft.

[4] The British never discriminated clearly between their sphere and the rights of Egypt; they certainly did not regard them as excluding each other. Fashoda

For Hanotaux the answer was both irrelevant and provocative. Though the British had regarded themselves as free to
lease this area to Leopold, they had also asserted in it as against
France 'the rights of Great Britain, of Egypt, and the Porte'.
He was therefore being asked 'to trench on the Egyptian
question'. He had asked to be told the southern limit of Egypt,
not the northern limit of the British sphere; and this the British
would not tell him. On 30 September he himself attempted a
practical definition. The Franco-Congolese arrangement of 14
August, by allowing the Belgians to advance as far north as
Lado, had implicitly acknowledged that the rights of Egypt on
the west bank ended at latitude 5° 30′ N. Hanotaux now
offered to recognize the British sphere on the east bank to the
same northern limit. Since the Belgians were already excluded
from the rest of the British 'sphere' by the promise made to the
French on 14 August, the alleged immediate object of British
policy would be attained. Further, to avoid an Anglo-French
conflict, he proposed 'a self-denying ordinance'; France would
promise for the moment not to pass the Nile-Congo watershed;
England would not advance beyond her present posts in
Uganda and Unyoro. Once Egypt could take action, there
would be a new agreement between the two governments.[1]
Phipps was delighted. He put the proposal into diplomatic
form[2] and, after securing Hanotaux's approval of this on 5
October,[3] telegraphed to Anderson on 6 October:

---

was named as the northern limit of the British sphere simply because it was
believed that the French could not reach the Nile farther north, if they recognized
the British sphere of influence; but there was never any intention of admitting a
'no man's land' between the confines of Egypt and the British sphere. The entire
Nile valley was regarded by the British as being included in one or the other; though
they were sometimes doubtful which a particular place was in. They certainly
never admitted that Egyptian rights ended at Khartum. The elaborate speculations
of Langer (*Diplomacy of Imperialism*, i, 260–2) therefore fall to the ground.

[1] Note by Hanotaux, 29 September 1894, *D.D.F.*, no. 237. Phipps to
Kimberley, no. 225, 29 September 1894; to Anderson, private, 30 September
1894, F.O. 27/3186. There is also a retrospective account of the negotiations in
Hanotaux to d'Estournelles de Constant, 28 October 1894, *D.D.F.*, no. 257.

[2] This enabled Hanotaux to father the idea on Phipps; later, on 10 October, he
admitted that he had originated it.

[3] Note by Hanotaux, 7 October 1894, *D.D.F.*, no. 249. The footnote in
D.D.F. errs in referring to the conversation of 29 September; that of 5 October
(not described in *D.D.F.*) is meant. Phipps to Kimberley, telegram, no. 49,
5 October 1894, F.O. 27/3188; no. 263, 5 October 1894, F.O. 27/3187.

Surely my dispatch of yesterday offers, if not a solution, an indica
tion. Is there not something anomalous in asking for the recognitio.
as a British sphere of a territory admittedly accruing to Egypt
Would it not intrench dangerously on the Egyptian Question prope
which I hear privately the greedy Colonials wish to disturb? W
might try define and restrict French sphere.[1]

Moreover, with that human failing of not hearing the unwel
come, Phipps ignored Hanotaux's limitation 'for the moment'
he assumed, in complete honesty, that France had agreed to
recognize the British sphere, and transmitted the offer in thi
form to the British government. Admittedly, the British woulc
be barred from entering the Nile valley without French permission. But if, as Phipps had been told, the British objec
was to prevent by diplomacy a French expedition to the Nile
which they had no means of stopping otherwise, that objec
had been attained. With each inquiry from London, Phipps
became increasingly emphatic. On 11 October he telegraphed
France would declare 'the territory east of the Congo as absolutely outside the sphere of French influence';[2] and in a further
telegram of the same date: 'there was certainly no question of
any such counter-declaration from us'.[3] Of course he did not
conceal that there was a condition: 'we declaring that we will
not advance into that Egyptian territory from the south without previous understanding with France'. This condition he
treated as temporary; 'by negotiations this difficulty may be
surmounted'.[4]

Thus Phipps supposed that he had succeeded. On 9 October
he transmitted the draft 'entente'-agreement to London for
approval.[5] The Foreign Office was not impressed with Phipps's

[1] Phipps to Anderson, private telegram, 5 October 1894, F.O. 27/3188.

[2] Phipps to Kimberley, telegram, no. 55, 11 October 1894, F.O. 27/3188.

[3] Phipps to Kimberley, telegram, no. 56, 11 October 1894, F.O. 27/3188.

[4] Phipps to Anderson, private, 15 October 1894, F.O. 27/3187. 'Hanotaux
seems to be ready . . . to agree that the Nile valley is *without* the French sphere of
influence and not to demand from us a declaration that it is "without" ours. They
declare that they respect Egyptian rights and pretend they only wish us to do the
same.'

[5] *D.D.F.*, no. 243, 245, 246; Phipps to Kimberley, no. 266, 9 October 1894,
F.O. 27/3187. The agreement covered nine points: compensation for French
missionaries in Uganda; frontier settlement at Sierra Leone; conflicts between
British and French forces at Waïma and N'Compabo; frontier settlement west of
the Niger; interpretation of certain points in the Anglo-French convention of
1890; the Mizon expedition; commercial agreement between certain adjacent

chievement. Intoxicated with the victory of forcing the pro-
ctorate over Uganda on a reluctant cabinet, Rosebery and
nderson dreamt of marching from Uganda to Fashoda, and
ere unwilling to agree to even a temporary suspension of this
dvance. Rosebery drafted a contemptuous telegram of rejec-
on to Phipps on 10 October:

> On the face of it, it appears to be an attempt to debar us from enter-
> ing on our sphere on condition that the French do not enter it. This
> seems a somewhat one-sided arrangement considering that our sphere
> is recognized by three out of the four Great African Powers.[1]

nderson noted: 'I fear Phipps has been much too sanguine';
nd Kimberley echoed him loyally: 'much what I expected'.[2]
wo days later Anderson produced a more detailed criticism:

> In the watershed of the Nile Great Britain and France are placed
> on the same footing. The question of its administration is kept open
> for future negotiation. Our present claim is to be extinguished. There
> is no recognition of any part of our sphere. The Anglo-Congolese
> Agreement is torn up. . . . We are offered nothing beyond the partial
> abandonment of extravagant pretensions which we are well able to
> resist.[3]

till, in Anderson's words, 'to keep France entirely off the
Nile would be a triumph for British diplomacy and might
ustify a surrender elsewhere'. He did not attempt to suggest
vhat this surrender might be. Instead he devised an alternative
proposal, by which Great Britain would get her hands on the
ıpper Nile, under cover of Egyptian authority:

---

olonies; the hinterland of Ashanti; and, finally, the upper Nile. Agreement,
more or less acceptable even to Anderson, was reached on all points except the
ast; when this fell through, only the frontier settlement at Sierra Leone was
aved. This agreement has been the subject of much speculation; date and con-
ents were unknown until the opening of the archives. Even Hanotaux was
ɔewildered, and ascribed it later to December 1894. The agreement was a formal
draft accepted by Hanotaux and Phipps, except for the final point of the upper
Nile. Phipps recognized that it was useless to formulate this, until the British
government gave its consent in principle; instead this consent was refused.

[1] Kimberley to Phipps, telegram, no. 60, 10 October 1894, F.O. 27/3188,
draft by Rosebery.

[2] Minutes on Hanotaux to Phipps, 10 October 1894 (*D.D.F.*, no. 245), F.O.
27/3187.

[3] This comes towards the end of comments on the Phipps-Hanotaux agreement which seem to have been written on 12 October and were printed for
circulation to the cabinet on 16 October 1894, F.O. 27/3209.

France admits her sphere is bounded by the Congo-Nile watershe
Great Britain gives assurance that it is not her intention directly
govern or to administer that part of the Nile watershed, mentioned
the Anglo-Congolese Agreement, which lies to the north of the
30′ parallel.

Anderson added: 'This would leave us a free hand to the ea:
of the Nile and would involve an indirect recognition of ou
sphere by the reference to the Agreement with the King.'[1]

Anderson thought that Hanotaux would agree to this onl
if he were treated roughly. 'M. Hanotaux would require to b
hard pressed to concede it and hitherto Phipps has not presse
him at all. A different tone would have to be used in the negc
tiations from Phipps' apologetic, almost supplicatory, lar
guage.' Kimberley once more agreed: 'It seems to me tha
Phipps has got to the length of his tether and that it is necessar
for Lord Dufferin to take up the matter.'[2] Phipps was therefor
told on 12 October that he was not to see Hanotaux again.
Hanotaux meanwhile was being hard pressed, though not i
the direction that Anderson desired. On 15 October he wa
warned that the Colonial ministry did not accept the self
denying proposal; and a few days later Delcassé told him tha
the French expeditions on the Ubanghi could race the Britisl
to the Nile.[4] Hanotaux needed an early reply from the Britisl
in order to fight his battle with Delcassé in the Council o
Ministers; and he appealed to Phipps on more than on
occasion.[5] Phipps could only tell him that he had been in
structed to suspend negotiations.

Dufferin returned to Paris at the end of October; he had
had to cut short his holiday, and was in a bad temper. Wher
he met Hanotaux on 31 October, he tried threats, as Andersor
had recommended: the British government, he said, would no
agree to the settlement of West African affairs unless France

[1] Anderson first devised this formula as a minute on Phipps' telegram, no. 56
Its final form appears in the comments mentioned in the previous note.

[2] Minutes by Anderson, 9 October, and by Kimberley, 10 October 1894, F.O
27/3209.

[3] Anderson to Phipps, telegram, 12 October 1894, F.O. 27/3188.

[4] Note by Hanotaux, 30 October 1894, D.D.F., no. 260.

[5] Phipps to Kimberley, telegram, no. 57, 18 October 1894, F.O. 27/3188
no. 280, 24 October 1894, F.O. 27/3187. Hanotaux mentions a meeting on 2c
October; he probably meant the meeting of 18 October. Hanotaux to d'Estournelles de Constant, 29 October 1894, D.D.F., no. 258.

dhered to the Anglo-German convention of 1890. Hanotaux
eplied that France was willing to do this, once the British
efined 'the confines of Egypt'. Discussion was back at its
tarting-point.[1] Anderson, late in the day, now attempted a
efinition of 'the confines of Egypt'. These, he wrote on 2
November, were laid down in the Hatti-Sherif of 1841; very
onveniently, their southern limit was parallel 10° N., and thus
with a little adjustment', Fashoda was in the British sphere.
As to the equatorial provinces, these were unknown in 1841.
They were 'temporarily occupied and then abandoned by
Egypt'; but 'we recognize the contingency of the resumption
f these abandoned rights'.[2] In other words, the rights of
Egypt, though ineffective against the British 'sphere', could
till be invoked against anyone else. This definition was passed
n to Dufferin on 3 November. Dufferin was further told that
he British government would not accept the mutual self-
denying proposal: 'it would amount practically to the abandonment by them of a large portion of the British sphere which
has been formally recognized by Germany and Italy and
ecently by the Congo Free State'. A last formula was produced
nore futile than its predecessors:

> In case, however, the French Government display an insur-
> mountable reluctance to formally recognize our sphere but should
> be disposed to give an assurance that they would not advance beyond
> the watershed of the Nile we on our side might take act of such an
> assurance and thus arrive at a practical settlement.

Dufferin was to insist that there could be no agreement on
ther African questions without a recognition of the British
sphere. At the same time he was not to press Hanotaux, 'as the
result might be that he would be led to make declarations,
denying our right to the sphere instead of leaving the matter,
as he appears at present inclined to do so, open for possible
negotiations at some future time'.[3]
 Dufferin and Hanotaux had a final, decisive interview on
7 November. Dufferin was by now in a better temper, and
perhaps even a little ashamed at having to break off negotiations. At any rate, he agreed that the frontier settlement at

[1] Note by Hanotaux, 1 November 1894, *D.D.F.*, no. 263. Dufferin to
Kimberley, telegram, no. 58, 31 October 1894, F.O. 27/3188.
[2] Memorandum by Anderson, 2 November 1894, F.O. 27/3257.
[3] Kimberley to Dufferin, no. 390, 3 November 1894, F.O. 27/3183.

Sierra Leone should be salvaged from the general wreck. O
the Nile, however, deadlock had been reached. Dufferin aske
for recognition of the Anglo-Congolese treaty of 12 Ma
Hanotaux quoted against it the Franco-Congolese conventio
of 14 August, and observed that the Congo State had con
sulted England before signing this. Dufferin, at sea as eve
asked Hanotaux if he could see a solution to the Sudanes
conflict. Hanotaux replied that 'the proposition of provision:
mutual disinterestedness or desistence' was all that occurre
to him. This was rejected by Dufferin: 'Phipps had advance
too far, and the views that he had expressed were not at a
those of the London Cabinet.' Dufferin then demanded th:
Hanotaux should take an engagement in the name of Franc
'not to extend our sphere of influence beyond the basin c
the Congo'. Hanotaux refused. There was no more to b
said.[1]

Ten days later the French Council of Ministers decided t
suspend negotiations regarding the upper Nile; and th
Colonial ministry was instructed to ensure that France shoul·
occupy as much as possible of these territories ahead of Col
ville, who was preparing to advance from Uganda. Delcass
claimed that Liotard, the explorer who had taken the plac
of Monteil, could be on the Nile within a year.[2]

(IV)

Diplomacy had ceased; the race to the Nile had begun
Each side was a little frightened by what it had started
Hanotaux still hankered after negotiations, and in Decembe
sent Courcel, the best French diplomat of his day, as ambassa
dor to London. Kimberley, sandwiched between Anderson and
Rosebery, had not been allowed much say in the previous nego
tiations, and was perhaps glad to do a little diplomacy on hi
own. On 18 December Kimberley and Courcel ranged onc
more over the question of the upper Nile. Kimberley inquire·
whether it would help things if Great Britain declared th
contested territory to be Egyptian—this might even be a sig
that England and France were drawing nearer on the Egyptia

---

[1] Note by Hanotaux, 7 November 1894, D.D.F., no. 272; Dufferin t
Kimberley, no. 293, 7 November 1894, F.O. 27/3187.
[2] Note by Hanotaux, undated [17 November 1894], D.D.F., no. 285.

question. Courcel did not care for this idea: it would not do to settle the first chapter of the Egyptian question unless they were willing to go on to the second. He took up Kimberley's suggested promise 'not to annex any part of this territory' and asked whether he would promise not to occupy it. Kimberley answered: 'No, for that would in effect be to relinquish the sphere altogether to which we could not consent.' Courcel then suggested a British promise not to enter the disputed territory for a given length of time, say for ten years. This also was too much for Kimberley; but he added, in his weak way, 'I don't think we shall be led to enter the territory concerned for a long time. We have quite enough to do in Unyoro.'[1] Agreement was still out of sight.

Kimberley, during the conversation of 18 December, mumbled the usual warning against any French attempt to enter the upper Nile. The warning was delivered in a friendly tone, and he added: 'Do not even say that I have told you that we do not want you to enter the disputed territory; these are things that are not said to a friendly Great Power.' Kimberley had reckoned without Rosebery. The distracted Liberal cabinet was moving towards its fall; and Rosebery, always nervous and irritable, wished to explode against someone. At the end of March 1895, he exploded against the French. There had been further disputes with the French on the Niger; there was no recent or reliable information regarding any French expedition towards the Nile—and in truth the French plans had fallen through. The only spur to action was a report from the Intelligence Department of the War Office, made on 6 March: the department had just come across a German map of the Sudan, showing the effects of the Franco-Congolese agreement of 14 August 1894, and their penetrating military minds deduced from this that the French route to the Nile was still open.[2] No other background for the 'Grey declaration' is to be found in the Foreign Office papers. However, for whatever reason, Kimberley was pushed into action by Rosebery on 28 March. Simulating an unusual indignation, he complained to Courcel about French encroachments on the Niger, and added a general reference to difficulties with France elsewhere. Courcel,

[1] Courcel to Hanotaux, 19 December 1894, *D.D.F.*, no. 319; Kimberley to Dufferin, no. 434A, 18 December 1894, F.O. 27/3183. Kimberley, not surprisingly, did not record this last remark.

[2] Intelligence Department to Foreign Office, 6 March 1895, F.O. 27/3257.

though he caught the word 'Siam', seems to have missed th
Nile altogether.[1]

The same evening Grey, the under-secretary for foreig
affairs, spoke in the House of Commons on the Foreign Offic
vote. He disclaimed knowledge of any French expedition to th
upper Nile, and said, in a famous phrase, that any such expedi
tion would be 'an unfriendly act'.[2] This was no more than ha
been said repeatedly to the French in private, and simila
warnings would have appeared in the promised Blue book o
the Anglo-Congolese treaty if it had ever been published.
Only in that case the warnings would have been accompanie
by the French answer. As it was, the Grey declaration—lackin
any justification of a specific French act—was surely a way c
trying to get by public statement what the British governmen
had failed to get by diplomacy, a legacy to the succeedin
government that was visibly in the offing. It would have bee
sharp practice for the French to send an expedition to the uppe
Nile while negotiations were proceeding, if, in fact, they ha
been; it was equally sharp practice for the British governmen
to bring the issue into the open without warning to th
French.

Courcel at once lodged a written protest with Kimberley;
he followed this up in person on 1 April. Kimberley, on whom
no doubt the Grey declaration had been sprung unawares,
reverted to his most apologetic mood. Grey, he said, was ':
simple Under-Secretary', whose declaration had less weigh
than if it had been made by the foreign secretary or the prime
minister; he had merely repeated the British thesis or 'claim'

[1] Kimberley to Dufferin, nos. 111 and 111A, 28 March 1895, F.O. 27/3229
Courcel to Hanotaux, telegrams, 28 March 1895, *D.D.F.*, nos. 412 and 413.

[2] The F.O. papers contain the drafts of Grey's answers to questions. The Grey
declaration, however, was made in the course of debate, not as an answer to a
question; and no draft has been preserved.

[3] Grey intended to promise papers 'if pressed' when he was questioned abou
the Franco-Congolese agreement on 16 August 1894. But no demand was made
(F.O. 10/625). The government announced a Blue book on 23 August 1894.
but never proceeded with it—a unique case.

[4] Courcel to Hanotaux (with enclosures), 29 March 1894, *D.D.F.*, no. 419

[5] Grey's own version, according to which he was told by Kimberley to us
strong language about the Niger and accidentally transferred the strong language
to the Nile (*Twenty Five Years*, i, 18), has been rejected by more than one
historian. Langer, *Diplomacy of Imperialism*, i, 265; Temperley and Penson,
Foundations of British Foreign Policy, p. 501.

d France was free to reject this thesis—'the question there-
re remained open to debate', and the only object of Grey's
eclaration was to prevent a French occupation while the
ebate was proceeding. Further, the British government had
) intention of taking any action at present (this was true—
ence their hostility to French action): 'We shall not have
e intention of attacking the Sudan for a long time, nor even
entering the regions which you dispute to our sphere of
fluence; we are not now planning to go into the Bahr el
hazal.' Finally he said that even if the Sudan were recovered,
would be occupied by Egyptian troops and administration,
d would be associated with 'the destiny of Egypt itself'.[1]

Hanotaux certainly did not wish to respond to Grey's chal-
nge. He had written sharply on 29 March: 'I cannot admit
at points which are the subject of diplomatic dispute shall be
eclared *indisputable* in the British parliament.'[2] Kimberley's
ology gave him, however, a way of escape; Kimberley him-
lf had said: 'the question remains open to debate', and this
as all that Hanotaux claimed when he spoke in the French
nate on 5 April. In the end, he declared, 'two great nations
ill know how to find formulas which will reconcile their
terests and satisfy their common aspirations towards civiliza-
on and progress'. Kimberley praised Hanotaux's conciliatory
ne to Courcel the following day. In an excess of conciliation
e now proposed something like the standstill agreement which
e British government had rejected when Hanotaux had
roposed it the previous autumn—'a tacit agreement implying
modus vivendi acceptable to the two countries and excluding
ny unilateral act which could prejudice the rights or claims
f one or the other'. Courcel did not respond to this suggestion.
t the end of the conversation Kimberley remarked that Grey's
eclaration was merely a reply to Hanotaux's speech of 7 June
f the previous year, and that 'he quite agreed with us not to
ttach any importance in diplomatic negotiations, to parlia-

[1] Kimberley to Dufferin, no. 112A, 1 April 1895, F.O. 27/3229. Courcel to
Hanotaux, telegram, 2 April 1895; 2 April 1895, *D.D.F.*, nos. 423 and 429.
Kimberley's account is naturally less apologetic, but Courcel read him the telegram to Hanotaux (Courcel to Hanotaux, 3 April 1895, *D.D.F.*, no. 430), and
e confirmed it except (i) he would not bind himself for the future so far as the
ahr el Ghazal was concerned; (ii) he had not meant to imply that British troops
ould not co-operate with Egyptian troops in reconquering the Sudan.
[2] Hanotaux to Courcel, private, 29 March 1894, *D.D.F.*, no. 416.

mentary declarations'.[1] Kimberley at any rate had done h
feeble best to erase the effects of the Grey declaration.

However, it was not only Kimberley who had secor
thoughts. By now the dream of conquering the Sudan fro
Uganda had proved unworkable, and it had become obvio
that the Sudan could only be entered from the north. Th
British were thus belatedly willing to leave the Nile alone sou
of Fashoda if the French would do the same. On 6 Ma
Anderson minuted that Rosebery wished to renew negoti
tions with the French about the 'projet de désistement
Anderson produced a new formula: 'the two Powers recogni
that they cannot make acquisitions in, or infringe upon th
Provinces of Darfur and Kordofan.[2] . . . They agree that the
will not make acquisitions in, nor infringe upon, the territor
adjoining these provinces (i.e. the territory as defined in th
lease which Leopold had not been allowed to take up). I
this arrangement Great Britain, acting in the name of Egyp
would have had exclusive control of the Nile as far south a
Fashoda; beyond that would have been a no man's land, whic
both France and Great Britain would be pledged not to ente
while all other neighbours would have recognized it as
British sphere of influence.[3] On 10 May Kimberley timidl
sounded Courcel along these lines. Courcel rejected 'the cor
nection which it was sought to establish between our occupa
tion of Egypt and the sphere of influence which we claime
on the Upper Nile'.[4] The conversation ended: it was the la
which took place during the tenure of the Liberal governmen

The objection which ended the negotiations had over
shadowed them from the beginning: it was impossible t
separate the upper Nile from the Egyptian question. At th
start, the British had tried to draw a line between their spher
of interest and the rights of Egypt; this line could never b
found, and the 'Grey declaration' completed the entanglemer
of British and Egyptian rights. For Leopold II the upper Nil
was, no doubt, valuable in itself; for the French it was a mean
with which to 'trench upon the Egyptian question'. Th
French were not concerned to establish themselves in the valle
of the Nile, nor even to eject the British from Egypt. Th

[1] Courcel to Hanotaux, telegram, 6 April 1895, *D.D.F.*, no. 435.

[2] These provinces were included within the Hatti-Sherif of 1841, and wer
therefore indisputably Egyptian.

[3] Memorandum by Anderson, 6 May 1895, F.O. 27/3257.

[4] Kimberley to Dufferin, no. 151, 10 May 1895, F.O. 27/3229.

gyptian question was for them a matter of internal politics—
find some compromise which would reconcile French public
inion to the loss of Egypt, and so enable good relations
tween England and France to be restored. In 1898 the
itish 'solved' the question of the upper Nile: by superior
rce, not argument, they compelled the French at last to
cognize their 'sphere of influence'. Though this deprived
ance of a bargaining counter, it did not settle the Egyptian
estion. The question of Egypt could not be solved by force;
could be solved only by compensation and goodwill. In 1894
anotaux alone had the goodwill, and even in his case it
cked urgency; at any rate he made no serious effort to formu-
.e the price at which France would accept British primacy in
gypt. At most, he sought to postpone Fashoda, not to avoid
It needed the decay of Morocco and a shift in the balance of
e Great Powers to bring Great Britain and France together.

XIV

BRITISH POLICY IN MOROCCO, 1886–1902

On 1 July 1886 Drummond Hay retired from the position
British minister at Tangier. He had held the post for more th[a]
forty years.[1] Like Stratford de Redcliffe at Constantinop[le]
under whom he had begun his diplomatic career, Drummo[nd]
Hay had aspired to be at once protector and reformer of t[he]
Moorish empire. Certainly British policy had held off t[he]
encroachments of others: it had checked France in 1847 a[nd]
Spain in 1860. It had been less successful in reform. Mul[ey]
Hassan, the Sultan of Morocco, had no more desire to [be]
reformed by the British than by anyone else; besides—wis[er]
than Drummond Hay—he realized that France and Spai[n,]
the two Powers who coveted his territory, would tolera[te]
Moorish independence only so long as Morocco remain[ed]
unreformed. They might postpone encroachment; they wou[ld]
not see the chance of it removed. In practice, Muley Hassa[n's]
policy of evasion suited British interests. Though Great Brita[in]
had the largest share of what Moorish trade there was, t[he]
essential British interest was negative: to keep the coastli[ne]
opposite Gibraltar out of the hands of a Great Power, not [to]
acquire this coastline for herself. Since Ceuta—directly opp[o-]
site Gibraltar—was already Spanish, this meant principal[ly]
preserving the independence of Tangier; and for British poli[cy]
Tangier and Morocco were almost interchangeable terms.

This was not so for France; hence the troubles which ha[d]
begun with the conference at Madrid in 1880. Moroc[co]
for France was an African problem, the anarchic neighbo[ur]
of Algeria, and the missing piece in her North Africa[n]
empire. In 1880 Great Britain, largely on Drummond Hay[']s
prompting, had taken the lead in summoning a conference [at]
Madrid, which should regulate 'protection'—the system b[y]
which Moorish subjects could virtually escape from th[e]
authority of their own government by becoming the agents [of]

[1] His work is described in F. R. Flournoy, *British Policy towards Morocco [in]
the Age of Palmerston* (1935).

114

e of the foreign ministers.[1] This conference had been
signed as a first step in a programme of reforms. Instead
ance diverted it into legalizing and extending 'protection';
d Bismarck, as part of his policy of conciliating France,
cured for her the backing of the other European Powers.
nly Spain had been timidly on the British side; but Spanish
pport was equivocal. The Spaniards were always conscious
at they already held in Morocco fragments of a vanished
frican empire; and therefore, though they were anxious to
eck the encroachment of France, they looked forward to a
stant day when they might renew their own.

Thus the Madrid Conference was a decisive defeat for
rummond Hay's dreams of reform. He was too old to devise
new policy, even if one could have been found. He continued
urge on the British government the impossible project of
forming Morocco with the general agreement of the Powers.
is political testament was to propose that the Great Powers
ould reach a formal understanding to maintain the inde-
endence of Morocco; thereupon the foreign representatives
ould move from Tangier to Fez, so as to be able to press
forms upon the Sultan.[2] This advice assumed that the Powers
ould co-operate in Morocco, that is, it assumed that there was
o Moroccan problem. The history of the next sixteen years
as to show repeatedly that this assumption was false. Drum-
ond Hay's prestige had cloaked the decline in British security
Morocco. With his retirement Great Britain began to search,
ough with little success, for a Moorish policy. Incidentally,
rummond Hay spent his last years in Tangier, at once
valuable and a great nuisance to his successor.

This successor, Kirby Green, at once rejected Drummond
[H]ay's proposal for a co-operation of the Powers. The Sultan,
e insisted, would ignore advice and would be driven to reform
nly by threats; nor was there any chance of a general agree-
ent among the Powers. 'For Her Majesty's Government to

[1] For the Madrid Conference see E. F. Cruickshank, *Morocco at the Parting
of the Ways* (1935).
[2] Drummond Hay to Rosebery, no. 24, 13 May 1886, F.O. 99/228. Hay had
ade a similar proposal to Granville in 1884. The F.O. 99 series, from which
e new material for this article is taken, though described as 'Morocco', contains
uch more than the correspondence with Tangier. It was an early experiment
he Suez Canal was another) in the system of filing according to subject, instead
f according to country, which was generally adopted in 1906.

conjure away these dangers by simply deciding upon mai
taining the *status quo* is impossible.' A force should therefo
be stationed at Gibraltar ready to seize Tangier at a momen
notice.[1] The project of seizing Tangier overnight was
become a constant refrain in the next few years. It was, a
remained, a piece of 'diplomatic' strategy. The garrison
Gibraltar was never increased so as to have men to spare f
the purpose; nor did the naval authorities make any effort
have ships ready to carry a landing-force. It certainly appea
from the scraps of evidence available that the naval authoriti
desired to acquire Tangier if Morocco broke down;[2] such
project is indeed inescapable from the most hasty glance at
map. But the naval authorities expected to be provided wi
Tangier by diplomatic means; whereas the diplomats alwa
spoke of 'seizing' Tangier, since they knew of no way
acquiring it by negotiation. In short, though 'seizing' Tangi
sounded more realistic than Drummond Hay's project
co-operating with the other Great Powers, it was open to tl
same objection. If the policy had been practicable, it wou
not have been necessary; if the British could truly seize Tangi
at any time, they would not need to worry about excludir
others. Alternatively, if Tangier could be obtained by dipl
macy, it did not represent a potential danger to Gibraltar.

Early in 1887 it seemed as though the question of Moroc
was to be decisively posed. The French secured from tl
Sultan a rectification of the frontier between Algeria ar
Morocco. It was feared that the next 'rectification' would be
French demand for Tuat. This was the principal oasis betwee
Algeria and Morocco; though once disputably Moorish, it w
now treated by the French as a no man's land, whereas othe
held that its seizure by the French would be the signal for
partition of Morocco. The Spaniards had a vague unde
standing with France, made in 1884, that the two would a
together in Morocco to maintain the *status quo*—this, when
was made, was a gesture against Drummond Hay's policy
reform; but the French always insisted that, since Tuat was n
in their view part of Morocco, they were not threatening tl
status quo by excluding the Moorish authorities from it. More
the Spanish foreign minister, was greatly alarmed and appeale

[1] Kirby Green to Iddesleigh, no. 73, 14 November; no. 77, 8 December 188
F.O. 99/299.

[2] Marder, *British Naval Policy*, 1880–1905, p. 580.

r British support. Salisbury gave a cautious reply. He
inuted the British ambassador's dispatch: 'He may assure
gnor Moret of our moral support in any effort he may make
secure the independence and integrity of Morocco' and
lded the advice that Moret should consult with the Italian
overnment.[1] For Italy, too, was now asserting herself as a
Iediterranean Power, and was as eager to play a part in
Iorocco at one end of the Mediterranean as in Turkey at the
her. Kirby Green disliked this reliance on diplomacy: 'we
iould always be ready for energetic and independent British
ction'.[2] However, he received no encouragement from
ilisbury in this course and, *faute de mieux*, joined with the
alian and Spanish ministers at Tangier in drafting a Note, in
hich the Sultan was urged to pledge himself not to alienate
Ioorish territory further.[3] The outcome of this would have
een to push Muley Hassan into the front line against France;
was thus implicitly a confession by the three Powers that
iey did not wish to find themselves in this position. Its effect,
i any case slight, was weakened still more when Salisbury
eleted the offer of support (*appui*) to maintain the indepen-
ence and integrity of Morocco and substituted *bons offices*.[4]
he Spaniards would have liked to involve Germany and
aimed that they had German backing. It soon turned out that,
iough the Germans encouraged a collective Note by Great
ritain, Italy, and Spain, they themselves intended to keep on
ood terms with France.[5] The German minister at Tangier told
irby Green that 'he was directed to observe the greatest
serve in his political conduct here, so long as friendly rela-
ons existed between France and Germany'.[6]

The collective note was dispatched to the Sultan on 12
Iarch 1887. Kirby Green followed hard after it in order to
ay his inaugural visit to the Sultan, who was at Marrakesh.
he visit was not a success. Muley Hassan was as unwilling
i Salisbury to be pushed into the front line of resistance

[1] Ford (Madrid) to Salisbury, no. 11, 1 February 1887, F.O. 99/241.
[2] Kirby Green to Salisbury, no. 15, 1 February 1887, F.O. 99/241.
[3] Kirby Green to Salisbury, no. 18, 7 February 1887, F.O. 99/241.
[4] Minute by Salisbury on Kirby Green's no. 27, 23 February 1887, F.O.
)/241.
[5] Ford to Salisbury, no. 20, 13 February 1887, F.O. 99/241; Malet to
.lisbury, no. 60, 19 February 1887, F.O. 99/241.
[6] Kirby Green to Salisbury, no. 30, 24 February 1887, F.O. 99/241.

against France. Certainly he wished the European Powers
defend the independence and integrity of Morocco; but
did not intend to debar himself from negotiating with tl
French and, if necessary, making concessions to them. Kirl
Green wrote irritably: 'the Sultan's uneducated mind is n
very capable of taking a broad view of the political position
exigencies of his country. His only motive is fear, mostly
France and Spain, who have given him more frequent pro
of their power to injure him.' The Sultan alleged that he ha
sent the Note to one of his most trusted counsellors in Fe
Green suspected that this counsellor was, in fact, the Frenc
minister. When Kirby Green showed, to his own satisfactio
that Morocco was doomed unless it co-operated with the thr
Powers who had signed the Note, Muley Hassan only replied
'But if God wished it otherwise all you have said could no
take place.' Kirby Green returned to Tangier with the gloom
conviction: 'conversation with eastern rulers is barren of result
because the will of the individual is allowed to override logic'[1]

Muley Hassan refused to give a binding answer to the co
lective Note. Instead he proposed that the three Powers shoul
obtain from all the Powers interested in Morocco a gener:
guarantee of its neutrality, similar to the guarantee of Belgiun
Kirby Green suspected that this idea had originated with Spair
the Spaniards, he thought, wished to retard the Frenc
encroachments, but without themselves taking sides agains
France. He told the Spanish minister impatiently: 'If ever th
integrity of Morocco came to be seriously menaced, the matte
would be treated as one of vital importance to British interest:
and not as a side question capable of half a dozen solutions
As to neutralization, general discussion would at once show it
impossibility and would thus be an encouragement to Franc
to renew her encroachments.[2] Salisbury also dismissed the ide
of neutralizing Morocco. He wrote on 7 September 1887
'European Powers would only neutralize a Power which by th
excellence of its internal constitution is incapable of givin
offence' and therefore inquired what reforms were contem
plated by the Sultan.[3] The proposal was not raised again.

Thus Salisbury's policy in 1887 was defined by its negations

[1] Kirby Green to Salisbury, no. 54, 25 April; no. 62, 7 July 1887, F.C
99/241.

[2] Kirby Green to Salisbury, no. 84, 22 August 1887, F.O. 99/236.

[3] Salisbury to Kirby Green, no. 68, 7 September 1887, F.O. 99/234.

He wished to encourage Muley Hassan in independence, without promising him British support; and similarly urged cooperation between Spain and Italy on a basis of vague British approval. In fact Spain and Italy made an agreement on 4 May 1887, pledging themselves to maintain the *status quo* in the Mediterranean: Spain undertook not to make any agreement with France, especially in regard to North Africa, directed against any of the Powers of the Triple Alliance.[1] The agreement was shown to Salisbury, who expressed 'full sympathy' with it. However, the Spanish government lived in constant apprehension of committing itself decisively to one side or the other; and in the autumn of 1887 stirred up the Moroccan question with the vague hope of escaping from its difficulties. Moret, the Spanish foreign minister, proposed to summon a new conference to revise the system of protection in Morocco; and he tried to frighten or persuade the rival Powers into this conference by telling them lies about each other. On the one hand he told the French chargé d'affaires that 'no discussion concerning the maintenance of the *status quo* in Morocco had taken place between Spain and other Powers than France' and that he was ready to continue the co-operation with France to maintain the *status quo* which had been agreed on in 1884.[2] On the other hand he told the British and Italian ambassadors that Paul Cambon, the French ambassador, was interpreting the agreement of 1884 as preparing the way for a partition of Morocco between France and Spain.[3] The Italians, of course, affected to believe the story, in the hope of drawing Salisbury into some commitment; the hope was disappointed. Cambon, no doubt, hit on the truth when he remarked to Sir Clare Ford that the Spaniards were building up alarms in Morocco 'in order to hold out hopes to their over-officered army of the near prospect of a campaign'.[4] Moret himself retreated and made out that the alarm was due to the blundering of Cambon: 'M. Cambon is a fool and no diplomat. I like to draw him out.'[5]

[1] Pribram, *Secret Treaties of Austria-Hungary*, i, 116–22.

[2] Belle to Flourens, telegrams, 8 October, 11 October 1887, *Documents Diplomatiques Français* (hereafter cited as *D.D.F.*), first series, ix, appendix, nos. v and vi, p. 691.

[3] Egerton (Paris) to Salisbury, telegram, no. 17, 14 October; Ford to Salisbury, no. 121, 16 October 1887, F.O. 99/241.

[4] Ford to Salisbury, no. 122, 18 October 1887, F.O. 99/241.

[5] Ford to Salisbury, no. 135, 28 October 1887, F.O. 99/241.

E

On 1 December 1887 the Spanish government issued invita
tions to the proposed conference. The British governmen
wished to add the question of commercial relations generally
the French government insisted on a defined programme
Finally, in the summer of 1888, the Spanish government—
with a new foreign minister—lost interest in the conference and
no more was heard of it.

There followed two years of quiet, almost unbroken till afte
the fall of Bismarck. Kirby Green was left to occupy himsel
with complaints about the state of the Moorish prisons and
about alleged sales of slaves which were made by the anti
slavery society in England. In the autumn of 1888 there was a
renewed alarm from Italy of an agreement between France and
Spain to divide Morocco.[1] Kirby Green was told to hold
'unreserved intercourse with his Italian colleague'; on the
other hand he received no encouragement when he urged tha
Great Britain and Italy should prepare to counter Franco
Spanish plans by occupying Tangier, Casablanca, Mazagan
and Mogador.[2] There was an alarm of a different kind in 1889
when Muley Hassan sent a special mission to congratulate
William II on his accession. The Moors insisted that thi
mission was a simple act of courtesy and in no way connected
with the German request for a Moorish port which—according
to Muley Hassan—had been made in 1886 or 1887. The
French thought that the mission might be intended on the
German side to frighten Spain into committing hersel
more firmly to the Triple Alliance.[3] Probably these elaborate
speculations were unfounded; it flattered the German govern
ment to be treated as a 'world power', but so long as Bismarck
ruled, Germany would not behave as one. The mission to
Germany, and its warm reception, was, however, a preliminary
announcement that one day Germany, too, would aspire to play

[1] Kirby Green to Salisbury, telegram, no. 13, 2 November 1888, F.O. 99/270
Kennedy (Rome) to Salisbury, no. 43, 14 November; Ford to Salisbury, 1.
November 1888, F.O. 99/270.

[2] Kirby Green to Salisbury, no. 93, 12 July; no. 130, 6 November 1888
F.O. 99/251.

[3] Herbette to Goblet, 7 February 1889, *D.D.F.*, first series, vii, no. 322
telegram, 17 February 1889, no. 327; Spuller to Herbette, 1 March 1889, no
336. The French give the name of the port alleged to be sought by the German
as Adjeroud; Kirby Green (to Salisbury, no. 36, 6 March 1887, F.O. 99/235
as Aggirud.

a part in the Moroccan question—and probably an erratic one.

The period of quiet in Morocco resulted, as on other occasions, in England and France drawing closer together. Morocco was for the other Powers mainly a question of prestige. The Spaniards had certainly the interest of propinquity and were resolved not to be left out in any partition; but they had virtually no trade with Morocco, and their fortresses on the coast—Ceuta and the rest—were too decayed to do more than produce occasional disputes with the neighbouring tribes. Italy had no interest in Morocco except to show that she was a Mediterranean Power; Germany had no interest except to make mischief. Only Great Britain and France were concerned with practical questions—France with the Algerian frontier, Great Britain with Moorish trade and the neutrality of Tangier. Therefore, when not actually quarrelling, they tended to establish an unacknowledged condominium, much to the annoyance of the other Powers.[1] It is true that early in 1890 Kirby Green at last extracted from the Sultan a grudging adherence to the principles of the collective Note of 1887—that is, he would not alienate Moorish territory;[2] but as the French were at this moment not demanding anything, the gesture was empty. In any case Kirby Green had lost faith in Moorish powers of resistance and even began to hanker after a partition agreement with France. He placed his fragile hope of saving Morocco in opening the country effectively to European trade. He therefore drafted a commercial treaty for which he got the approval of his French, German, Spanish, and Italian colleagues,[3] and then proposed to press this treaty on Muley Hassan by collective action. This scheme was wrecked by the dishonesty of Tattenbach, the German minister, who visited Fez in May 1890. Tattenbach seems to have been motivated solely by the desire (common among German envoys) to display his strength. According to Moorish reports, he repeated the German request for a port near Melilla; then, although he had promised to leave the commercial treaty to collective action,

---

[1] The Germans complained of Kirby Green's friendship with France in December 1890. Marschall to Hatzfeldt, 25 December 1890, *Die Grosse Politik der Europäischen Kabinette* (hereafter cited as *G.P.*), viii, no. 1914, p. 293.

[2] Kirby Green to Salisbury, no. 20, 27 February 1890, F.O. 99/275.

[3] Kirby Green to Salisbury, no. 22, 13 March; no. 34, 16 April; Salisbury to Kirby Green, no. 29, 27 March; no. 39, 20 May 1890, F.O. 99/275.

he demanded and secured a commercial treaty to Germany's exclusive benefits, in exchange dropping his request for a port.[1] The Moors, who knew everything that went on among the foreign ministers at Tangier, were aware that collective action for an effective commercial treaty was being prepared; and they were glad enough to get the Germans out of step. Tattenbach, on his return to Tangier, had to admit that he could not join in a collective action, though he denied that he had asked for a port; and the German commercial treaty was to raise still more difficulties for the British two years later. Kirby Green decided to attempt to carry the commercial treaty by his own persuasion. He paid a long visit to Muley Hassan at Marrakesh, and died there suddenly on 25 February 1891, with nothing accomplished.

Kirby Green's initiative over the commercial treaty would probably have ended the 'truce' between France and Great Britain which had lasted since 1887; in any case, the question of Morocco was revived early in 1891 by a new alarm over Tuat. In May 1891 the French warned Muley Hassan that, though they were not yet prepared to occupy Tuat, they would oppose any Moorish attempt to do so; and in August the Moorish government appealed to Great Britain, Spain, and Italy.[2] The diplomacy of the Tuat affair, for the next twelve months, parodied the diplomacy of the Bulgarian question in 1887, which had culminated in the Mediterranean *entente* between Great Britain, Italy, and Austria-Hungary. Italy tried to be the link between Spain and Great Britain, as she had been the link between Austria-Hungary and Great Britain; and Germany tried to act as patron of this new triple *entente*, while insisting that she was not concerned in the affair. Just as Salisbury had answered Bismarck's promptings in August 1887 by hinting at a British deal with Russia,[3] so he brushed off German warnings over Morocco by declaring that he had

---

[1] There is no reference to Tattenbach's visit to Fez in *G.P.* Kirby Green to Salisbury, no. 44, 18 May; no. 48, 11 June; no. 49, 13 June; no. 50, 25 June 1890, F.O. 99/275. The French and Spanish ministers both believed that Tattenbach had indeed asked for a port; Kirby Green accepted Tattenbach's denial and was approved by Salisbury (to Kirby Green, no. 41, 22 May 1890, F.O. 99/275).

[2] White (chargé d'affaires) to Salisbury, telegram, no. 9, 20 August 1891, F.O. 99/284.

[3] Hatzfeldt to Bismarck, 3 August 1887, *G.P.*, iv, no. 907, p. 336.

un bon appetit' there.[1] This lighthearted remark presumably pointed to a possible partition with France, to the detriment of Spain. The Germans affected to welcome this evidence of an active British interest in Morocco, believing, no doubt, that British and French interests there could never be reconciled.[2]

The attempt to build up a western Mediterranean *entente* was not successful. For one thing, Spain was not in the same position as Austria-Hungary. Spain was not an essential German interest; and the Spaniards had to get along without the ultimate security of a German backing. If the Spaniards could have had some defensive guarantee against France, as the Habsburgs had against Russia by the treaty of 1879, they might have been as anti-French as the Austrians were anti-Russian, though even this is doubtful: the Spaniards were at once weaker and more cunning than the Austrians. As it was, the Spaniards played persistently with both sides and would commit themselves to neither. On 4 May 1891 they had renewed with the Italians the Mediterranean agreement of 1887.[3] Though this was certainly directed against France, the Spaniards now added to it a declaration that the *status quo* was not to be interpreted as a bar against future Spanish action in Morocco to assert their ancient *de jure* claims; thus the Spaniards still had it both ways—they could call on Italy to oppose France, yet were themselves free to devise a partition at some time in the future. Further, the Spaniards ran over with friendly statements to France. Thus on 21 June the Duke of Tetuan, Spanish foreign minister, told Paul Cambon that he regretted the intrusion of other Powers than France and Spain into the affairs of Morocco, but assured him that on coming into office (in 1890) he had not found 'any written trace of the interference of the Powers into Moorish affairs'—an odd statement to be made only six weeks after the renewal of the Italo-Spanish agreement.[4] On 14 August he said in regard to Tuat: 'If you do not have an armed conflict with the Sultan; if he resigns himself, as I expect, to your occupation, we shall have nothing to say; but if he resists the question of the main-

---

[1] Metternich to Caprivi, 10 June 1891, *G.P.*, viii, no. 1918, p. 297.

[2] Marschall to Hatzfeldt, 13 June 1891, *G.P.*, viii, no. 1919, p. 299.

[3] Pribram, *Secret Treaties of Austria-Hungary*, i, 142–9.

[4] Paul Cambon to Ribot, 22 June 1891, *D.D.F.*, 1st series, viii, no. 385, p. 513.

tenance of the *status quo* will be raised.'[1] The French had n
intention of having 'an armed conflict' with Muley Hassan
therefore they knew from the first that they were safe fror
united opposition.

Salisbury clearly understood Spain's equivocal position. Hi
own was much the same—this was the second essentia
difference from the affairs of the Near East. British policy wa
resolutely anti-Russian—or as resolute as it ever was; it wa
never uncompromisingly anti-French. Besides, on the othe
side, the French were unwilling to provoke their own isolatio
—they had quite enough on their hands with Egypt. Th
Russians had been ready to face this risk. Thus Salisbury, toc
hung back, as the Spaniards had done. The only difference wa
that he did not actually reveal the lack of united opposition t
the French until he had clearly ascertained that the Spaniard
would not commit themselves. He met the Italian proposa
for a joint protest in Paris very coolly: 'It would be more likel
to precipitate sudden action than to prevent it.'[2] The Italian
returned to the attack in October, this time with German back
ing. Salisbury replied: 'though Great Britain was less interestec
in North-west Africa than Spain or Italy, he was disposed t
support their views diplomatically' and agreed to inquire as t
Spain's attitude.[3] In conversation with Hatzfeldt, the Germar
ambassador, he went further and said that, if consulted, h
would advise the Sultan against giving up Tuat[4] but thi
remark was never made to either the Italians or the Spaniards

The Duke of Tetuan refused to be drawn. He proposed tha
the Sultan should be advised to ask the French governmen
on what grounds they claimed Tuat and that, if the reply wa
unsatisfactory, Muley Hassan should appeal to the good office
of the interested Powers[5]—thus the responsibility for raising
the question of Morocco would rest on Muley Hassan, anc
Spain would, no doubt, be free to promote her own designs
The answer did not satisfy the Italians; and they renewed thei

[1] Paul Cambon to Ribot, 15 August 1891, *D.D.F.*, 1st series, viii, no. 502
p. 668.

[2] Salisbury to Dering (chargé d'affaires, Rome), no. 160A, 7 September; no
165, 16 September 1891, F.O. 99/284.

[3] Salisbury to Ford, telegram, no. 6, 28 October 1891, F.O. 99/284.

[4] Hatzfeldt to Foreign Office, 23 October 1891, *G.P.*, viii, no. 1925, p. 303

[5] Ford to Salisbury, telegram, no. 10, 30 October 1891, F.O. 99/284.
Marschall to Hatzfeldt, 2 November 1891, *G.P.*, viii, no. 1930, p. 307.

pressure on Salisbury, with German support, on 3 November.
Salisbury was too clever for them. He replied:

> The matter concerns Italy and Spain rather than Great Britain and
> we did not propose to express any opinion, either at Tangier or at
> Paris, unless asked by those immediately concerned. It was the opinion
> of Her Majesty's Government that Tuat was part of the Empire of
> Morocco and that any possible alienation would prejudice the integrity
> of that Empire. If the Government of Spain should think it important
> to express this opinion, we were prepared diplomatically to support
> them.[1]

Italy and Germany were thus directed back to Madrid, where
their effort proved vain. The Duke of Tetuan would give
advice in Tangier; he would not join in a protest at Paris. The
affair 'was of small importance and not the subject of active
resistance; it would give France the great opportunity of ad-
ministering a diplomatic check to the three Powers'.[2] Salisbury
at once used the excuse of the Spanish refusal to retreat in his
turn. On 13 November 1891 he told Hatzfeldt that a diplomatic action 'would not prevent a French move against the
oasis, that this latter was worth little in itself, and that the
interested Powers would perhaps do better to keep their strength
for the serious question later, that is when it concerned
Morocco itself and especially the coast'.[3] The Germans now
made out that they had never cared about Tuat;[4] and the
Italians had to be content with the advice of the three Powers to
Muley Hassan, as originally suggested by the Duke of Tetuan.[5]
The Moorish Note, which did not altogether conform to the
advice of the Powers, was handed to the French chargé
d'affaires on 11 January 1892.[6]

Meanwhile, Salisbury was covering himself on the French

[1] Salisbury to Dufferin (Rome), no. 197, 3 November 1891, F.O. 99/284.

[2] Salisbury to Ford, telegram, no. 7, 13 November 1891, F.O. 99/284;
Marschall to Stumm (Madrid), 5 November, G.P., viii, no. 1934, p. 311;
Stumm to Foreign Office, 10 November 1891, G.P., viii, no. 1936, p. 312.

[3] Hatzfeldt to Foreign Office, 13 November 1891, G.P., viii, no. 1940, p.
314.   [4] Malet to Salisbury, no. 219, 28 November 1891, F.O. 99/284.

[5] Salisbury to Ford, no. 94, 4 December; Ford to Salisbury, telegram, no. 11,
7 December; Salisbury to Ford, telegram, no. 9, 8 December, F.O. 99/284;
Salisbury to Euan Smith, telegram, no. 10, 11 December 1891, F.O. 99/279.

[6] The Powers had advised Muley Hassan to ask the French their grounds for
claiming Tuat; instead he asked the French their grievance against the tribes
there. Souhart to Ribot, telegram, 11 January 1892, D.D.F., 1st series, ix, no.
138, p. 206.

side. On 22 December 1891 he said to Waddington, the
French ambassador: 'I know by experience that a great
civilized nation in contact with barbarism is always obliged to
advance', and added: 'be cautious and do not raise a Moroccan
question'.[1] On 22 January 1892 he told Waddington he had
put the damper on the Moroccan question: 'You can tell M
Ribot that I shall do everything I can to extinguish this so-
called Moroccan question.' As to Tuat, 'England has certainly
no interest in Tuat and I have told everyone that I consider
the question as trivial. . . . I don't claim to give an opinion
on your rights or on those of the Sultan; I do not know them
either the one or the other.' Waddington: 'All we ask is not
to concern yourself with them. You have only to say, if the
Sultan consults you, that the question does not concern you.'
Salisbury: 'I recognize and have already declared that it is a
trifling question.'[2] This was all that the French required. On
31 January 1892 they replied to Muley Hassan that the claim
of Morocco to Tuat was founded neither on right nor on fact
and therefore refused to discuss the question with him.[3]
Although Muley Hassan replied to the French in another
argumentative Note on 13 April,[4] he had too much sense to
appeal to the good offices of the interested Powers, who were
too much interested in Morocco for his liking. Euan Smith,
the British minister, did not learn of the French reply until the
end of May and was then told by the Moorish foreign minister
that if the Moorish agent at Tangier had not communicated
this to him earlier 'it was probably from forgetfulness'.[5]
Euan Smith wished to show the French Note to the Italian and
Spanish ministers, but was instructed by Salisbury not to do
so. By now, even the Italians realized that nothing could be
made of the Tuat question. In June, Brin, lately become
Italian foreign minister, said: 'while his Government would
have confidently followed the lead of England, they would

[1] Waddington to Ribot, 23 December 1891, *D.D.F.*, 1st series, ix, no. 113,
p. 176.
[2] Waddington to Ribot, 22 January 1892, *D.D.F.*, 1st series, ix, no. 169, p
239.
[3] Souhart to Si Feddoul Gharnit, 31 January 1892, *D.D.F.*, 1st series, ix, no
194 annexe, p. 289.
[4] Si Feddoul Gharnit to Souhart, 13 April 1892, *D.D.F.*, 1st series, ix, no.
286 annexe, p. 415.
[5] Euan Smith to Salisbury, no. 104, 31 May 1892, F.O. 99/296.

hesitate to embark with Spain alone in an attempt to arrest French designs';[1] and again, 'Italy was prepared to join in opposing the danger which confronted all the Mediterranean powers, but would not take the initiative or move except in concert with England and Spain'.[2] The conclusion suited Salisbury's book: he could call on Italy, and perhaps even on Spain, if it were necessary, yet was not committed himself.

By the spring of 1892 the Tuat question was safely out of the way; and all seemed quiet in Morocco. There followed a sudden explosion, one of the oddest episodes in British diplomacy. Sir Charles Euan Smith had been hurriedly chosen for Tangier in May 1891 after Kirby Green's sudden death. Euan Smith was not a professional diplomat: he had spent his life in India and had entered the service of the Foreign Office only when he succeeded Sir John Kirk at Zanzibar. There he had achieved some diplomatic reputation, by imposing a British protectorate on the Sultan; but the real diplomatic work, as regards France and Germany, had been done for him in London by Salisbury. He came out to Tangier only with the vague instruction that British policy aimed 'to preserve the independence and territorial integrity of the Empire of Morocco, while neglecting no favourable opportunity of impressing upon the Sultan and his Ministers the importance and advantage of improving the Government and administration of the country'.[3] For the first few months he was occupied with the Tuat question, which effectually estranged him from the French chargé d'affaires; while the caution of Salisbury estranged the Italian minister on the other side. Euan Smith had been told at the outset that Kirby Green had failed to get general backing for his draft commercial treaty; but this did not alarm him. He was quite confident that he could by his own resources pull off the success which had eluded both Drummond Hay and Kirby Green.

In February 1892 Euan Smith prepared to visit Fez on a lavish scale. As the French minister remarked afterwards, he took with him 'amateurs, historiographers, prestidigitateurs, et musiciens'.[4] He wrote on 13 February that he proposed to press the draft commericial treaty on Muley Hassan:

[1] Vivian (chargé d'affaires, Rome) to Salisbury, no. 119, 13 June 1892, F.O. 99/296.   [2] Vivian to Salisbury, no. 132, 30 June 1892, F.O. 99/296.
[3] Salisbury to Euan Smith, no. 1, 16 May 1891, F.O. 99/279.
[4] D'Aubigny to Nisard, 31 July 1892, D.D.F., 1st series, ix, no. 429, p. 627.
E*

In view of the hideous misgovernment of the country the only way of improvement is by the introduction of drastic commercial reform which, by gradually throwing open the interior of the Empire to the operations of legitimate commerce and materially benefiting the inhabitants will insensibly raise them, under the stimulus of the new influence that will be brought to bear upon them, to demand *for them selves* a greater measure of justice and humanity at the hands of their Rulers.

A commercial treaty would also be 'the most efficient bulwark against any schemes of territorial aggrandisement on the part of other Powers' by identifying Morocco 'with the great commercial interests of the British nation'. The inducements he would hold out to Muley Hassan would be a promise to try to secure the abolition of the system of 'protection' (as established by the Madrid Conference of 1880); the prospect of the reception of a Moorish mission by Queen Victoria; and the gift of a female elephant. If these failed, he 'should be authorized to hold language to His Majesty of a character more vigorous than that of mere remonstrance and disappointment'. He should warn Muley Hassan:

Her Majesty's Government would in the future feel themselves compelled to withdraw from the position they have hitherto held of being his most solicitous friends and to adopt in all future arrangements that line of policy alone which might seem best suited for the maintenance and encouragement of British interests in Morocco.[1]

Salisbury ought to have taken alarm at this dispatch. But a general election was approaching and he had other things on hand. Besides, he admitted that 'co-operating with all the Powers is an impossibility'. He therefore contented himself with the warning:

I wish you to abstain from anything in the nature of a menace which would be doubly dangerous, because if resisted it might bring about serious crisis and, if successful, would place Her Majesty's Government in the position of having undertaken the protection of Morocco.

[1] Euan Smith to Salisbury, no. 29, 13 February 1892, F.O. 99/286.

[2] Even more revealing of the storm to come was Euan Smith's no. 28 of 1 February, in which he asked to be allowed to object to the ceremony of reception at which 'the Minister has to stand bareheaded in a square (like a Pasha or chief while the Sultan addresses him from horseback, and presents are exposed to the crowd, who think they are tribute'. Salisbury merely minuted: 'What a tiresome man he is!'

[3] Salisbury to Euan Smith, no. 22, 2 March 1892, F.O. 99/285.

A little later, when Euan Smith asked for full powers to sign a commercial treaty, Salisbury telegraphed:

> Full Powers will be given, but must be used circumspectly, so that other Powers, especially Italy and Spain, will not think you are getting exclusive advantages; and there is a danger that the Sultan may think we have sent you to Tangier to establish another protectorate over a Moslem Ruler, as under our instructions, you did at Zanzibar.[1]

Euan Smith answered that he was 'deeply imbued with the sense of responsibility to do nothing to weaken the Sultan's authority or to awaken the just susceptibilities of the foreign Powers'.[2]

On 27 April Euan Smith left for Fez. The French chargé d'affaires did not accompany the other diplomats who came to see him off; the absence was deliberate.[3] At Fez Euan Smith displayed to the full the qualities he had learnt from the empire-builders of India.[4] He wrote of the ceremony of reception: 'it served to remind us strongly of the scenes which one is accustomed to associate with the performance of a pantomime at Drury Lane'. He had not brought the customary presents, and declined to receive any. He raised at once the question of the commercial treaty and claimed that it had been approved by all the Powers (this was true only in the sense that the ministers at Tangier had not objected when it had been shown to them two years before by Kirby Green). Muley Hassan proved 'extraordinarily obstructive and unyielding'; he also proved extremely ingenious. His first argument was that the commercial treaty which he had made with Tattenbach in 1890 secured him against any further demands for five years and that this treaty had been approved by all the Powers. This argument was overthrown only by a direct British appeal to Berlin. Muley Hassan also learnt at once from the French that Euan Smith was not entitled to speak in the name of all the Powers. Indeed the French agent at Fez warned Muley Hassan: 'If the English obtain the little finger, we shall claim

[1] Salisbury to Euan Smith, telegram, no. 12, 28 March 1892, F.O. 99/290.
[2] Euan Smith to Salisbury, telegram, no. 34, 29 March 1892, F.O. 99/291.
[3] Euan Smith to Salisbury, no. 84, 27 April; no. 85, 28 April 1892, F.O. 99/286.
[4] I have not thought it necessary to particularize Euan Smith's reports from Fez. His reports are in F.O. 99/286–8, his telegrams in F.O. 99/291.

the hand.'[1] Thus from the outset there was no chance that
Euan Smith's demands would be granted.

Negotiations at Fez dragged on throughout June. At one
moment Muley Hassan tried to scare Euan Smith by organizing a riot outside his house. Euan Smith answered by riding
through the 'rioters' to the palace and declaring that, if he were
killed, 'within a month there would be another British minister
in Fez, but there would not then be a Sultan', a statement
strengthened by referring to the fate of Cavagnari at Kabul.
Euan Smith also announced that, if there were more riots, he
would hoist the Union Jack over his house with his own hands.
As a further challenge to the Sultan, Euan Smith provocatively
appointed a British merchant in Fez vice-consul.[2] Muley Hassan
then tried conciliation: he dismissed the Pasha of Fez for allowing
the riot and offered Euan Smith £20,000 if he would go away.
His principal resource, however, was an inexhaustible diplomacy. The commercial treaty was endlessly discussed—clauses
modified, withdrawn, conceded, and then withdrawn again.
The Grand Vizier, with much mystery, submitted to Euan
Smith an alleged compromise which, on translation, turned out
to be no compromise at all; Euan Smith tore it up and returned
it in fragments to the Vizier. Euan Smith also played at diplomacy on his side. On 19 June he approached the French military mission and said that it was time England and France
settled the Moroccan question together: England should have
Tangier and a commercial treaty, and France could take the
rest.[3] The French did not respond; they were convinced that
England was trying to raise the Moroccan question on a grand
scale and began to enlist Spain in a common resistance.[4]

Euan Smith's patience gave out, and he left Fez on 12 July

[1] D'Aubigny to Ribot, 1 June 1892, D.D.F., 1st series, ix, no. 330, p. 472
[2] Euan Smith had been authorized to appoint a vice-consul at Fez in December
1891, but had held up the appointment so as 'not to embarrass my negotiations',
and Salisbury had forgotten that he had authorized it. Euan Smith, when rebuked,
alleged that he had appointed the vice-consul 'after consulting the Sultan and with
his concurrence and with the proviso that he should not fly the flag for the present'
The Foreign Office had some doubt whether the clause of the treaty of 1856
authorizing the appointment of vice-consuls in the 'ports and cities' of Morocco
covered appointments inland. At any rate the Moorish government refused to
acknowledge the appointment (F.O. 99/333).
[3] D'Aubigny to Ribot, 26 June 1892, D.D.F., 1st series, ix, no. 374, p. 536
[4] Ribot to Waddington, 4 July 1892, D.D.F., 1st series, ix, no. 390, pp
566–8; to Roustan, 4 July, no. 391 and 392, pp. 569–72.

ursued to the last by Moorish 'commissioners' who offered
im further compromise if only he would stay. He now de-
ıounced Muley Hassan as 'faithless and dishonourable'; but
n fact Muley Hassan had behaved very reasonably. He had
aid frankly that he would give way 'only if the British fleet
vas sent to Tangier to enforce the Commercial Treaty'. Unless
England could threaten him, there was no need to give way;
noreover, unless England could threaten him and so show her
strength against the other Powers, he dared not give way—
his only line was to balance between the competing Powers.
The Euan Smith episode, unimportant in itself, was a striking
lemonstration that the Moroccan question could not be solved
'on the spot'—neither by England nor, for that matter, by
France. It could be settled only by diplomacy, as in fact Zanzibar (which had so misled Euan Smith) had been. Euan Smith
understood nothing of this. He returned to Tangier well
pleased with his work. Muley Hassan, he telegraphed on his
arrival, was frightened and unhappy: 'If Your Lordship sees
fit to support my action, I have no doubt whatever the Sultan
will conclude the treaty at once, satisfy our just demands and
give such other satisfaction as Your Lordship may deem
necessary. . . . French influence and prestige will decrease
in the same proportion as those of Great Britain will *increase*.'
Euan Smith had a good press, mainly with information supplied by himself or by one of his entourage, and enjoyed a brief
fame as a builder of empire. Salisbury did not share this
delight. The Foreign Office sent repeated demands to Euan
Smith for an explanation. On 8 August Salisbury repudiated
Euan Smith's proposal of menaces:

> They might or might not extract from the Sultan of Morocco a
> consent to the commercial reforms which he has just refused; but
> they would revive and to many minds would seem to confirm the
> reports which have been circulated that Her Majesty's Government
> entertain projects inconsistent with the independence and integrity of
> that Empire.[1]

A Blue book was hastily put together to show Salisbury's
innocence;[2] and Salisbury told Waddington that Euan Smith

---

[1] Salisbury to Euan Smith, no. 82, 8 August 1892, F.O. 99/285.

[2] Morocco, no. 1 (1892), C. 2815; and Morocco, no. 2 (1892), C. 6281.
Owing to haste, Ribot's approval for one of Dufferin's reports was not obtained,
and he protested (*D.D.F.*, 1st series, no. 439, p. 638). Euan Smith's report of

was 'too keen to advertise himself' and had not been authorize
to carry things so far.[1] The French hardly believed Salisbury'
explanations: they thought the Euan Smith mission had been
'try-on' and this view was shared by the other Powers
Hence Euan Smith helped to consolidate the myth of Salis
bury's policy as anti-French and based on co-operation with th
Triple Alliance; and the fact that the repudiation of Eua
Smith virtually coincided with the change to the Libera
government strengthened the further myth that the Liberal
were pro-French—as a consequence of which the French buil
up groundless hopes in regard to Egypt. In reality, Salisbury'
only concern had been to keep the Moroccan question quie
and he had done little to encourage a triple *entente* with Ital
and Spain (no doubt because, in view of Spain's position, it wa
impracticable). Euan Smith had simply created embarrass
ment for him. The affair had also an awkward sequel for th
French. The French government had been quite ready to mak
a diplomatic complaint to Salisbury; they were taken abac
when Muley Hassan wrote a letter of complaint and requeste
the French to forward it to Queen Victoria. Waddingto
especially objected: he hoped that the new Liberal govern
ment would be willing to co-operate with France and Spain, i
trying to negotiate a commercial treaty with Morocco. Mule
Hassan, however, threatened to give the letter to the Germans
if the French would not transmit it; and Ribot would not allo
the Germans to act as the protectors of Morocco. Waddingto
therefore hastened to give the letter to Salisbury before he lef
office, so that 'Gladstone should be presented with a *fai
accompli*, and it would be easier for him to put a damper o
Euan Smith by putting the blame for the mistakes on hi
predecessor'.[3]

Muley Hassan's offer of a bribe also gave great offence to Tattenbach, who had
no doubt, accepted one himself. Kirby Green had also been offered a bribe i
1887, but had the sense not to report it. (Euan Smith to Rosebery, no. 163,
September 1892, F.O. 99/288.)

[1] Waddington to Ribot, 29 July 1892, *D.D.F.*, 1st series, ix, no. 426, p. 622
[2] For example, Tattenbach to Foreign Office, 27 July 1892, *G.P.*, viii, no
1948, pp. 320–2.
[3] D'Aubigny to Ribot, 24 July, *D.D.F.*, 1st series, ix, no. 419, pp. 608–10
Ribot to Waddington, 28 July, no. 422, pp. 616–18; Waddington to Ribot
29 July, no. 620, p. 620; Salisbury to Phipps (Paris), no. 199, 12 August 1892
F.O. 99/296.

Rosebery, the new foreign secretary, did not come up to Waddington's expectations. On 29 August, he listened to Waddington's insistence that France desired the *status quo* in Morocco, but did not respond to the suggestion that England and France should co-operate to obtain a commercial treaty, nor did he endorse Waddington's criticisms of Euan Smith. According to Waddington, Rosebery said that Euan Smith was going on leave to Carlsbad: evidently Rosebery disliked even this scrap of apology for he did not record it in his own account.[1] Two days later, Rosebery drafted a reply to Muley Hassan, which insisted sharply on the commercial treaty: 'It is a matter of surprise that the treaty proposed by Sir Charles Euan Smith has not yet received the approval of Your Imperial Majesty.' Euan Smith's last fling was to hold up this letter, on the ground that it would be a sign of weakness to send it during the visit of the French minister to Fez. It was only forwarded by Eliot, the chargé d'affaires, on 21 October, after Euan Smith's departure.[2]

D'Aubigny, the French minister, had naturally an easy time of it at Fez, after the alarm of Euan Smith's visit, especially as he was instructed to emphasize French anxiety for the *status quo*. Muley Hassan said: 'Every time Great Britain was concerned he would take our advice and follow it faithfully.' When the letters from Rosebery and Queen Victoria arrived, Muley Hassan got D'Aubigny to draft the answers (which the Moors then characteristically held up in order to inflict a slight on the British).[3] Finally, convinced that Euan Smith was about to return, Muley Hassan asked for some written definition of French policy—a declaration that they were opposed to *all innovation* in Morocco and a promise not to support any foreign demand for a concession which Muley Hassan should judge a *vital injury*.[4] This was asking a good deal more than the French were prepared to grant. In fact, the odd result of D'Aubigny's visit was to restore good relations between England and France.

D'Aubigny's visit to Fez alarmed his colleagues at Tangier,

[1] Waddington to Ribot, 29 August 1892, *D.D.F.*, 1st series, x, no. 10, p. 15; Rosebery to Dufferin (Paris), no. 219, 30 August 1892, F.O. 99/296.

[2] Eliot to Rosebery, no. 188, 21 October 1892, F.O. 99/289.

[3] D'Aubigny to Ribot, 14 October 1892, *D.D.F.*, 1st series, x, no. 30, p. 50.

[4] D'Aubigny to Ribot, 21 December 1892, *D.D.F.*, 1st series, x, no. 70, pp. 18–20.

especially the Italian. Italy and Spain had been frightened by
Euan Smith's activity into an anti-British line; but they were
much more permanently frightened of French ambitions, and
the Italians in particular repeated alarmist rumours about
D'Aubigny's demands.[1] No doubt this was part of Italy's
general campaign to get from Rosebery some endorsement of
Salisbury's Mediterranean *entente*. Eliot, in Tangier, denied
all these rumours and reported, correctly, on D'Aubigny's
modest aims.[2] These reports may have affected Rosebery's
attitude. Besides, it is clear that the Foreign Office did not
share Rosebery's enthusiasm for empire-builders, at least so
far as Euan Smith was concerned; the permanent officials
seem to have made up their minds that Euan Smith should not
return to Tangier. More generally, Rosebery was sobered by
the opposition inside the Cabinet to his imperialist policy:
probably he thought he had better reserve his energy for the
decisive question of Uganda. At all events, British policy in
Morocco made a fresh start in 1893. To spare Euan Smith's
feelings, Sir West Ridgeway, permanent under-secretary for
Ireland,[3] was sent to Tangier on a temporary mission; but
Rosebery told Waddington that Euan Smith would not be
returning to Tangier. The French were further told that Ridgeway had been instructed to co-operate with the other foreign
representatives, especially the French:[4] 'in the delicate and
critical state of the Moorish empire, a favourable result is
possible only by a sincere and unselfish co-operation of all the
Powers'. These British assurances gave the French an excuse
for evading Muley Hassan's request for any written guarantee.[5]

[1] Culminating in the rumour that D'Aubigny had offered Muley Hassan an
alliance with France, Russia, Turkey, and Belgium.

[2] Eliot to Rosebery, no. 235, 5 December 1892, F.O. 99/289. Cf. Eliot to
Rosebery, no. 198, 31 October; no. 214, 14 November; no. 256, 26 December
1892, F.O. 99/296.

[3] There is no explanation in the F.O. records of this odd choice. Waddington
believed it was to get Ridgeway out of Irish affairs, 'since he is devoted to the
Unionist cause and Mr. John Morley is very anxious to be rid of him'. (To
Develle, no. 107, 17 January 1893, *D.D.F.*, 1st series, x, no. 107, p. 164.)

[4] Rosebery to Dufferin, no. 6, 9 January 1893; no. 16, 16 January, F.O.
99/309; to Eliot, no. 7, 13 January 1893, F.O. 99/299. It is characteristic of
Rosebery that, in the dispatch to Eliot, he deleted the words 'especially the
French'.

[5] Develle to D'Aubigny, 30 January 1893, *D.D.F.*, x, no. 149, p. 214.

Ridgeway's main task was to put things right with the Moors: to restore the ancient friendship which has so long existed between Great Britain and Morocco to the mutual advantage of both countries'. He was to warn the Moors that there could be no mission to London during the present 'conspicuous absence of good will'. Similarly he was not to go to Fez without a 'cordial and spontaneous invitation' from the Sultan.[1] As this was not forthcoming, his experience of Morocco was confined to Tangier and the towns of the coast. Nevertheless he managed to demonstrate to the Moors that he was not concerned to bully them, as Euan Smith had been.[2] Ridgeway refused to be moved by the usual Italian alarms; and when Tattenbach seconded Italian anxiety Ridgeway silenced him with the question whether Muley Hassan should be encouraged to resist the annexation of Tuat by force.[3]

Ridgeway completed his report on Morocco early in July: it is the most detailed discussion of British policy in the records of these years. British influence, he pointed out, had been paramount so long as Great Britain had been content to leave Morocco alone; it had begun to decline as soon as British merchants pressed for the opening of Morocco to British trade —here he instanced the establishment of a cable between Tangier and Gibraltar in 1888, the endless bickering over the commercial treaty, and the opening of a vice-consulate at Fez. The Moors would not reform voluntarily; reform by order was impossible. 'Who is to be the mandatory of Europe? Certainly not England.' The only British concern was Tangier; but it was impossible to hold Tangier in isolation. Great Britain, Italy, and perhaps Germany had some interest in maintaining the *status quo*; but neither Italy nor Germany could be counted on to be of use against France. Spain was interested in the *status quo* only so far as it was binding on others, not on herself; her forts on the coast were a perpetual reminder of her past (and future) claims. Thus Ridgeway was brought back to the idea

[1] Rosebery to Ridgeway, 18 January 1893, F.O. 99/299.

[2] When in May some English travellers to Fez had a tiff with the Moorish authorities, the vice-consul exacted an indemnity which Ridgeway ordered him to return. Rosebery approved his action as 'a complete confirmation of the principles on which the policy of H.M.G. is based' (to Ridgeway, no. 68, 19 May 1893, F.O. 99/299.)

[3] Ridgeway to Rosebery, no. 102, 19 June 1893, F.O. 99/309; Marschall to Hatzfeldt, 21 June 1893, *G.P.*, viii, no. 1953, p. 324.

of an agreement with France: 'if the eastern frontier of Morocco could be defined [i.e. French encroachments limited] England might make this a condition antecedent to the evacuation of Egypt'. This was a striking anticipation of the *entente* actually concluded with France eleven years later, except that Ridgeway proposed a negative bargain—Great Britain and France were to take their hands off Egypt and Morocco, whereas in fact they acquired them. Ridgeway further pointed out that the hackneyed solution of 'seizing Tangier' did not avoid the need for agreeing with France:

> France must be allowed to encroach or she must be resisted. The alternative policy is to temporize until the long-expected European war takes place, and the Map of Europe is remade. . . . When war breaks out England must take Tangier; and therefore it will still be necessary to fix a limit to French encroachment in time of peace, and to prevent her occupation of the zone which is necessary for a British occupation of Tangier.

This argument was reinforced by a memorandum by Count Edward Gleichen, who had accompanied Ridgeway as military attaché. Gleichen showed convincingly that Tangier could not be seized by a scratch force from Gibraltar and that it could not be held at all unless the hinterland was in friendly hands. In fact, a British occupation of Tangier, far from making agreement with France unnecessary, was only possible with French consent and support.[1]

Ridgeway's report exposed the futility of the assumption on which British policy in Morocco had been based. There was no hope that the Moorish empire would, by reform, become capable of maintaining itself; and the seizure of Tangier by a *coup de main*, which the British had kept up their sleeves as a device for meeting all emergencies, was shown to be impracticable. Thus the only sound policy was agreement with France, first to leave Morocco alone, ultimately to partition it. It would be pleasant to record that Ridgeway's report marked an epoch in British policy in Morocco, the first step towards the agreement of 1904. There is, however, no evidence that it was considered seriously by the Foreign Office or by the government. It was printed and circulated; no comment was made and no action followed. Advocacy of an approach to France came at a bad moment in July 1893; it coincided with the dispute over Siam.

[1] Ridgeway, Report on Morocco, 10 July 1894, F.O. 99/304.

Satow, Ridgeway's successor, left for Tangier before Ridgeway's report had been received. He was instructed to follow 'a firm but conciliatory course' and to say that a Moorish mission would be welcomed in London 'once the relations of the two countries should permit it'.[1] Satow limited himself to this modest role. He made no suggestions concerning general policy during his two years in Tangier. He did not visit Fez until November 1894, and then only advised the new Sultan to keep down the taxes, to have regular returns made of the number of prisoners in his jails, and to build bridges.[2]

As in each period of negation, Great Britain and France tended to draw together over practical questions. Thus, when a dispute between Spain and Morocco arose in the autumn of 1893 as the result of a brush between the Spanish garrison at Melilla and the neighbouring tribes, England and France acted virtually as mediators, averted a war, and persuaded the Maghzen to agree to the payment of an indemnity.[3] Similarly, in 1894, when the Maghzen tried to persuade the British to withdraw their vice-consul from Fez (on the characteristic ground that he was liable to be murdered at any moment), Kimberley, now become foreign secretary, at once inquired what line the French were taking;[4] and Hanotaux replied that 'he would wish to hold precisely similar language to that of the British government'.[5] This was the more remarkable in that Hanotaux was being pressed by the men on the spot to encourage the Moorish action against the British.[6] Instead the French insisted on full recognition of their vice-consul in Fez; and this recognition, obtained early in 1895, covered the British vice-consul also, who thus remained as the only concrete relic of Euan Smith's stormy episode. Anglo-French

[1] Rosebery to Satow, 18 July 1893, F.O. 99/299.

[2] Satow to Kimberley, no. 43, 15 April 1895, F.O. 99/326.

[3] Rosebery to Dufferin, telegram, no. 95, 30 October; Dufferin to Rosebery, telegram, no. 100, 31 October 1893, F.O. 99/309. It was characteristic of Rosebery to represent this co-operation as his answer to Waddington's approach of 29 August 1892.

[4] Satow to Kimberley, no. 83, 16 August; Kimberley to Phipps, no. 391, 10 September 1894, F.O. 99/333.

[5] Phipps to Kimberley, telegram, no. 73, 12 September 1894, F.O. 99/333.

[6] De Monbel to Hanotaux, 17 October 1894, D.D.F., 1st series, xi, no. 251, p. 375. De Monbel had been sent to Tangier with instructions to co-operate with England and Spain (Hanotaux to de Monbel, 28 August 1894, D.D.F., 1st series, xi, no. 229, pp. 338–40).

co-operation was shown still more sharply on the death of
Muley Hassan in June 1894. Great Britain and France consulted Spain alone before deciding to recognize Abdul Aziz.
The other ministers at Tangier dragged sulkily in their wake,
Tattenbach, the German, keeping ostentatiously out of step 'in
order to preserve his independence *vis-à-vis* the Representatives
of the Powers which have political interests in Morocco'.[1]

This development of British policy was not to the taste of
the Italians. In the autumn of 1894 they complained strongly
to the Germans that England and Spain were co-operating
with France instead of with Italy;[2] and the Germans tried to
oblige the Italians by whipping up the Tuat question.[3] The
Italians also played at being a Moorish Power by compelling
the Maghzen to order a cruiser in Italy, as a compensation
for their arms-purchases from France—this proved a great
embarrassment, as the Moors had no sailors with which to man
the ship when it was completed, and it had finally to be sold
off as a job-lot in part payment to Spain of the indemnity of
1893. Even the Germans played at Moorish politics and
staged a naval demonstration against Saffi in May 1895; this
had the curious result that the Maghzen appealed to Great
Britain and France as the guardians of Moorish independence.
These trivial manœuvres did not incline the British towards
co-operation with the Central Powers. One of Salisbury's first
acts on returning to office in June 1895 was to send British
warships to Moorish waters as a gesture against the German
demonstration.[4] In regard to Tuat, Sanderson, the permanent
under-secretary, wrote in July 1895, 'Hitherto we have been in
the habit of dealing with the French claim to Tuat in concert
with Spain and Italy. But the way in which the Italians have
been forcing the Italian-built cruiser down the throats of the
Moors—and the attitude of Germany have made the Spanish
suspicious and restless.'[5] When Sir Arthur Nicolson visited
Abdul Aziz at Marrakesh in the spring of 1896, he advised

[1] Satow to Kimberley, no. 56, 13 June; no. 61, 18 June 1894, F.O. 99/317.
[2] Bülow to Caprivi, 7 October, 8 October 1894, *G.P.*, viii, no. 1961, 1962,
pp. 330–2.
[3] Gosselin to Kimberley, no. 149, 14 September 1894, F.O. 99/352. Marschall said Tuat was 'the black spot at the present moment of European politics'
(Marschall to Tattenbach, 12 January 1895, *G.P.*, viii, no. 1968, p. 337).
[4] Salisbury to White (chargé d'affaires), telegram, no. 33, 3 August 1895, F.O.
99/329.   [5] Minute by Sanderson, July 1895, F.O. 99/352.

he Maghzen 'to take no action which would be likely to
nduce the French authorities to raise the question in a form
which might have unpleasant consequences'.[1] Nicolson found,
ather to his surprise, that the Moors were not worrying about
Tuat; they confined their complaints to the rude and bullying
conduct of Tattenbach, the German minister.[2] Nicolson sympathized with their complaint. On his arrival at Tangier he had
been told by Tattenbach that 'the French would never be
allowed to occupy Tangier, so long as the German Legation
were in Morocco'[3]—not a welcome remark to the representative of a Power which was supposed to have earmarked Tangier
for itself.

Nicolson, like his predecessors, began by despairing of
Morocco and continued the policy of practical co-operation
with France. He said to the French minister in July 1896: 'It
seemed to be necessary to keep matters as quiet as possible in
this country, as I was sure that both he and I would be carrying
out the wishes of our Governments in so doing.'[4] The French
responded in the same spirit. This partnership was not to
Moorish taste, and the Maghzen attempted to play off one
country against the other by proposing at one time to send a
mission to Paris, at another to London. Nicolson and his French
colleague stood firm, and each gave the same reply: if a mission
went to one capital, it must go to the other. The real Moorish
concern seems to have been to receive an invitation to Queen
Victoria's diamond jubilee; but Salisbury would not have them,
and the Moorish mission had to wait in Paris until the jubilee
celebrations were over. The leader of the mission then fortunately went mad; and the visit to London was cancelled.
The Moors returned from Paris with stories of having offered
the French a protectorate over Morocco, stories which Nicolson
half-believed;[5] these stories were ignored by Salisbury. His
only concern, it is clear, was to keep the Moroccan question
quiet; and this concern was strengthened in 1898, when the
Hispano-American war threatened to raise the problem of the
security of Gibraltar in an even more acute way. The offers

[1] Nicolson to Salisbury, no. 10, 23 January 1896, F.O. 99/336.
[2] Nicolson to Salisbury, no. 58, 27 April 1896, F.O. 99/336.
[3] Nicolson to Salisbury, no. 12, 31 January 1896, F.O. 99/352.
[4] Nicolson to Salisbury, no. 82, 3 July 1896, F.O. 99/338.
[5] Nicolson to Salisbury, no. 23, 15 February; no. 66, 16 May 1897, F.O.
99/345, 346.

of alliance which the Spaniards made, sometimes to the British, sometimes to the Franco-Russian partners, had no serious purpose except to tide over the crisis, and certainly no relevance to Morocco.

The Moroccan question was brought back to life in 1899, as part of the German policy of exploiting the supposed difficulties of the British. In February 1899 Hatzfeldt told Salisbury that Germany would expect a share in any partition. Salisbury replied cheerfully, 'Divisions, divisions', but, when asked what points on the Moorish coast other than Tangier concerned England, evaded any answer other than that his knowledge of geography was too slight for him to express an opinion.[1] At a further conversation in June (which Hatzfeldt does not seem to have reported) Salisbury warned the Germans off the Atlantic seaboard; and as the British had already claimed the Mediterranean seaboard there was not much left for a partition.[2] Salisbury followed this up by staging a naval visit to Tangier in July as a demonstration against the Germans.[3] Salisbury's attitude was not shared by Chamberlain, who repeatedly hinted at a partition with the Germans;[4] and Nicholson, too, seems to have begun to favour partition. He wrote to Gosselin in September 1899 that the British government, in case of the Sultan's death, should show foreign Powers that no sudden 'rushes' were permissible and should themselves be ready to send two or three ships to Tangier and a ship to Rabat, Casablanca, Mazagan, and Mogador. He continued:

> The wisest course for us to follow is to leave matters—bad and deplorable as they are, alone; and endeavour to postpone the day of division as long as possible. In the meantime we should come to a clear decision as to what we must not, and cannot, allow to fall into the hands of others; and be perfectly ready to secure that when the final moment arrives.[5]

[1] Hatzfeldt to Bülow, 8 February 1899, G.P., xvii, no. 5152, p. 296.

[2] Salisbury to Lascelles, 7 June 1899, B.D., ii, no. 307, p. 356.

[3] Nicolson complained of this visit: 'the ships may excite comment. Are they necessary?' and Gosselin, the under-secretary to whom he had written, passed on his protest to the Admiralty. Salisbury wrote: 'I am sorry you have done that—for they have been sent at my request. Sir A. Nicolson has not the German part of the question clearly before him.' F.O. 99/361.

[4] In November 1899: Hatzfeldt to Foreign Office, 3 November 1899, G.P., xvii, no. 5153, p. 297; in May 1900: Hatzfeldt to Foreign Office, 27 May 1900, G.P., xvii, no. 5162, p. 309.

[5] Nicolson to Gosselin, private, 23 September 1899, F.O. 99/361.

This was the old idea of laying hands on Tangier which Ridge-way had exploded in 1893; it was an idea to which Salisbury showed no sympathy.

The conflict of opinion between Nicolson and Salisbury was shown more clearly when the question of Tuat reappeared at its most serious: this time a French expedition was really under weigh. On 22 April 1900 Nicolson passed on sympathetically an anxious appeal from the Grand Vizier.[1] Salisbury merely minuted: 'he should consult his colleagues especially those of France and Italy as to the best course to pursue'. When the Foreign Office did not make Salisbury's meaning plain enough Salisbury himself added some discouraging words.[2] On 1 May Nicolson received an assurance from Révoil, the French minister, that France 'had no deep designs against the integrity of Morocco'.[3] Salisbury approved of Nicolson's suggestion that he should pass on this assurance to the Maghzen.[4] When, however, Nicolson further suggested advising the Moors to address themselves to the other legations, Salisbury rejected the idea: 'He need not be in a hurry to make suggestions.'[5] Salisbury also suppressed Nicolson's proposal to advise the Moors to ask France for a direct assurance of the security of Tuat.[6] Finally, when Nicolson proposed assuring the Sultan privately 'that the French have no schemes against Tafilelt [the neighbouring oasis to Tuat] and that if he keeps the tribes quiet the French will not encroach', Salisbury deleted the first part of the assurance.[7] In other words, Salisbury refused to be alarmed about French plans and thought that the wisest policy was to let them make frontier gains. Nicolson must have received a hint from someone in the Foreign Office that Salisbury was emasculating all his suggestions, for on 22 May he wrote an argumentative private letter, which was clearly intended for Salisbury's eyes:

> Personally I think it would be of advantage not to throw too much cold water on the Moors. . . . We are in reality the dominating and

[1] Nicolson to Salisbury, no. 55, 22 April 1900, F.O. 99/367.

[2] Salisbury to Nicolson, telegram, no. 9, 28 April 1900, F.O. 99/369: 'Any isolated intervention by Great Britain is, of course, out of the question.'

[3] Nicolson to Salisbury, no. 58, 1 May 1900, F.O. 99/367.

[4] Salisbury to Nicolson, no. 44, 16 May 1900, F.O. 99/366.

[5] Nicolson to Salisbury, no. 63, 5 May 1900, F.O. 99/367.

[6] Nicolson to Gosselin, private, 18 May 1900, F.O. 99/367.

[7] Nicolson to Salisbury, telegram, no. 26, 26 May 1900, F.O. 99/369.

restraining Power in Morocco. No Power could undertake any operation of a serious nature against our wish. . . . A word or hint from us carries great weight. . . . The abandonment of this country would, I think, entail dangers to our Mediterranean position.[1]

Salisbury initialled this letter without comment. Later in 1900 Salisbury received from Delcassé a further assurance that France 'had no intention of attacking Morocco';[2] and this assurance was passed on to Nicolson for the benefit of the Moors.[3] It gave them little satisfaction.

Nicolson, it is clear, was drifting out of sympathy with Salisbury's policy, or lack of policy, a change of sentiment shared by other members of the foreign service. Nicolson was becoming more suspicious of the French; he was succumbing to the local disease of wanting to reform Morocco (though earlier he had dismissed this hope); and he was on friendly terms with Kaid Maclean, the Scottish subaltern who had been for many years employed by the Sultan as a military adviser. Maclean's influence with the young Abdul Aziz was now at its height; and Nicolson would not have been human if he had not welcomed this opening for giving unofficial advice. Nicolson was too loyal to go against his instructions. In February 1901, when the Sultan asked him to draft a letter for the French concerning Tuat, Nicolson replied: 'the question is one which the Sultan and his Government must decide for themselves and I regret I am unable to give any advice'.[4] Nevertheless Nicolson soon began to give advice when he received further requests. This advice was cautious and sensible: the Sultan should introduce reforms;[5] he should deal directly with France over Tuat without asking for the assistance of any third party.[6] For the Maghzen the important thing was not the moderation but that they had got advice at all. For some time they had been pressed by the German minister to seek German protection;[7] now they decided to play off Germany against England. At the end of March 1901 Maclean told Nicolson that El Menebhi, the minister of war, was to go on a mission to

---

[1] Nicolson to Gosselin, private, 22 May 1900, F.O. 99/367.
[2] Monson to Salisbury, 17 October 1900, B.D., ii, no. 313, p. 259.
[3] Salisbury to Nicolson, no. 92, 24 October 1900, F.O. 99/366.
[4] Nicolson to Lansdowne, no. 16, 13 February 1901, F.O. 99/380.
[5] Nicolson to Lansdowne, no. 43, 9 April 1901, F.O. 99/380.
[6] Nicolson to Gosselin, private, 13 May 1901, F.O. 99/380.
[7] Nicolson to Gosselin, private, 10 December 1900, F.O. 99/368.

London and Berlin: 'He is going to Germany after England and is to be guided by what he does in England. If we will not receive him he is in any case to go to Germany.' Nicolson welcomed the idea of Anglo-German co-operation, 'we must not try to obtain a monopoly of any concession as that would wreck the whole scheme'.[1] He also informed the German minister of the Moorish plans;[2] and the Germans began to consider what advantage they could get from the situation— they wished to push Great Britain forward without becoming involved themselves. In Bülow's words, 'In this affair we must be completely reserved and behave like the Sphinx'.[3]

Nicolson also began to prepare the Foreign Office for a change of emphasis in British policy. He wrote on March 29:

> Personally I do not quite see what the Sultan can do alone and unsupported to resist the French advance. . . . Moreover on broad grounds of general welfare I question whether it would be easy to justify the maintenance of this Government unless the Sultan really reforms his administration.[4]

Implicitly, this was a defence of his participation in the schemes for Moorish reforms. In London, too, the climate was changing. Lansdowne, who had become foreign secretary at the end of 1900, had neither Salisbury's distaste for cooperating with Germany nor his readiness to accept the drift of French policy. When, in February 1901, Nicolson reported that Révoil, the French minister, 'was emphatic in regard to the French authorities having no designs on Tafilelt but this view, he admitted, was not shared by the military authorities', Lansdowne commented, 'The military view is I feel sure that which will prevail'.[5] This remark would never have been made by Salisbury.

El Menebhi therefore was given a friendly reception when he came to London at the end of June. He was received by the King. He was advised to improve the prisons, roads, and harbours of Morocco, and to construct telegraph lines. In return

[1] Nicolson to Gosselin, private, 1 April 1901, F.O. 99/380.
[2] Nicolson to Lansdowne, no. 44, 10 April 1901, F.O. 99/380; Richthofen to Hatzfeldt, 13 April 1901, *G.P.*, xvii, no. 5173, p. 327.
[3] Minute on Hatzfeldt to Foreign Office, 19 June 1901, *G.P.*, xvii, no. 5177, p. 332.
[4] Harold Nicolson, *Lord Carnock*, p. 138.
[5] Nicolson to Gosselin, private, 10 March 1901, F.O. 99/380.

he placed orders for 4,000 rifles, two steam launches and a tug, electric lighting plant, irrigation machinery, and agricultural machinery. He spoke generally of modernizing Morocco's economic life. Lansdowne noted of these economic reforms: 'if he says he will carry them out I might compliment His Excellency and wish him success. But the scheme should not go forth as originating with us, and pressed upon the Morocco Government in the same manner as we are pressing for commercial facilities.'[1] At the same time Nicolson busied himself in trying to persuade the Germans to invest also in the reform of Morocco.[2] But when El Menebhi went on to Berlin he got little satisfaction from the Germans. Certainly he was told that if the French had not encroached more this was due to German reserve; but to the question what would happen if the French took the aggressive, the secretary of state replied—the future lies in the hands of Allah.[3] It was not surprising that El Menebhi, on his return to Morocco, fell into disgrace; he was rescued from prison only by sharp British protests, in which the Germans conspicuously failed to join.[4]

The French had tried to set off El Menebhi's mission by insisting that a Moorish mission should also be sent to Paris; this was a far cry from 1897 when the French had received a Moorish mission only on condition that it proceeded to London. They were given fragmentary explanations of what had taken place in London. On 28 June Lansdowne told Cambon that the conversations had been limited to the difficulties of importing Moorish vegetables.[5] On 3 July he gave Cambon a memorandum enumerating as the subjects discussed the construction of bridges and improvements of roads; port improvements; freedom for the coasting trade; and the export of potatoes and tomatoes. Nothing was said of the far-reaching economic measures which Lansdowne had approved, though not advised. Cambon expressed himself satisfied and said that France had no desire 'to disturb the independence and integ-

---

[1] Minutes by Nicolson and Lansdowne, 13 June, 25 June, 13 July (retrospective) 1901, F.O. 99/381.

[2] The proposal for a partition of Morocco between England and Germany is probably a myth by Eckardstein; but Nicolson certainly sought German investment in Morocco. Nicolson, *Lord Carnock*, p. 141.

[3] Minute by Mentzingen, July 1901, *G.P.*, xvii, no. 5179, pp. 334–6.

[4] *G.P.*, xvii, no. 5182–5, pp. 338–42.

[5] Cambon to Delcassé, 28 June 1901, *D.D.F.*, 2nd series, i, no. 305, p. 355

ity of Morocco'.[1] Nicolson, on his return to Tangier, further
hinted that the Moors had been advised to seek a definition
of their frontier with Algeria[2]—a proposal which the French
had always resisted.

The French were much alarmed. They could allow Morocco
to drift so long as it remained in its existing backward state;
they could not allow reforms except under their direction.
Though Nicolson was quite right in believing that only reform
could enable Morocco to survive; yet his well-meant efforts,
with those of Maclean and El Menebhi, launched the French
on an active Moroccan policy which could only end in partition.
French alarm increased in the autumn of 1901 with the
mounting rumours that Abdul Aziz intended to seek a loan
from the British.[3] At the beginning of 1902, a new French
minister, Saint-René-Taillandier, arrived in Tangier; he came
out with instructions to fight the 'English protectorate'[4]
and, immediately on arrival, he let it be generally known that
he was determined 'to break through the English ring round
the Sultan'[5] and that 'if His Majesty continued to be guided
by British advisers France would take extremely disagreeable
measures on the frontier'.[6]

Nicolson, however, managed to get in first with a visit to
the Sultan. According to his biographer, 'Nicolson, realizing
that His Majesty's Government would in the last resort leave
Morocco in the lurch, decided himself to visit the Court and to
clear the atmosphere'.[7] This modest policy does not appear in
his contemporary correspondence. Certainly he advised the
Sultan 'not to give the slightest ground for complaint on the
part of the French authorities' and to reduce the number of
British employees in subordinate positions. He further advised

---

[1] Minute by Lansdowne, 3 July 1901, F.O. 99/381; Cambon to Delcassé,
July 1901, *D.D.F.*, 2nd series, i, no. 315, p. 374.

[2] De la Martinière (chargé d'affaires) to Delcassé, telegram, 15 July 1901,
D.D.F., 2nd series, i, no. 326, p. 387.

[3] De la Martinière to Delcassé, telegram, 2 December; telegram, 29 December;
31 December 1901, *D.D.F.*, 2nd series, i, no. 547, p. 647; no. 583, p. 688; no.
588, pp. 693–5.

[4] Saint-René-Taillandier, *Les Origines de la Maroc française*, p. 13.

[5] Information from the German minister, Nicolson to Lansdowne, no. 9, 19
January 1902, F.O. 99/394.

[6] Information from the Austro-Hungarian minister, Nicolson to Lansdowne,
no. 11, 20 January 1902, F.O. 99/394.   [7] Nicolson, *Lord Carnock*, p. 144.

the Sultan against seeking a loan and against any railway
building except a light railway inland from Casablanca. On the
other hand he said: 'the recent acts of the Sultan invite
approval and encouragement'. He advised the Sultan 'to steer
a straight course'. 'If he followed this line I did not see how
any difficulties could arise or any obstacles be placed in his
path by foreign nations.' Finally, if the Sultan insisted on a
loan, 'it was desirable if the Sultan were to apply to us in the
first place before entertaining any other proposal'.[1] In fact
Nicolson was still hoping that Morocco might reform itself
with disinterested British advice and perhaps some British
money.

Saint-René-Taillandier followed close on Nicolson's heels.
His prolonged visit saw a series of conflicts with the Maghzen.
Like Euan Smith ten years before, he refused to accept the
first Moorish Note; unlike Euan Smith he remained until he
had got his way. Finally the Moors promised not to engage
new foreigners 'except for a very limited period'; and they
added this verbal declaration: 'The Sultan especially informs
you that concerning innovations such as the making of a railway, telegraphs, etc., absolutely nothing has been done till
now and that he promises, when there is a question of it, to
inform you before anything is done.'[2] Saint-René-Taillandier
regarded this negative result as a defeat for France; and certainly it was the lowest point of French influence for many
years. On the other hand the Maghzen had virtually renounced
(no doubt with relief) the programme of reform on which
Nicolson placed all his hopes; Morocco drifted helplessly; and
the way remained open for France once her international position enabled her to follow it. Nicolson did not appreciate that
the Maghzen had gone back on its good intentions; he
remained confident that Morocco could be saved. In May he
was shown a report from Troubridge, the British naval attaché
at Madrid, who, after a visit to Tangier, argued that partition
was inevitable. Nicolson wrote in reply:

> Troubridge is unaware that the Sultan has taken seriously in hand
> the reform of his administration. . . . A Fresh spirit has been infused
> into the government. . . . I am fairly confident that . . . order and

[1] Nicolson to Lansdowne, no. 15, 23 January; no. 19, 29 January; no. 22,
31 January; no. 24, 2 February; no. 26, 10 February 1902, F.O. 99/394.

[2] Saint-René-Taillandier to Delcassé, 9 March 1902, D.D.F., 2nd series, ii,
no. 125, pp. 146–50.

security will be established, taxes will be justly and fairly collected, exactions and oppressions of provincial officials will be finally checked. ... Any other course than the maintenance of the *status quo* will hardly permit of a peaceful solution.[1]

In French eyes, however, the reform of Morocco was a decisive alteration of the *status quo*; and Saint-René-Taillandier was anxious to counter this danger by some violent measure such as a military demonstration on the Algerian frontier. Delcassé rejected this proposal: it would not be effective so long as Morocco was receiving British patronage.[2]

The time had arrived for the French to deal with the question of Morocco on an international scale. Italy had been already bought off by the agreement of December 1900; and now Delcassé proposed to negotiate with Spain.[3] Great Britain would thus be finally deprived of her former associates and would be brought to negotiate in her turn. The alarming reports from Saint-René-Taillandier upset this time-table. Early in July 1902, Delcassé consulted Paul Cambon as to the right line to follow, and agreed to try conciliation rather than the military action which was being urged by Saint-René-Taillandier.[4] Cambon approached Lansdowne, allegedly on his own initiative, on 23 July; and, receiving an encouraging reply, repeated his proposals more officially on 6 August. The gist of Cambon's offer was that if Great Britain would drop Maclean, and therewith the programme of reform in Morocco, France would promise in return the neutralization of Tangier; freedom of trade in Morocco for a limited period; and a share of the Mediterranean hinterland for Spain. Lansdowne tried to play down Maclean. 'What we had most enjoined upon the Sultan was that he should not get into debt and that he should keep his prisons cleaner' (it is surprising that he did not mention the export of vegetables). On the proposed 'liquidation' Lansdowne, according to his own account, took up a reserved attitude and spoke of the 'serious complications' concerning other Powers. Nevertheless he gave Cambon some encouragement; for he discussed such details as neutralizing a zone of territory round Tangier and the exact share to be allotted to

[1] Nicolson to Lansdowne, no. 76, 14 May 1902, F.O. 99/395.
[2] Saint-René-Taillandier, *Origines*, pp. 66 and 85–8.
[3] Note on the Moroccan Question, 15 July 1902, *D.D.F.*, 2nd series, ii, no. 33, pp. 397–400.
[4] Saint-René-Taillandier, *Origines*, pp. 85–8.

Spain. Cambon and Lansdowne promised to renew the discussion after the holidays.[1]

A mysterious leakage followed. W. B. Harris, self-appointed
patron of Morocco and *The Times* correspondent at Tangier
learnt the terms of Cambon's offer in accurate detail.[2] Harris
according to his own account, got his information while on
holiday in London; he even claimed to have had it confirmed
by Lansdowne himself, after making out that Nicolson (also
on holiday in England) had let him into the secret. Harris was
certainly on friendly terms with Nicolson, with whom he had
often travelled in Morocco. Nicolson admitted the accuracy
of Harris's information and later surmised that the French
must have shown him the correspondence. It is difficult to
understand the French interest in a leakage; and Saint-René
Taillandier himself says that Harris brought the information
from London.[3] On the other hand there were certainly those
in the British foreign service who had faith in the Moorish
plans of reform; and for them the prospect of a deal with
France must have been unwelcome. Harris was, no doubt, an
unreliable witness; but there is every ground for supposing
that he received his information either from a member of the
Foreign Office—or from Nicolson himself.

Harris at once returned to Morocco and raised the alarm at
the Sultan's court. He wrote to Nicolson on 9 September that
the Sultan felt himself 'betrayed by his best friends'. On 21
September Nicolson showed this letter to Sanderson, the permanent under-secretary; and the two drafted a telegram to the
British chargé d'affaires at Tangier: 'you may authorise the
vice-consul at Fez contradict any such report in the most
positive terms'.[4] The denial, though a little strong, seems to

---

[1] Lansdowne to Monson, 23 July, 6 August 1902, *B.D.*, ii, no. 321, 322
pp. 263–8. Cambon to Delcassé, 9 August 1902, *D.D.F.*, 2nd series, ii, no. 369
pp. 437–43.

[2] Harris wrote to Nicolson on 9 September, according to Nicolson to Sanderson, 21 September 1902, F.O. 99/395. Mentzingen to Foreign Office, 1.
September 1902, *G.P.*, xvii, no. 5188, p. 344. The only point added by Harris
which was not in the official record was that England was offered compensation
'in Egypt and Hither-India'. The latter may be a reference to Siam which was
certainly discussed.

[3] Saint-René-Taillandier to Delcassé, telegram, 17 October 1902, *D.D.F.*,
2nd series, ii, no. 443, p. 546.

[4] Lansdowne to White, telegram, no. 16, 23 September 1902, F.O. 99/395

ave been not unwelcome to Lansdowne. On 24 September
Maclean arrived in England, where he stayed more than a
month. He was sent on a visit to the king at Balmoral and
nighted, perhaps in an effort to avoid political conversations.
The effort did not succeed. Nicolson saw him repeatedly and
eported the results in four long sympathetic memoranda.
According to Cambon, there was now an estrangement
•etween the two men;[1] this estrangement does not appear in
Nicolson's reports. Cambon probably got his information from
•anderson, who, as the only surviving remnant of the Salisbury
ra in the Foreign Office, may well have regarded the 'active'
•olicy in Morocco with distaste.

Maclean brought with him an offer and a threat. The Sultan
vas 'desirous of placing himself entirely under the protection
nd guidance of the King and the British Government'. He
sked for a loan of £300,000 and offered the prospect of large
ailway concessions. Further, in return for a British guarantee
•f the integrity of Morocco he would promise to carry out
eforms within seven years. If the British did not care to act
lone, the loan and the guarantee could be shared with Ger-
nany. The threat was more serious: if the British would not
telp him, the Sultan would turn to Germany. Maclean was
rmed with a letter from the Sultan to the German emperor;
nd the Sultan was confident 'that Germany would be inclined
o accord the support which the Sultan and his Government
re seeking'. Nicolson was most urgent in warding off this
hreat. He said at his first meeting with Maclean that 'it would
•e better not to deliver the letter to William II'.[2] After a
nonth of discussion the Foreign Office finally produced a
nemorandum which Lansdowne authorized and which
Nicolson passed on to Maclean. The British government
lodged the request for a guarantee: 'it does not seem to His
Majesty's Government to be well calculated to achieve the
•bjects which his Shereefian Majesty has in view'. The French,
t was asserted, 'do not desire to raise issues involving the
•artition of Morocco, or to threaten the integrity of the
•ultan's Empire . . . there is not the slightest chance of any one
•ower being given a free hand in that country. Great Britain

[1] Cambon to Delcassé, 23 October 1902, *D.D.F.*, 2nd series, ii, no. 456, p.
61.

[2] Memoranda by Nicolson, 24 September, 25 September, 3 October, 8
October 1902, F.O. 99/395–6.

will not acquiesce in any such attempt.' As to the loan and the railway concessions, these should be shared between Great Britain, France and Germany: 'this method of procedure seems well calculated to prevent rivalry between the Powers' (a remark contradicted by all experience of such financial partnerships).[1] Maclean regarded these assurances as adequate; at any rate he did not proceed to Berlin.

Yet Maclean's visit had its effect. Lansdowne did not renew with Cambon the discussions which had been broken off in August. Morocco was not mentioned between them until the middle of December; and then Lansdowne spoke with much reserve. Cambon surmised that he had been checked by the cabinet; Nicolson's notes of his conversations with Maclean offer another explanation. Lansdowne spoke slightingly of Maclean: 'this person did not concern himself at all with politics and his only ambition was to create a good personal situation for himself, in other words to make his fortune'[2]— it is curious that such a person should have been recently knighted and received by the king at Balmoral. However, Lansdowne's opinion of Maclean was no longer of much moment. Throughout the autumn of 1902 there had been tribal revolts in Morocco; at the end of December the Sultan's army was decisively defeated. The capital of prestige which Abdul Aziz had inherited from Muley Hassan was exhausted; though he retained a shadowy position for another five years, he ceased to be the effective ruler of Morocco at the end of 1902. Maclean's brief importance ended; and with it ended the British project of reforming Morocco under the Sultan's authority. The collapse of this policy was complete; and soon Lansdowne, Nicolson, and the Foreign Office forgot that they had ever contemplated it. The alternative of resisting French encroachments with the assistance of others was perhaps briefly considered. This policy, too, proved hopeless when, in the spring of 1903, the British learnt of the French offers of partition to Spain. Cambon had already made it clear that Italy had been bought out; and the Germans showed repeatedly that their support was not for sale. Thus only the policy of settlement with France remained.

[1] Memorandum for Kaid Sir H. Maclean, 24 October 1902, *B.D.*, ii, no. 328, p. 272.

[2] Cambon to Delcassé, 17 December 1902, *D.D.F.*, 2nd series, no. 529, pp. 660–2. Cambon does not give the date of this conversation; it was 'recently'.

It would be tempting to read into British policy regarding Morocco a consistent pattern and to present it as moving steadily from supporting the *status quo* in co-operation with Spain and Italy to preserving British interests by a bargain with France. Close examination shows that no such simple development took place. Salisbury was nearest to a full triple *entente* against France in 1887, though even then with caution; he had lost faith in this policy by 1891 and made no effort to renew it between 1895 and 1900, when indeed his only gestures were against Germany. Salisbury was never as much alarmed at French encroachment as the Germans, and others, thought he ought to be; and it is difficult to see how his policy could have ended in anything other than a bargain with France. Besides, Salisbury favoured keeping things quiet; and every quiet period in Morocco brought Great Britain and France on to terms of day-to-day co-operation. The Liberals and Lansdowne are sometimes supposed to have been more friendly than Salisbury towards France. This was certainly not shown in Morocco. Rosebery behaved as grudgingly to France as he could and held back only because he had been placed in an impossible position by Euan Smith; he made no attempt to reach an agreement with France, even when Ridgeway, his own special envoy, showed that this was the only sensible policy. The Anglo-French *entente* over Morocco in 1893, like that over the upper Nile in 1894, remained one of the might-have-beens of history.

Lansdowne readily fell in with the impatience at Salisbury's temporizing which had been growing at the Foreign Office. This, far from leading him towards France, made him the only foreign secretary of the period who took co-operation with Germany seriously. Great Britain developed a Moroccan policy in 1901, after years of neglect. This policy was actively to promote reform in Morocco and to maintain the independence of Morocco against France with German assistance. This policy survived repeated rebuffs from the Germans. It broke down only when Morocco broke down. There was in British policy no foresight, no calculation, no preparation. There was certainly an object: to keep Tangier harmless. The practical implications of this were never considered, except in Ridgeway's report which was first ignored and soon forgotten. The British continued to repeat to the end the meaningless phrases about being prepared to 'seize' Tangier. The

F

solution of keeping Tangier harmless by agreement with th
French, which Ridgeway had propounded, was put forwar
independently by the French in the summer of 1902; it had t
be imposed on the British by events. But for French initiativ
and the rebellious tribesmen of Morocco, British policy migh
well have continued to drift along in feeble dependence o
Germany, paying out the *pourboires* of Lansdowne's phrase
Thought and action on the French side, lack of an alternativ
on the British—these brought into being the Anglo-French
entente.

XV

THE JAMESON RAID

HE Jameson Raid of 29 December 1895 is one of the most
controversial episodes in recent British history. Was Joseph
Chamberlain implicated in it? For many years it was thought
that the answer might be found in the 'missing' telegrams,
exchanged between Cecil Rhodes and his London agents,
which were produced before the Select Committee of Inquiry.
Garvin published extracts from these in the third volume of his
Life of Chamberlain and argued that while Chamberlain knew
that a revolution against Boer rule was being prepared at
Johannesburg (a revolution which never came off) he never
knew that Rhodes and Jameson were gathering a force outside
the Transvaal to go to the aid of the rising. This, though
damning enough, was still inconclusive; and it was supposed
that a final verdict could never be reached. A South African
scholar has now opened a new source.[1] Sir Graham Bower,
Imperial Secretary to Robinson, the High Commissioner, was
the 'fall-guy' of the Jameson affair. His official superiors persuaded him to admit his own complicity but to deny that of
Robinson or of Chamberlain. He had his career ruined as a
reward. Though he loyally kept silence until death, he left
his papers and a full record for future historians. They are
decisive: the mud sticks to Chamberlain, and to others besides.

The idea of engineering a rising in Johannesburg was
devised by Rhodes in the days of the Liberal Government.
It was approved by Rosebery; and Sir Hercules Robinson,
a shareholder and director of Rhodes's concerns, was appointed
High Commissioner in the belief that he would be clay in
Rhodes's hands. Bower was sent out with him to keep the
technical side of things in order. When Chamberlain took over
the Colonial Office in July 1895, Rhodes was in high hopes.
It was the essence of his plan that a force should be stationed
outside the Transvaal, ready to make a dash for Johannesburg;
and territory in Bechuanaland Protectorate had to be handed

[1] Jean van der Poel, *The Jameson Raid.*

over to Rhodes's company in order to make this possible. Th
is the key-point: if Robinson and Chamberlain knew wh
Rhodes wanted this land, they condoned and encouraged th
raid.

It is now clear that they both knew. Robinson said to Bowe
after a talk with Rhodes: 'The less you and I have to do wit
those damned conspiracies of Rhodes and Chamberlain th
better. I know nothing about them.' But, adds Bower, 'h
ordered me to allow the troops to come down to Pitsani' (th
jumping-off ground for the raid). As to Chamberlain, he wrot
to Robinson on 2 October asking for his views on a rising :
Johannesburg, 'with or without assistance from outside'.

In December 1895 the conspirators at Johannesbur
began to falter. Fairfield, Assistant Under-Secretary at th
Colonial Office, told Bower later 'he had written to M
Chamberlain at Birmingham suggesting that the revolutio
be damped down. Chamberlain had replied telling him to hurr
it up on account of the Venezuela dispute [with the Unite
States]. He had therefore instructed Lord Grey and Maguir
accordingly and they had telegraphed in the sense I have given
Bower saw Rhodes show this telegram to Robinson on 2
December. It has been alleged by Garvin and others that th
telegrams urging Rhodes to hurry came only from Rutherfoor
Harris, his shady man-of-affairs, and that they were designe
to blackmail Chamberlain. This will not do for Earl Grey an
Maguire, a Fellow of All Souls. Chamberlain later intende
to put the blame on Fairfield, who wrote to Bower that 'he wa
to be the scapegoat of the Colonial Office and was to be di
avowed'; he would be required 'to conform his evidence to tha
of the others'. Fairfield, however, died suddenly before h
could have the pleasure of perjuring himself for the sake c
Joseph Chamberlain. Rhodes, at any rate, had no doubts
When Bower expostulated, Rhodes replied, 'Then you are di
loyal to your chief, Chamberlain, who is hurrying me up'.

Of course part of Chamberlain's defence is technically tru
He did not know that there would be a raid without a revolu
tion. But no one knew this, neither Rhodes nor Jameson him
self. The latter decided on it spontaneously when the revolutio
in Johannesburg 'fizzled out'. But that there was to be a raid a
well as a revolution was planned by Rhodes, authorized b
Chamberlain, and known to Robinson. The raid did immeas
urable harm in South Africa. More than any other single even

caused the Boer War; and it left an estrangement between Boer and Briton which is not yet removed. The authors of the Jameson Raid were those two builders of Empire Cecil Rhodes and Joseph Chamberlain.

Why did this not come out at the time? Far from Rhodes blackmailing Chamberlain, it was Chamberlain who black-mailed Rhodes. He threatened to take away the charter of the British South Africa Company if the telegrams came out; and Rhodes paid the price of silence. According to Bower the Attorney-General thought that the only telegram that 'could not be explained away' was the Grey-Maguire message. It was not produced at the inquiry, nor has it been published by Garvin. Bower would not 'fling all the mud at Rhodes and Jameson'. Therefore he was instructed to confess that he had known of the preparations for the raid but had not told either Robinson or the Colonial Office. Rhodes said to him: 'If you branch off and divulge this correspondence old Robinson will be carried into the box in his bandages like the dying Chatham and will give you the lie. He will be backed by Chamberlain, and at the day of judgement those two old men will shake hands and say they did the right thing.'

Why did the Liberals on the Select Committee swallow this suppression? Miss van der Poel suggests that they knew that Rosebery had been involved in the original plans for a rising and were afraid to discredit their former leader. This seems unlikely. It appears from Harcourt's 'Life' that they were content to have secured a unanimous condemnation of Rhodes. No doubt they did not realize the weight of evidence against Chamberlain, nor appreciate how he had behaved. For, in fact, Chamberlain stood in exactly the same relation to Rhodes and Jameson as Hitler stood to Henlein and the Sudeten Germans in 1938. Perhaps it was this which made Neville Chamberlain listen so sympathetically to Hitler's tales of innocence. They were no worse than those which Joseph Chamberlain had dished up to the Committee of Inquiry.

XVI

THE BOER WAR

On 11 October 1899 the Boer ultimatum expired and Boer forces crossed the frontier into Natal. The Boers hoped to over run all South Africa before British forces arrived; more remotely, they had hoped for the intervention of European Powers. The British, on their side, had expected the Boers to give way without a struggle; at worst, in Milner's words, 'an apology for a fight' would be necessary. 'A slap in the face would do the business. Though Boer hopes were disappointed British hopes were disappointed also, The war dragged on for three years, and by the end the eclipse of Boer independence was of less importance than the deflation of British Imperialism. In fact, the Boer War had a more decisive effect on British politics than on Imperial history. It brought first the culmina tion and then the end of an arrogant, boastful epoch, in which British public opinion seemed to have abandoned principles for power—the political equivalent of that *fin de siècle* spirit in art and literature which produced decadence and Oscar Wilde.

The Boer War caused a bitterness in British politics without parallel since the great Reform Bill and never equalled since except in 1914, during the Ulster rebellion (and perhaps briefly at the time of Munich). 'Pro-Boer' was a more oppro brious epithet than ever 'pro-German' became in either German war. No Minister during these later world conflicts openly regretted the escape of an opponent from physical violence or even death as Chamberlain regretted Lloyd George's escape from Birmingham Town Hall. His comment was: 'What is everyone's business is nobody's business.'

This bitterness had many causes. Every dispute in which Chamberlain was involved was conducted in a savage, scurri lous way (on both sides); the Boer War gave the cheap press its first chance to display its quality; most of all, the war had the bitterness of a family quarrel—not merely a quarrel within the Empire but a quarrel in England between politicians of the same party origin. Imperialism and anti-Imperialism were both advocated by men of Liberal background. Even Disraeli had been originally a Radical; Milner, Chamberlain, and their

associates had all started as Liberals; and Milner's friends
were still mostly Liberals—it was Grey, Haldane, and Asquith
whom he visited when he came to England. In the same way
Rosebery, not Salisbury, had been the most Imperialist of
Prime Ministers. Old Toryism, with its roots in the country-
side, had little sympathy with the aggressive and optimistic
spirit of Imperialism. In August 1899 Salisbury passed this
verdict on the coming war: 'We have to act upon a moral field
prepared for us by Milner and his Jingo supporters. And therefore I see before us the necessity for considerable military
effort—and all for people whom we despise and for territory
which will bring no profit and no power to England.'

Salisbury was dragged into war by Chamberlain; and
Chamberlain was dragged into war by Milner. Certainly
Chamberlain wanted to establish British supremacy in South
Africa; this he had hoped to do gradually, by persuasion and the
passage of time. But Chamberlain was fatally compromised
by his association with the Jameson Raid, the greatest blunder
in his career. The Raid ruined the chance of the Boer moder-
ates and made it certain that Milner would have to deal with
Kruger and his associates, men as violent and as obstinate as
himself. Milner was a great administrator, but no statesman
and no diplomatist. He hated inefficiency and delay; most of
all, he hated compromise. With German dogmatism he wrote
on 16 August 1899: 'They will collapse if we don't weaken,
or rather if we go on steadily turning the screw.' Milner had a
great vision of a British South Africa, which would escape
dependence on the goldmines by wise economic planning and
by raising the standard of life of the native population; he
destroyed this vision by his impatience with the Boers. After
the Jameson Raid the Boer War was probably inevitable; but it
was Milner who determined that it should come when it did
and in the way it did.

Milner made a mistake not uncommon among civilian politicians: he supposed that the soldiers would conduct the war
as competently as he had brought it about. The early disasters
could be repaired; what could never be repaired was the prestige of Imperialism, on which Milner and Chamberlain had
staked their political existence. Even worse than the blow to
prestige was the damage to England's moral position on the
continent of Europe. No war has been so unanimously condemned by enlightened European opinion. Even forty years
afterwards, every European, though few Englishmen, recog-

nized the taunt in the Nazi 'concentration camps', which
deliberately parodied in name and nature the British 'method
of barbarism'. Yet it will not do for the later historian to reac
against this by idealizing the Boers, as the pro-Boers did at the
time. Though the Boers fought to preserve their independence
they were even more concerned to preserve other, and les
admirable, things: their policy of racial exclusion; their shar
of gold profits; and their tyranny over the natives.

Fifty years afterwards, it is clear that victory has gone to the
worst elements on both sides. Milner got his war, with
out achieving his vision; the Boers lost their independence
without being won for progress and civilization; soon the
British citizen in South Africa will be again an *uitlander*, as he
was before the Boer War. The mining houses and the mos
narrow-minded Boers, Johannesburg and Pretoria, have
joined hands to oppress and exploit the native peoples who are
the overwhelming majority of the population; and Smuts, the
last General of the Boer war, lived to accuse the Prime Ministe
of South Africa of using 'the methods of Fascism'. If Milne
could see the results of victory, or Campbell-Bannerman the
results of Boer self-government, would either have reason to
be proud of his handiwork?

The pro-Boers were wrong about the Boers; they were
right about the war. The great underlying issue at stake was
not whether the Boers stood for a moral cause but whether the
British Empire stood for one. Milner and Chamberlain had
appealed from principles to power; the pro-Boers reasserted
the claims of principle, and four years after the end of the war
this despised minority received at the polls the greatest
majority that any party had won since the Reform Act. Many
men fought bravely in the Boer War; but none acted more
bravely or served his country better than the politician who
declared in the St. James's Hall on 15 September 1899:

> You may make thousands of women widows and thousands of
> children fatherless. It will be wrong. You may add a new province to
> your Empire. It will still be wrong. You may give greater buoyancy
> to the South African stock and share market. You may create South
> African booms. You may send the price of Mr. Rhodes's Chartereds up
> to a point beyond the dreams of avarice. Yes, even then it will be wrong.

The outbreak of the Boer War were better passed over in
silence, were it not for the occasion it gives of reprinting
Morley's words.

XVII

'JOE' AT HIS ZENITH

WE have had to wait a long time for the Life of Joseph Chamberlain. The late J. L. Garvin gave up after publishing three volumes which carried the story to the end of 1900. Mr. Julian Amery is to complete the task in the present[1] and a subsequent volume. 'Joe' will receive five volumes where Mr. Gladstone had to be content with three and most Prime Ministers with two or even one. Though Chamberlain's political importance does not justify this excessive length it was inevitable once Garvin was given the job; he was incapable of writing concisely, and the three volumes were composed in the oracular style of his famous 'Observer' articles. Mr. Amery was bound to follow the Garvin pattern of treatment, though not, fortunately, the Garvin style. The best that can be said of his book is this: since someone had to wield Garvin's bow, Mr. Amery is to be congratulated on having done it successfully.

The present volume runs only from the end of 1900 until the spring of 1903, when Chamberlain returned from his visit to South Africa. He was overworked and getting old; as a result, the revelations in this volume are fewer and less interesting than previously. For instance, in spite of a valiant attempt by Mr. Amery to build up Chamberlain as 'the chief author of the revolution in British foreign policy', there is nothing of importance on foreign affairs; the bulk of the story is taken from German documents long published. There is one document of interest: a memorandum of 10 September 1900 naïvely proposing to play off Germany against Russia in the Far East:

> Both in China and elsewhere it is our interest that Germany should throw herself across the path of Russia . . . the clash of German and Russian interests, whether in China or Asia Minor, would be a guarantee for our safety.

The other curiosity is the comment of Paul Cambon when he

[1] Julian Amery, *The Life of Joseph Chamberlain*, vol. iv, 1901–1903.

learnt that Chamberlain had become the advocate of friendshi
with France:

> It must not be forgotten that Mr. Chamberlain has no politica
> principles. He lives in the present and changes his opinions with in
> credible ease; he is not in the least embarrassed by his own statement
> and contradicts himself with extraordinary ease. He has a very accurat
> sense of what public opinion wants and follows its fluctuations whil
> having the air of guiding them—hence his popularity.

Mr. Amery calls this judgement 'myopic'.

The two principal themes of the volume are South Afric
and the origins of Tariff Reform. South Africa bulks the larger
though here again there is not much to add, especially to th
material published from the Milner Papers. It is clear tha
Chamberlain meant ultimately to give self-government to th
Boers; equally clear that he meant to humiliate them first
There is an account here of the lamentable scene when he me
the Boer generals who had come to Europe to seek help fo
their women and children:

> A launch swept them out to Nigeria [the Colonial Secretary's ship]
> There, on the deck, they came face to face, for the first time, with
> Chamberlain. The Colonial Secretary, immaculately dressed as ever
> was accompanied by Roberts and the colonial dignitaries assembled
> for the Coronation. Behind him the battle fleet of Britain stretched
> out in four grey lines to the horizon. Amid the pageantry of Empire
> the generals seemed awkward in their crumpled country clothes. For
> all their valour and cunning they were only simple farmers seeing the
> world for the first time.

This is how German historians used to write of Bismarck;
but one of the Boer generals was called Botha. Would it have
increased their faith in Chamberlain if they had known that
Milner, his chosen pro-consul to whom he gave 'a Roman
welcome', was writing in 1902:

> What I have seen of the working of 'responsible government' in
> South Africa makes it wholly impossible for me to labour for its
> extension with any sort of zeal;

or that Chamberlain himself, who had once denounced the
population of Johannesburg as 'devoted to money-making and
their own interests', should write after his visit there:

> The population of this city . . . is keen, intelligent, and responsive,
> with an inclination to be too impatient and critical but still at the
> bottom intensely loyal and Imperialist.

In fact, Chamberlain, once a social reformer, even—as Mr. Amery calls him—a revolutionary, had energy without principle and became the willing prisoner of the most energetic men of his time, the great capitalist magnates, whether in London or Johannesburg. He thought of the Empire as power or as an undeveloped estate, not as a moral cause; and he said, with profound misjudgement: 'The days are for great Empires and not for little States.'

This led him to Imperial Preference and so, ultimately, to Tariff Reform. Mr. Amery has been able to use the unpublished minutes of the Colonial Conference of 1902; and these show how Chamberlain's plans for Imperial Federation and for military unity broke on colonial resistance. The great Colonies, Canada in particular, wished to be equal nations, not daughters of the Mother Country; and Chamberlain, without sentiment himself, could not conceive of a Commonwealth held together by sentiment alone. Imperial Preference seemed to be the answer; and it suited Canada's needs.

But there were also motives of domestic politics. As Mr. Amery shows in the most interesting part of his book, Imperial Preference was taken up by Chamberlain in order to put new life into the dying party of Liberal Unionism. This had been essentially the party of the industrial middle class, which needed a separate organization so long as the Tory party was ' a predominantly landed interest'. But now the Tory party, too, had become a party of business men; they could promote their interests there without paying the price of social reform, on which Chamberlain had previously insisted. Hence, as Mr. Amery points out, Chamberlain had to drop his advocacy of old-age pensions if he was to keep his followers. The one thing which discriminated the Liberal Unionists from the Tories was their Nonconformity, and here the Education Bill of 1902 was decisive. Chamberlain supported the Bill so as to have his hands free for South Africa, and he rammed it down the throats of his Nonconformist followers. Also, in part, he wanted to pay the Nonconformists out for having supported Gladstone. He said to a leading Nonconformist Liberal:

Had the Nonconformists supported me, they would have had Disestablishment long ago. Now they have got nothing. When Mr. Gladstone suddenly sprang his Irish policy upon the country after consulting Morley, it was not so much to satisfy Ireland that he did so as to prevent me placing the Disestablishment of the Church of

England in the forefront of the Liberal programme, as Mr. Gladston
knew and feared I meant to do.

Since Chamberlain could no longer use a sectarian appea
for his party, he sought something else; and believed tha
Imperial Preference would do the trick. In the words of Lor
George Hamilton, 'If we had had no Education Bill of 1902
we should have had no Tariff Reform in 1903'. The move wa
not designed only to salvage the Liberal Unionist party; it wa
designed ultimately to oust Balfour from the leadership of
great party of Imperial Union. As it was, Chamberlain onl
managed to destroy the Unionist party, as he had earlie
destroyed the old Liberal party. Like all men who split thei
party, he was a failure, slightly above the level of Ramsa
MacDonald, a great deal below that of Lloyd George.

XVIII

QUEEN VICTORIA AND THE CONSTITUTION

A MONARCH who occupies the throne for fifty or sixty years becomes inevitably a symbol of stability, and at the end of his or her death an age seems to end. So it was long foretold that the Habsburg monarchy would not survive the death of Francis Joseph; so Mrs. Arbuthnot felt that the old world had passed away with the death of George III, even though he had been hopelessly insane for nine years; so, most of all, the Victorian age was universally felt to end on 22 January 1901. It is easy to agree that the symbolic character of the British Crown was greatly strengthened during the reign of Queen Victoria, especially in relation to the self-governing Dominions; it is more difficult to assess the individual behind the symbol. Yet the Crown is not just a symbol in the British Constitution; it plays an individual and sometimes a decisive part.

The reputation of Queen Victoria has known some sharp vicissitudes since her death fifty years ago. At the time of her death, and indeed for many years before it, she was popularly regarded as the perfect constitutional sovereign, discharging with impartiality the tasks defined by Bagehot: 'To advise, to encourage, and to warn.' The publication of her letters, which began in 1907, revealed a different picture of a sovereign more active but more partisan than had been supposed. The first series, which ran to 1861, was edited with an excess of tact, and it needed the genius of Lytton Strachey to bring them to life. The later volumes were increasingly frank and there was little left of the impartial Queen when readers learnt of her ceaseless conflicts with Gladstone or of her intrigues with the leader of the Opposition to overthrow the Liberal Government in 1893.

Historical authorities of the Left, such as Harold Laski and Berriedale Keith, spoke sternly of her unconstitutional actions. The phrase seems meaningless: in our flexible system any practice is constitutional which is tolerated by contempor-

163

aries, and these authorities, to adapt a phrase of Romney Sedgwick's, were condemning Queen Victoria for acting like George III when she should have been acting like George VI. It is more important for the historian to discover what Queen Victoria did than to condemn her for doing it, and we have enough material to form an estimate of her position in constitutional history, though the royal archives at Windsor will no doubt reveal more.

The essential prerogative of the British Crown is the appointment of the Prime Minister, and this was exercised as a matter of personal choice by the four Georges and even by William IV. The great Reform Bill itself owed its origin to the fact that William IV preferred Lord Grey as Prime Minister, not to any violent swing of public opinion. Queen Victoria meant to continue the same system and regarded Melbourne as her personal appointment. The general election of 1841 marked an epoch in British history; in Croker's words, 'For the first time the people chose the First Minister for the Sovereign'. Peel, a Conservative, managed to perform the feat that had been beyond all the great Whigs of the eighteenth century and 'forced the closet'. The last Government to be brought into existence by the independent initiative of the Crown was Aberdeen's coalition of 1852, and royal favour could not sustain it against the stresses of the Crimean War.

Thereafter, as party feeling solidified the Crown could occasionally choose between individuals but no longer between parties. The essential condition here was rigid party organization; when this weakened or broke down initiative returned to the Crown. It was not unreasonable for Queen Victoria to suppose in 1886 that, with the split in the Liberal party, it was her duty to promote a Unionist coalition rather than to let Home Rule be carried by a minority Government. George V certainly did not take the advice of the outgoing Prime Minister when he appointed Lloyd George to succeed Asquith in December 1916; he acted, as his ancestors had done, according to his independent judgement of what would be best in the national interest.

In 1940 Neville Chamberlain advised George VI to send for Mr. Churchill; but this advise was tendered at the King's request, and the subsequent discussion between Chamberlain, Mr. Churchill, and Lord Halifax was an informal meeting between friends, not of Ministers formally advising the Crown.

The old Whigs sometimes dreamt of turning the Cabinet into an autonomous body which should elect its own head. This was not what happened in 1940. The King retained the initiative; only, being anxious to save time in view of the military crisis in France, he himself asked for Chamberlain's opinion, instead of leaving inquiries to his private secretary, and Chamberlain gave his opinion as leader of the Conservative party, not as outgoing Prime Minister.

Queen Victoria also refused to accept certain individuals as Cabinet ministers; sometimes she objected to their views, more usually she was offended by their having opposed the grants to her sons and daughters—an intrusion of maternity into politics. George V excluded Lansbury from the first Labour government; and George VI is said to have intervened in Cabinet-making on one occasion. But this was influence rather than prerogative. It has been used discreetly, and there is no doubt that the Prime Minister can get the Cabinet of his choice if he insists on it.

It seems clear that the Prince Consort early foresaw the approaching change in the British system and intended the Crown to exert its influence on policy rather than on personalities. Disraeli indeed said that if the Prince Consort had survived 'we should have enjoyed the blessings of absolute monarchy': all he meant by this was that the Crown would have made an independent contribution to policy, as it has done in other constitutional monarchies, successfully in Sweden, less successfully in Belgium. This is probably the greatest importance of Queen Victoria's reign: the Crown failed to establish its claim to a share in policy-making. After the death of the Prince Consort, Queen Victoria was at first too withdrawn and then too erratic in her interventions to count for anything.

One of the greatest legends of our recent history is that the Queen's favour was an advantage to Disraeli. He enjoyed flattering elderly ladies and got this pleasure in high degree from his relations with the Queen; apart from this, her criticisms were as much trouble to him as they were to Gladstone or to Lord Salisbury. Dr. Hammond preserved a tradition from Gladstone's last Government that the Prime Minister would open almost every Cabinet meeting by saying, 'Gentlemen, I have a message from the Queen'. He would then read a letter full of violent criticism and complaint. At the end he would fold the letter and put it back in his pocket; there would be a

short silence; then the old man would exclaim, 'And now
gentlemen, to business'. This, in fact, is all that the Queen'
influence amounted to. There is nothing to suggest that Home
Rule would have been carried if she had been as strongly in it
favour as she was against; nor would the Queen's support have
made the Liberal Government of 1892–5 anything other than
a collection of warring elements.

The system envisaged by the Prince Consort demanded a
ruler who should be intelligent as well as industrious; this was
beyond Queen Victoria. While the Prince Consort lived all
the greatest figures of the age were to be found at Court—
artists, scientists, philosophers, novelists; after 1861, the Court
became the centre of society in the formal sense and has so
remained. A woman on the throne must always find it difficult
to establish personal contacts with her subjects; and Queen
Victoria did not make the attempt. Moreover the reign of a
woman always involves a decline in the power of the Crown.
The reign of Queen Elizabeth, in spite of Mr. Rowse, is no
exception to the rule. English history would have been very
different if Edward VI, instead of Elizabeth, had reigned for
fifty-five years.

Queen Victoria did not by any means intend to create a new
type of monarchy; to adapt Romney Sedgwick again, she tried
to carry on the system inherited from her grandfather to the
best of her limited ability. These very limitations made it
easier, as well as more necessary, for statesmen to exclude her
from the practical workings of politics; and the effect was completed when she was succeeded by a king too lazy, and too
elderly, to make any serious attempt at recovering the lost
ground. In short, our modern constitutional monarchy was
devised by accident and much against the will of the Queen
who made it.

XIX

NORTHCLIFFE AND DAWSON

POWER, no doubt, corrupts; the illusion of power corrupts still more, and nothing feeds that illusion so much as directing the policy of a great newspaper. Those who conduct *The Times*, like those who have written its history, are always conscious of their national importance; and even a reader who believes that the greatest newspaper in England is not published in London must acknowledge that *The Times* has played a vital part in modern British history. But what is the part that a great newspaper of this kind should play? This is the fundamental question which shapes the last volume of *The History of The Times*.[1] It opens in 1912, with Northcliffe securely in control, an editor of his own choice just appointed. It ends virtually in 1939, when Geoffrey Dawson had held unchecked sway for seventeen years. Barrington-Ward's brief tenure of the editorial chair from 1941 to 1948 is given personal mention; but nothing is said of the great issues of policy raised in those years—they are too recent and perhaps too controversial to be tackled even by the self-confident, dogmatic writers (or 'compilers' as they describe themselves) of this final volume.

The conflict which shook *The Times* and which reached its climax in 1922 can be expressed in many forms. It was a conflict of personalities. On the one side was Northcliffe, the Ogre, the Napoleon of Fleet Street, irresponsible, inconsistent, a man of torrential opinions and undisciplined mind, with no formal education, and—when all is said and done—a genius. On the other side Dawson—cultivated, cautious, a Fellow of All Souls and a member of the Athenæum, fancying himself as a country squire, but safely tied up, too, with the mining interests of South Africa; second-rate himself, except in obstinacy, he preferred the second-rate in others. Northcliffe was dynamic, with infinite faith in British greatness and creative power; he represented, though he would have hated the description, the

[1] *The History of The Times*, vol. iv. *The 150th Anniversary and Beyond*, part i, 1912–20, part ii, 1921–48.

era of Lloyd George. Dawson was intent only to preserve, to settle questions without sharp disturbance; it would have pleased him to be told that he represented the era of Baldwin

The conflict of personalities merged into something bigger the conflict between Proprietor and Editor. Though North-cliffe had bought *The Times* in order to preserve it as a national institution, he meant it to be also the instrument of his will Lord Beaverbrook has said of him: 'he was the greatest figure who ever strode down Fleet Street'; and the present *History* adds the firm verdict, 'he and he alone had transformed the early Victorian survival into a contemporary newspaper with a prospect of a commercial future not less impressive than its past'. But Northcliffe was not content to save *The Times* com-mercially; he wished it to become his personal organ, express-ing his policy and making, or more often unmaking, govern-ments. It would be wrong to think that he had political ambi-tions in the ordinary sense. He knew few politicians and did not get on with them; he did not aspire to high office. As for his title, 'When I want a peerage I will buy one, like an honest man'—and so he did. His sole ambition was to dictate policy to *The Times* and, through *The Times*, to the country. The Editor was simply his agent, his mouthpiece, until such time as he might become Editor-Proprietor in one. Against this stood the tradition of *The Times* as an anonymous 'companion-ship' headed by the Editor, the 'gentlemen scholars of Printing House Square' as they are described here. This battle waged continuously throughout the years when Northcliffe was Chief Proprietor. When he made Dawson Editor in 1912 he thought that he had found a new broom, and an amenable one at that. Instead the two men grew increasingly estranged; and Dawson resigned in 1919. Northcliffe then appointed Wickham Steed, who was undoubtedly more congenial to him—dynamic, adventurous, and ready enough to revive the old line of *The Times* as 'the Thunderer'. Nevertheless, the conflict between Proprietor and Editor was repeated. Northcliffe intrigued against Steed, humiliated him, and in 1922 acquired the re-maining shares of his co-Proprietor, John Walter, so as to make himself all-powerful.

At the very moment of dismissing Steed and forcing *The Times* under his will, Northcliffe went mad. Within two months he was dead. The most dramatic part of the present *History* deals with the financial battle that followed. John

Walter, though he had parted with his shares, had a somewhat disputable option to re-purchase the property from Northcliffe on his death; others had the money, but no option. Endless schemes were aired—the most fascinating and far-fetched, one by which Lloyd George should resign as Prime Minister and become Editor of *The Times* instead. This would certainly have enlivened the drab inter-war years. Lord Rothermere believed that he could outbid all competitors.[1] Walter managed to get the backing of 'a New College man', John Astor; and Rothermere was beaten at the last moment. By an appropriate chance, *The Times* returned to its traditional Proprietor on the very day that Bonar Law became Prime Minister. Steed was dismissed, Dawson restored. It was his duty to give *The Times* a period of steadiness, 'even of stodginess'; he certainly succeeded. Dawson came back on new terms. Previously there had been no written agreement between Proprietors and Editor; after the Northcliffe experience, Dawson was determined to make his position 'bomb-proof'. He laid down terms which ensured that '*The Times* is being run by the Editor and no one else'; and these terms were accepted by the new Proprietors. They never attempted to influence policy. Walter expostulated once at the height of the Czech crisis; Dawson disregarded him. John Astor apparently did not get even this far. Moreover, the Proprietors allowed Dawson complete freedom also in conducting the office and acquiesced, for instance, in his calamitous abolition of the post of Foreign Editor. As the *History* observes, Dawson had a position which had not been held 'by Barnes, Delane, Buckle, Dawson in his early period, or even Steed; or by any former Editor of *The Times*'. Dawson, in fact, achieved Northcliffe's ambition: he became dictator. There is a loose assumption nowadays that the freedom of the press is synonymous with dictatorial powers for the editor; but it is difficult to resist the feeling that *The Times* would have been freer, as well as a better, paper if Dawson had possessed only the limited powers of his predecessors. In the press, as elsewhere, there is something to be said for constitutional monarchy—a system of checks and balances. Dawson, however, was a mayor of the palace; the Proprietors *rois fainéants*.

The results, as the *History* argues, were baleful. The con-

[1] Or so *The Times* circle thought. Rothermere, as administrator of his brother's estate, may, however, have been concerned only to push up the purchase price. Perhaps, after all, he was the bluffer, not the bluffed.

flict between Dawson and Northcliffe had been far more than
a clash of personality between Editor and Proprietor. It was
the clash between two fundamental conceptions of journalism.
Northcliffe wanted his papers, and especially *The Times*, to make
policy. Though he was also anxious to maintain the sales of the
paper, he never shrank from unpopularity: he would rather
lose readers than fail to advocate the causes which he believed
to be right. No doubt he sometimes abused his power and
attacked governments from motives of personal dislike rather
than public policy. But usually he was patriotic as well as courageous, as when he preached conscription during the First
World War or settlement with Ireland after it. Dawson, on the
other hand, claimed to express public opinion, not to lead it.
What is more, he meant by public opinion that of men in his
own class and to his own taste. He went from his club to his
college and from his college to his country house, listening to
the slow, the cautious, the timid; avoiding the dynamic and
adventurous, the 'viewy' men. The writers of the *History*
emphasize Dawson's fault, perhaps even exaggerate it. But
they attribute it to a strange motive—the mass-electorate.
'The act that brought the number of voters at the 1929 election to 28,500,000 was unaccompanied by any move to instruct
them in issues of national significance.' Northcliffe would have
welcomed this challenge; Dawson shrank from it. In any case,
the explanation is false. There was nothing wrong with the
British people in the inter-war years except its leaders. The
traditional governing class turned timid, failed to lead. Dawson
was a symbol of this. His claim to express public opinion was
fraudulent; he would only express the public opinion with
which he agreed. The *History* observes, 'He was close to
Baldwin and Chamberlain; he was intimate with Halifax.
There is no sign that he consulted statesmen, whether Conservative or not, who were known to oppose the policy of the
party.' Details are given here of the way in which Dawson,
himself as uninstructed in foreign affairs as his hero Baldwin,
inserted late at night the notorious sentence which advocated
the dismemberment of Czechoslovakia. This was not express-
ing public opinion; it was leading it—in the wrong direction.
Dawson was a gentleman; Northcliffe was not. Dawson was
restrained, courteous; he knew the Prime Minister and the
Archbishop of Canterbury; he had the approval of the Church
of England and of every respectable member of the University

of Oxford. The fact remains that he was a more powerful dictator than Northcliffe and that he used his power for evil purposes. He did his best to knock the guts out of the British people and British life. The one thing to be said for Dawson is that he had the courage of his convictions; he never wavered in wrongdoing or disclaimed responsibility for, say, the dismemberment of Czechoslovakia or the abdication of Edward VIII. His friends were more craven. They seconded him when he was alive and sought his favour; but when the present volume was published, the Bishops and Fellows of Colleges remained silent, and it was left to Wickham Steed, the man whom he had displaced, to speak in his defence.

The writers of the *History* themselves pass verdict against him. They speak with contempt of his 'simply advocating half-measures on every occasion, or sitting on the fence and softening rearmament into "re-equipment" or "the thorough organisation of British resources" '. But their criticism is narrowed to a single issue, which they seem to regard as the only problem of politics: that of resistance to Germany. Indeed much of this *History*, not only in this volume, is delayed revenge of the old Toryism against the new. The third volume, which was published in 1947, devoted a quite disproportionate space to discussing Anglo-German relations between 1901 and 1912; this was not so much a contribution to the history of *The Times* as a vindication of those of its staff who gave warning to the German danger. The present volume repeats the demonstration. The writers have no doubt that it was right to go to war against Germany in 1914 and wrong to hesitate in 1939. They like to imply that they are more aware of the problems of the modern world than were Dawson and Barrington-Ward; in reality all they mean by a modern policy is 'rearmament', and an anti-German coalition. Their argument is out of date; their younger, more 'realistic' colleagues are no doubt already projecting a further volume in which the present writers will be condemned for continuing to advocate resistance against Germany when they ought to have been preaching war against Russia.

This antithesis reveals the great weakness of *The Times*. Its only question has been—war against which rival? It has existed to serve 'the national interest', by which it has meant the interest of the British governing class. As this class has altered its character and changed its views, *The Times* has

altered too. Sometimes it has jumped too quickly, sometimes
not quickly enough. But always it has considered 'the Establishment' and its duty to it. Northcliffe did not belong to the
Establishment and cared nothing for it. The Establishment
thought that it had ensnared Northcliffe when he became proprietor of *The Times*. Instead, he nearly blew the Establishment sky-high; and what a sight it would have been! It is
difficult not to see the workings of Providence in the way in
which Northcliffe went mad at the exact moment when *The
Times* was at last firmly in his grasp.

XX

OLD DIPLOMACY—AND NEW

Diplomacy is the method by which sovereign states reach agreement with each other. The methods change; but so long as there are sovereign states and so long as they wish to agree, there will always be diplomacy—and even diplomats. What makes international affairs so bewildering at present is that the methods are changing and that the basic assumptions are being challenged at the same time. The change in methods can be exaggerated. It is true that things move faster nowadays. Diplomats telephone and send telegrams where they used to write dispatches; they listen for the ring of the telephone-bell where they used to wait for the arrival of the messenger. But what they say on the telephone is very much what they used to write in their dispatches; maybe the style is a little less elegant. In any case, the essential job of the diplomat is personal contact with the rulers of other countries; and this job has changed very little. It is still important to have an able British ambassador in Washington and an able American ambassador in London. A good diplomat cannot make two countries agree if they do not want to agree, but he can make their agreement easier if they want to agree.

A great change is often found in the way in which the man at the top—President, Prime Minister, or dictator—cuts across the work of the diplomats and does the job himself. But this is not new at all. In the nineteenth century, Tsars, Emperors, and Kings did a great deal of their own diplomacy, often to the annoyance of the professional diplomats. Napoleon and Alexander I met on a raft in the river Niemen and divided up the world even more casually than the 'Big Three' did at Yalta. A few years later Alexander I conducted his own diplomacy at the Congress of Vienna just as President Wilson did at Paris in 1919. Napoleon III conspired with Cavour, behind the back of his own Foreign Minister, to launch a war against Austria; just as Hitler conspired with Henlein against

Czechoslovakia in 1938, without informing the German Foreign Office. Even in England, Lord Salisbury said that Queen Victoria gave him as much trouble as parliament and foreign Powers put together when he was trying to conduct foreign policy. There is a difference all the same. The ruler, though a nuisance, was a tolerable nuisance, so long as he was a single man, an Emperor or a King. Now, in democratic countries, the people rule; and diplomacy has to keep in touch with public opinion. Sometimes public opinion causes unnecessary wars; and sometimes it prevents necessary ones. The British government, for instance, got itself involved in the Crimean war against Russia, mainly in order to show British public opinion that it was a resolute government, despite being a coalition. On the other hand, most people who knew England and France in 1938 will agree that it would have been impossible for the then governments to take an intransigent line with Germany even if they had wished to do so; their public opinion would not have supported them. It is useless for the diplomat to complain about the public demand to be kept informed. If the people are going to pay taxes and perhaps even to fight a war as the result of diplomatic action, they will want to know what it is about.

No one will pretend that this makes the task of the diplomat easier. It is difficult to negotiate with a foreign government if at every step, you have to explain in public the limit of your concessions and why you are prepared to make them. In the old days Great Britain and the United States would have kept quiet about the fact that they cannot agree whether to recognize Communist China; now they have to draw the attention of the Soviet Union to this cause of possible difference between them— though no doubt the Soviet Union had noticed the point already. One of the most curious legends of the twentieth century is that 'secret diplomacy' caused World War I. As a matter of fact, it would be more reasonable to argue that World War I was caused by the absence of secret diplomacy: that is, the Great Powers did not negotiate enough between the murder of Archduke Ferdinand on 28 June and the Austrian declaration of war against Serbia a month later. But there was nothing secret about the diplomatic background of World War I. Every one knew that France had an alliance with Russia and that Germany had an alliance with Austria-Hungary; therefore if Austria-Hungary and Russia went to war, France and Germany would come in. Everyone knew that Great Britain had guaranteed the neutrality of Belgium; even the German general staff assumed that the British government would declare war—their mistake was to suppose that British military intervention would be ineffective. Men blamed 'secret diplomacy' for World War I because they shrank from the true explanation. After thirty years and more of European peace that had followed the Congress of Berlin (1878), men had come to regard peace as 'normal'; they could not bring themselves to believe that there were tensions between states which could not be settled by agreement, and therefore fell back on the theory that World War I was a 'blunder' caused by the incompetence of diplomats. Yet the causes of World War I were there for all to see: the rivalry of Slav and German in the Balkans, the naval rivalry between Germany and Great Britain, fundamentally in fact the German determination to dominate the continent of Europe and, ultimately, the world. If proof were needed that World War I was not caused by secret diplomacy, this was provided by World War II. There was virtually no secret diplomacy before World War II: Hitler stated his demands in public and received replies in kind. The only secret diplomacy was with Russia; and this resulted not in war, but in the Nazi-Soviet pact—an agreement for neutrality, though no doubt on a somewhat cynical basis.

This suggests indeed one of the strongest grounds for the popular objection to secret diplomacy: the suspicion that every deal will be a dirty deal. And so in a sense it will. Agreement by diplomacy implies compromise; and compromise implies that you will get less than you want, probably indeed less than you think right. The alternative, however, is not to reach agreement, that is, to get nothing at all. The Hoare-Laval plan, for instance, was a reasonable, though discreditable, bargain by the standards of diplomacy, old or new. It would have saved part of Abyssinia for the Emperor, and perhaps even brought Mussolini back on to the Anglo-French side against Hitler. The British public rejected it as wicked; they would not have been so high-minded if they had understood the danger they were in from Germany. Similarly, in 1939, the French, being in mortal terror of Hitler, would have handed over the Baltic states to Stalin in exchange for a Soviet alliance; the British, still confident of their strength, would not. By 1942 it was the British who were ready to make territorial concessions in

Poland to please Stalin; and the Americans who held out. Bu
at Yalta, President Roosevelt outdid the British in concession
because he believed that he needed Russian help against Japan
Yet even these deals were not merely dirty deals. The Britisl
government, for instance, was willing to make concessions t
Russia partly because they wanted to keep her in the war
but partly too because there were good ethnic, or even moral
arguments in favour of her demands. The British were read
to agree to Russia's claims up to the Curzon line, their ow
proposal of 1919; they would not have conceded Polish terri
tory beyond that line even at the crisis of the war. Of course
the British would not have felt the weight of these ethnic an
moral arguments in favour of the Curzon line if they had no
been in desperate need of the Russian alliance. All this i
merely to say of diplomacy what Bismarck said of politics i
general: it is the art of the possible.

It would be tempting to add that those who dislike diplo
macy want the impossible; it is less controversial to say tha
they want something different. To go back to the definitio
in the first sentence of this article, those who dislike diplomacy
either want sovereign states to cease to exist or they want them
not to agree. So far the only alternatives discovered to diplo
macy are isolation or war. Isolation is a reputable alternativ
to diplomacy of long-standing. The old Chinese Empire befor
1840 refused to acknowledge the existence of any other state
than itself and therefore, logically enough, excluded al
foreigners from its territory. Once it let them in, diplomacy wa
bound to follow; and very unpleasant diplomacy it turned ou
to be for the Chinese. Isolationism, whether British, American
or Chinese, is a form of idealism: it rests on the belief that you
alone possess standards of right and civilization. In nineteenth
century England, for instance, Bright and Cobden argued that
once British steam-engines spread over the world, everyon
would be interested in getting rich and that therefore ther
would be no need for diplomacy; in fact they thought diplo
macy merely an excuse for giving well-paid jobs to members o
the upper classes. In Bright's words: 'the Balance of Power i
a gigantic system of out-relief for the British aristocracy'
But even the idealism of Bright and Cobden stopped short a
the British navy: they held, as American isolationists did later
that isolation was possible only so long as it was based on sea
power. This was a reasonable view so long as sea-power an

land-power did not overlap; once they did, the world was back at diplomacy—or war.

The idealism of isolation easily turns into its opposite: the desire that sovereign states should cease to exist. This idealism has come to dominate the policy of the Anglo-Saxon countries in recent times. President Wilson, for instance, believed at bottom that France and Germany were equally responsible for World War I; and he wanted to put them, and all other states, under the rule of law. The essence of the League of Nations was that it should be something other than a meeting-place for the representatives of sovereign states; it was to create a conscience of humanity to which all states would become obedient. This is the way the rule of law has grown up in the Anglo-Saxon world: legislation by consent springing from the conscience of the community. But it is not the way in which the rule of law has been established elsewhere in the world: there, in Europe or in the great Oriental empires, it has been imposed from above by authority. President Roosevelt took himself to be a more practical man than Wilson; therefore he accepted what Wilson had not, a world authority based on force. In his original conception of the United Nations, he proposed that every state in the world except the three Great Powers who had fought the war—Great Britain, the Soviet Union, and the United States—should be kept compulsorily disarmed for good. Moreover he assumed—and this was essential to the conception of the United Nations—that, as the three Great Powers were temporarily in agreement, they would remain agreed for ever. In other words, the United Nations was not a new method of diplomacy; it sprang from the belief that diplomacy was no longer necessary. As the assumption has not worked out, the nations are back at diplomacy with the added embarrassment of the United Nations on their hands. The delegates at the Security Council have to make fierce speeches against each other in public and then meet secretly in hotel bedrooms in order to get on with diplomacy, that is, with the task of reaching agreement. The only difference between the old diplomacy and the new is that nowadays the diplomats are ashamed of diplomacy and have to pretend that it is not happening. And of course it may not happen; in which case there is always the alternative of war.

It would be foolish to blame Anglo-Saxon idealism as the sole cause for the breakdown of diplomacy. As a matter of fact,

the Russians have exactly the same belief as western idealist
that the day of the sovereign state is over and that there shoul
be a single world community; only they expect this community
to be Communist and to be run from Moscow, not from Lak
Success. There is a three-volume *History of Diplomacy* i
Russian, edited by Potemkin, a one-time Vice-Commissar o
Foreign Affairs, and very scholarly in its way. This argues tha
there are two sorts of diplomacy: old-style *bourgeois* diplomacy
which does such wicked things as sharing out the colonia
areas of the world or making alliances against the Soviet Union
and new-style Soviet diplomacy, which is engaged in bringing
more and more of the world under the beneficial influence o
'the workers' state'. The object of this diplomacy is not t
reach agreement, but to manœuvre yourself into a more favour
able position for the ultimate and inevitable conflict. It is th
diplomacy of 'the cold war'. Even this is not as new as Potem
kin and his colleagues make out, or as is supposed by people i
the western world who find the cold war intolerable. Ther
have been plenty of occasions in history when two civilization
thought that they could not live side by side and believed that a
fight to a finish was the only solution. In the sixteenth century
Protestants and Roman Catholics thought that there was n
room for both religions in Europe and conducted 'cold war
even when Spain and England were not actually fighting. Ye
in the end the two had to put up with each other not only i
Europe, but even within Germany, after they had torn centra
Europe to pieces by a generation of war. The Chinese refuse
to admit the existence of any civilized Power except themselves
and they described all white men as 'foreign devils'—
phrase quite as offensive as anything coined by Mr. Vishinsky
The Ottoman Turks, in the days of their glory, knew only on
method of diplomacy: they imprisoned the foreign ambassado
in the Castle of the Seven Towers, often fory ears at a time
Even the western ambassadors in Moscow are still littl
better treated than that.

The closest parallel to the present deadlock of outlooks is
however, to be found in the French revolution. The Frencl
Jacobins, like the Bolsheviks, thought that they had discovere
a 'new diplomacy'; by this they meant that revolutionar
France should overrun Europe. The European states of the ol
order, on the other hand, regarded the Jacobins as criminals
apostles of universal destruction, with whom it was impossibl

to negotiate: when in 1797 delegates of revolutionary France
first attended an international conference they were assassinated on the way home. All the amenities of modern international
relations can be found in the dealings between old Europe and
revolutionary France. Napoleon called the British ambassador
a liar in public; the French ran a Jacobin 'fifth column' in
England (complete with peace propaganda and a Convention,
or front, of distinguished names) and the British government
subsidized monarchist risings in France. In the end the two
rival systems, which had intended to fight each other to the
death, had to settle down together. Kings survived in Europe,
and the ideas of the French revolution survived along with
them. A hundred and fifty years ago an Englishman could
have been sent to prison for speaking in favour of 'liberty,
equality, fraternity'; now the phrase could safely be used by a
Conservative Member of Parliament or by a Republican
Senator.

Thus when men say at the present time that diplomacy has
broken down or that new diplomacy is less successful than old
diplomacy, they really mean that the basis for diplomacy is
lacking. Diplomacy is merely a fine name for doing business;
and you cannot do business except with mutual tolerance and
a certain confidence that the other man will keep his bargain.
This is a very different thing from saying that you want the
other man to have things all his own way. When two business
men get together, each wants to make the bigger profit for
himself; but he also wants to reach agreement, though a
profitable one, with the other fellow. Or put it another way.
Diplomacy is a game with elaborate rules, which is played for
high stakes. The game has got more difficult in recent years
because the spectators now look over the shoulders of the
players and shout out the best, or more usually the weakest,
cards in their hands. You can win or lose quite a lot in this
game even if you stick to the rules. But the game becomes
really too difficult if the two principal players each suspect the
other of cheating and are resolved to kick over the table rather
than be beaten; add to this that many of the spectators and even
some of the players think that the game is wicked and ought
not to be played at all, and it will be clear why the new diplomacy is not so successful as the old one. For diplomacy can
work only when there are certain common aims and certain
common interests. At the Congress of Vienna, Russia and

Austria had many conflicts; in fact they almost went to war over the division of Poland. But when Metternich, the Austrian Chancellor, went to call on his mistress, he found the carriage of Tsar Alexander drawn up outside the door; and the two men had a very profitable discussion in the passage outside the lady's bedroom. It is difficult to think of a common ground where Mr. Acheson and Mr. Vishinsky could meet in this chance way.

XXI

SPAIN AND THE AXIS

THE third volume of documents[1] from the archives of the
German Foreign Ministry is sadly lacking in scandal and
sensation. Devoted to the Spanish civil war, it contains little evidence of a Fascist conspiracy and none at all of British or
French connivance in it. Either the Western friends of Franco
were discreet in their conversation or the German diplomatists
were discreet in their reports. There is a solitary sentence to the
contrary. On 16 October 1936 the German chargé d'affaires
with Franco reported from Alicante:

> England is supplying the Whites with ammunition via Gibraltar,
> and the British cruiser commander here has recently been supplying
> us with information of Russian arms deliveries to the Red Govern-
> ment, which he certainly would not do without instructions.

The first part of the sentence sounds like gossip; the second
may record only the aberration of a single officer. Perhaps
the British pro-Fascists let themselves go only in the more congenial company of the Italians. As to France, the one interesting
story is of an approach to Franco by Laval in April 1937, with
the programme of a Pétain Government which would work
for Franco's victory. This certainly blows on the current legend
of Laval as a maligned champion of democracy.

These are sidelines. The bulk of this inordinately long
volume sticks closely to German policy, or rather the lack of it.
For the Spanish civil war took the Germans entirely by surprise
and it was a long time before they decided what use to make of
it. The material here is, of course, drawn exclusively from the
diplomatic archives; there is very little from the military side,
and not a single directive from Hitler. No doubt wild ideas
were aired at Berchtesgaden and wild projects sketched. But
it certainly appears that the professional diplomatists were left
to deal with the Spanish affair as best they could, gathering
little prestige and improving the international situation for
Germany, but without risking a general war.

[1] *Documents on German Foreign Policy*, 1918–1945, series D, vol. iii, The
Spanish Civil War.

The German authorities on Spain at first expected Franco to be defeated, and therefore did not commit themselves deeply; they even welcomed the British proposal of non-intervention as a way of escape from an embarrassing situation. It is clear from this record that a firm French stand in the early autumn of 1936 would have settled the civil war to the advantage of the Spanish Government, without any risk of a general conflict; but of course the real French fear was of conflict within their own country. Another curious point is that in the opinion of the German Ambassador in Moscow (and of the French Ambassador also) the Russian Government, too, did not care much about the Spanish question, but was dragged into it in order to please the Communists of Western Europe.

Mussolini was Franco's real patron; and Italian zest outran German policy and patience. In December 1936 Mussolini made an agreement with Franco, securing economic and political advantages for Italy; the Germans were so annoyed that they cut down their aid to Franco and insisted that Italy carry the main burden of intervention. All the Germans secured during the civil war was an innocuous agreement of friendship made on 20 March 1937. The main concern of German policy was not directly with Spain: it was to keep Italy estranged from England and France, a purpose admirably served by the Italian intervention in Spain. Hence the Germans did not trouble themselves much about Franco or about the fortunes of war; they were ready to do anything which could keep Italy securely committed to intervention without unduly risking themselves. It was hopeless for the British to ask the Germans to exercise a moderating influence on Mussolini; this was the last thing that the Germans intended to do. But then the British Government hit on the strangest devices. In May 1938 according to Jordana, the Spanish Foreign Minister, they urged the Spanish rebel Government 'to use its influence with Mussolini to get him to take a stiffer attitude towards France' then the French frontier would be more rigidly closed and the civil war the sooner over.

German policy only came alive as the civil war drew to a close; after all, they wanted to have something to show for the activities of the Condor Legion. Throughout the war German adventurers—combining profit and Nazi principles—had been on the hunt for mining concessions; and Franco had held out grandiose prospects to them. But the concessions proved elusive

n November 1937, the Germans theatened 'to re-examine their
ttitude towards the Spanish Nationalist Government on various
uestions'. But, as they confessed to themselves, they could not
epudiate their political line for the sake of mining concessions;
nd Franco knew it. When told that he ought not to be surprised
t the German claims, he smiled and said in a conciliatory tone:
Well, when you're surprised, you're just surprised.' Efforts to
each a political agreement were equally fruitless; and Franco
ostentatiously announced his neutrality during the Munich
risis—according to one report, he even promised the French
o intern the Condor Legion if war broke out.

After the Munich crisis agreement was easier. It was now
obvious that France would never be provoked into action;
he Germans, on their side, realized that a Spain independent
f France, even if not hostile to her, was much to their advan-
age. Besides, Franco needed German capital equipment for
nternal reconstruction; and he paid the price in favoured
reatment for the German mining interests. It also suited
'ranco's book to be taken seriously as a Fascist leader. In
anuary 1939, he signed an agreement for cultural co-opera-
ion with Germany; this had no serious import and was never
atified, owing to the objections of the Vatican. In March, after
characteristic delay, he adhered to the Anti-Comintern Pact
nd renewed, in more formal shape, the friendship agreement
f March 1937. All along, Franco was quite as concerned to
ssert his equality and independence as to do anything to
lease the Germans. The volume ends with the vain endeavours
f Göring to meet Franco during his cruise in Spanish waters,
ust after the end of the civil war; Franco had no intention
f showing gratitude or subservience.

In short, there was no Fascist solidarity nor even any deliber-
te German plan. The Spanish affair came to the Germans by
ccident. Franco's victory gave the anti-democratic cause a
ertain prestige everywhere; it did not bring the Germans any
olid advantage—and the Italians seem to have done no better.
German intervention was not a success even as a venture in
economic imperialism'. As soon as Franco had won he cut
lown the German concessions and began to seek capital aid
rom the City of London. Those who argue that Franco tricked
Hitler are quite right; but this would not make him a reliable
nember of Western union. If he could trick Hitler, he could
ertainly trick us.

G

XXII

FULL SPEED TO MUNICH

THE unique feature of the Munich crisis is that everyone
expected it. Unlike most crises, it was announced months in
advance: it would begin on 12 September with the meeting of
the Nazi party in Nuremberg. The British government had
been caught out by the crisis over Austria in March; they were
determined not to be caught out again. They wanted to get
ahead of Hitler and of events. In March they had acquiesced
in a German act of violence: this had shaken the peace of
Europe. But if they could induce the Czechs to give way voluntarily and could prevent the French from supporting the Czechs
then there would be no humiliation. Hitler would get his way
as an act of justice and appeasement, not by conquest; and the
peace of Europe would be strengthened. Better to be seduced
than raped; better still to appear as the seducer. British public
opinion might suppose that the problem was how to resist
Hitler; official policy was concerned to offer him concessions
before he made demands. Germany was a secondary problem
so far as policy went. The overriding problem was to get the
Czechs launched on the path of surrender and then to keep a
tight rein on the French.

The object of the Runciman mission was to prove that the
Czechs were eager to yield. 'It will be less difficult for the
Czechoslovak Government to collaborate if it can be represented
that initiative in proposal had been theirs—and that his
Majesty's Government had acceded to it.'[1] Runciman doubt-
less acted in good faith, and genuinely believed that the
Sudeten Germans desired only a remedy for grievance. Mr
Ashton-Gwatkin, his assistant, wrote of Henlein, the Sudeten
leader (now known to have been acting throughout under
Hitler's orders), 'he is courteous, friendly and (I believe)
honest'. Again, 'he is simple and honest. . . . He is anxious to
dissociate his movement from identification with the Reich

[1] *Documents on British Foreign Policy*, 1919–1939, 3rd series, vol. ii, 1938
edited by E. L. Woodward.

184

Nazis and he repudiates absolutely the spirit of persecution.'
British pressure worked. On 5 September the Czechs accepted
the full Sudeten programme; instead of averting the crisis,
this precipitated it. Lord Runciman had, however, a more
pressing care than to reconcile Czechs and Germans; he had to
avoid committing Great Britain, however reasonable the
Czechs and however violent Hitler might be. He rejected the
suggestion made by Lord Halifax that he should appeal
directly to Hitler: 'Price of failure in Berlin would be to make
solution here impossible and in the event of hostilities morally
to commit Great Britain on the side of Czechoslovakia.'

All the same, Berlin was more important than Prague; and
for the Foreign Office, Berlin meant Nevile Henderson. Lord
Halifax wrote to Henderson on 5 August, 'Write as often as
you can or like. It is very helpful.' Two of Henderson's judgements were decisive—Hitler did not want war, and the German
claims were morally justified. He wrote on 26 July:

> War would doubtless serve the purposes of all the Jews, Com-
> munists, and doctrinaires in the world for whom Nazism is anathema,
> but it would be a terrible risk to-day for Germany herself. . . . That
> this is not apparent to Hitler, I cannot believe.
>
> The Czechs are a pig-headed race and Benes not the least pig-
> headed among them. . . . We shall have at long last to put our foot
> down very firmly and say to Benes, 'You must'.

On 12 August:

> I doubt if Germany would actually go to war this year with Czecho-
> slovakia if she was certain it meant British intervention. It might be
> a near thing but I think that Hitler's good sense would prevail. . . .
> I trust that we shall not use the definite menace of British participation
> in a war, unless our case is morally copper-bottomed. The British
> Empire cannot set its face against the principle of self-determination.
> Personally, I am sorry to say, I am convinced that we cannot per-
> manently prevent these Sudeten Germans from coming into the Reich
> if they wish it, and undoubtedly the majority to-day do so.

On 6 September:

> I do wish it might be possible to get at any rate 'The Times,'
> Camrose, Beaverbrook Press, &c. to write up Hitler as the apostle of
> Peace. It will be terribly short-sighted if this is not done.

Lord Halifax was necessarily influenced by Henderson and
accepted his arguments to a certain extent. He acted on the

theory that Hitler was a moderate man surrounded by extre-
mists such as Ribbentrop; hence the letter of 11 August, in
which Chamberlain and Halifax appealed directly to Hitler
'not to do anything which might sterilize Lord Runciman's
mission and prematurely and unnecessarily create a fresh
crisis in Europe'. But even if Hitler was an extremist there
was little to be done. 'I have always felt that to fight a war for
one, two, or three years to protect or recreate something that
you knew you could not directly protect, and probably could
never recreate, did not make sense.' In conversation with the
French Ambassador:

> The French Government felt that if this contemplated aggression
> were allowed to pass unresisted, their turn would come next. I said
> that this really was an argument in favour of a certain war now, against
> the possibility of war, perhaps in more favourable conditions, later.
> With that argument I had never been able to feel any sympathy.

For lack of anything better, Halifax followed traditional
British practice. He would not promise support to the Czechs;
he would not promise neutrality to the Germans. No attempt
was made to draw in the two Great Powers who were outside
Europe. On 17 August Mr. Maisky expressed disappointment
at the undue weakness of the Western democracies. He was
fobbed off with a reference to the definition of policy made in
Parliament on 24 March, and 'regretted that we had not
found it possible to be more precise'.

No explanations were given to the United States until 2 September; and these were provoked by a direct inquiry from Mr.
Kennedy. He asked should the President make another speech.
'The Prime Minister thought not, at any rate at present.'
Nothing was made of Mr. Kennedy's opinion 'that if France
went in and we had to go in too, the United States would
follow before long'.

But would France go in? On 31 August Bonnet said, 'France
would honour her engagements, but if what his Majesty's
Government considered a fair solution was refused by Czechs
that was their look out, *tant pis pour eux*'. Daladier was more
resolute. On 8 September 'Daladier declares most positively
that, if German troops cross the Czechoslovak frontier the
French will march to a man'.

When the crisis arrived on 13 September Bonnet 'said that
peace must be preserved at any price' and 'seemed genuinely

pleased at the negative nature' of Lord Halifax's reply to his query concerning British support. Daladier wavered longer; 'he said, but with evident lack of enthusiasm, that if Germans used force, French would be obliged also'.

Then, at 10 p.m., Daladier appealed to Chamberlain: 'Entry of German troops into Czechoslovakia must at all costs be prevented. If not, France will be faced with her obligation.' Daladier proposed 'a meeting of the Three Powers—namely, Germany for Sudetens, France for the Czechs, and Great Britain for Lord Runciman'.

Chamberlain, however, decided to carry out a plan which he had had in mind 'as early as 30 August'—he would visit Hitler alone. When told of Chamberlain's plan 'Daladier did not look very pleased'; Bonnet 'expressed the warm thanks of himself and of his Government for the magnificent gesture of the Prime Minister'.

There is not much to add to the story of Chamberlain's first visit to Hitler on 15 September. After a good deal of ranting from Hitler, Chamberlain said, 'On principle I had nothing to say against the separation of the Sudeten Germans from the rest of Czechoslovakia, provided that the practical difficulties could be overcome'; and he agreed to return home to persuade his colleagues.

Nevile Henderson at once underlined the implications of this policy. He telegraphed on 16 September, 'French Government should definitely notify Czechoslovak Government that the latter cannot count on French support if they decide to go to war rather than accept such a solution'. On the morning of 17 September, 'if we do accept the principle of secession we must be prepared to coerce the Czechoslovak Government or leave her to her fate'. And the same evening, 'If we decline to admit self-determination we must face world war: if we recognize it, we must coerce Czechoslovakia or sit by and watch her coerced by Germany'. The British Ministers (to say nothing of the French) were less honest: they still hoped to persuade the Czechs to commit suicide for their own good.

On 18 September Daladier and Bonnet came to London to meet the British Ministers. Chamberlain gave an account of his interview with Hitler and insisted that the question was whether to accept the partition of Czechoslovakia (or, as he called it, 'the principle of self-determination'). Daladier tried to shift the ground. 'He feared that Germany's real aim was the dis-

integration of Czechoslovakia and the realization of Pan-
German ideals through a march to the east.' He argued that
plebiscites could be used to disrupt every State in Eastern
Europe.

Lord Halifax now took a hand.

> Nothing was further from their thoughts than that the French
> Government should fail to honour their obligations to the Czecho-
> slovak Government. . . . On the other hand we all knew—and he
> certainly thought their technical advisers would agree with them in
> this—that whatever action were taken by ourselves, by the French
> Government, or by the Soviet Government, at any given moment, it
> would be impossible to give effective protection to the Czechoslovak
> State. We might fight a war against German aggression, but at the
> peace conference which followed such a war he did not think that the
> statesmen concerned would redraft the present boundaries of Czecho-
> slovakia.

Chamberlain seized on the Czech objection to a plebiscite:

> The idea of territorial cession would be likely to have a much more
> favourable reception from the British public if it could be represented
> as the choice of the Czechoslovak Government themselves and it
> could be made clear that they had been offered the choice of a plebis-
> cite or of territorial cession and had preferred the latter. That would
> dispose of any idea that we were ourselves carving up Czechoslovak
> territory.

Daladier had to give way, but he posed an essential condition—Great Britain must guarantee the Czechoslovakia that
remained. This was not for the sake of the Czechs—the British
and French Governments had already decided that they could
do nothing to help the Czechs either now or hereafter. The
British were being asked to underwrite Hitler's statement that
this was his last territorial demand in Europe. Daladier said:

> If he were certain that Herr Hitler were speaking the truth when
> he repeated the usual Nazi propaganda to the effect that nothing more
> was wanted than the Sudeten Germans and that German aims stopped
> there, then he would not insist upon a British guarantee. But he was
> convinced in his heart that Germany was aiming at something far
> greater. . . . A British guarantee for Czechoslovakia would therefore
> help France in the sense that it would help to stop the German march
> to the East.

The British Ministers withdrew for two hours, and on their
return Chamberlain said, 'If the Czechoslovak Government

accepted the proposals now being put to them and provided no military coup had taken place meanwhile, his Majesty's Government were prepared to join in the suggested guarantee'. The guarantee, that is, was to operate only after Czechoslovakia had been partitioned. All the same, Daladier had built better than he knew. He had committed Great Britain to oppose Hitler's march to the East; six months later the British public insisted on taking the promise seriously in spite of the wrigglings of Chamberlain and his associates. In fact, Daladier gave Great Britain the decisive, though delayed, push on the path of resistance to Germany.

Chamberlain had asked, What would be the position if Dr. Benes said 'No'? Daladier answered, 'If that situation arose, the question would have to be discussed at the Council of Ministers'. Events turned out differently. At 7.45 p.m. on 20 September the Czechs refused the Anglo-French terms and invoked their arbitration treaty with Germany. An hour later Newton, British Minister in Prague, telegraphed:

> I have very good reason from an even better source [than the Minister of Foreign Affairs] to believe that . . . if I can deliver a kind of ultimatum to President Benes, he and his Government will feel able to bow to force majeure.

Since this even better source can only be Hodza, the Prime Minister, Newton's telegram confirms Bonnet's story that the Anglo-French ultimatum was delivered at Czech request. But telegrams received in the Foreign Office from Paris at 6.20 p.m., 7.45 p.m. and 8.30 p.m. on 20 September show Bonnet was urging the threat of 'washing their hands of Czechoslovakia' long before the message was sent from Prague. Thus even if Hodza asked France to repudiate Czechoslovakia, Bonnet had already decided to do so. At 2 a.m. on 21 September Newton and the French Minister broke the resistance of Benes: 'We told him our démarche had character of an ultimatum.'

On 22 September Chamberlain met Hitler at Godesberg to announce that he had succeeded. Chamberlain concluded, 'The guarantee would not necessarily mean that the present Czech frontiers would be guaranteed in perpetuity. ['Present' means, of course, the new frontiers.] They could be altered by negotiation, as was being done in the present case.' Hitler rejected Chamberlain's offer, even with its invitation to further

plunder. Chamberlain wanted an 'agreed settlement' for the
sake of British public opinion and, perhaps, of his self-esteem
Hitler wanted a settlement by conquest to strengthen his posi
tion in Germany and perhaps for his self-esteem also. Chamber
lain cared nothing for the Czechs; Hitler cared nothing for the
Sudeten Germans.

After two days of argument, deadlock was reached. Meanwhile, in London, Lord Halifax had revolted. On 22 September the French urged that the advice given to the Czechs not to
mobilize should be withdrawn; Halifax agreed. Sir Horace
Wilson, however, telephoned from Godesberg against this
message and it was held up during the evening. On 23 September Halifax, prompted by Daladier, again insisted; and
Chamberlain gave way. 'In doing so, however, Prime Minister
thinks it should be pointed out that such action may very well
precipitate action by others.'

On the news of the failure at Godesberg only Nevile Henderson was undismayed, 'Only hope of preventing or at least
localizing war is for his Majesty's Government to make it
absolutely clear at Prague that they must accept German plan
or forfeit claim to further support from Western Powers.'
Henderson at least had the courage of his convictions. On 23
September Lord Halifax sent a message to Chamberlain at
Godesberg which concluded: 'It seems to your colleagues of
vital importance that you should not leave without making it
plain to Chancellor . . . that, after great concessions made
by Czechoslovak Government, for him to reject opportunity of
peaceful solution in favour of one that must involve war would
be an unpardonable crime against humanity.'

Halifax also sent a message to Geneva (where the League of
Nations was in session) asking Litvinov 'what action Soviet
Government would take in event of Czechoslovakia being thus
involved in war with Germany, and at what point they would
be prepared to take it'. On 24 September Litvinov answered,
'If French came to the assistance of the Czechs, Russia would
take action'. He added:

> He had for long been hoping for conversations between Great
> Britain, France, and Russia, and he would like to suggest . . . that a
> meeting of the three Powers mentioned, together with Rumania and
> any other small Power who could be regarded as reliable, should take
> place away from the atmosphere of Geneva, and preferably in Paris,
> and so show Germans that we mean business.

It was even more urgent to know French intentions. On 24 September Phipps wired from Paris, 'All that is best in France is against war, almost at any price', and he warned against even appearing to encourage small, but noisy and corrupt, war group here'. (In a later telegram he explained that by this he meant 'the Communists who are paid by Moscow'.) Phipps also reported the opposition to war voiced by Caillaux and Flandin. On 25 September he was instructed to make wider inquiries and replied the following day, 'People are resigned but resolute. . . . The "petit bourgeois" may feel disinclined to risk his life for Czechoslovakia, while most of the workmen are said to be in favour of France complying with her obligations.'

Meanwhile Daladier and Bonnet had come to London on 25 September for another meeting with British Ministers. Daladier was in fighting spirit. Hitler should be asked to return to the Anglo-French proposals of 18 September. If he refused 'each of us would have to do his duty'; and, again, 'each of us would do what was incumbent upon him'. Chamberlain answered, 'One could not go into so great a conflict with one's eyes and ears closed. It was essential to know the conditions before taking any decision. He would, therefore, like further information and would ask Sir John Simon to put certain points to M. Daladier.'

There followed an incredible scene in which the Chancellor of the Exchequer cross-examined the Prime Minister of France as though he were a hostile witness or a criminal. Daladier did his best to prove that war was possible and returned to the question of policy: 'There was one concession he would never make, and that was . . . the destruction of a country and Herr Hitler's domination of the world.'

It was finally decided to ask Gamelin to come over and to meet again the following day.

However, on 26 September, instead of producing Gamelin and plans for war, Chamberlain announced that he had sent Horace Wilson to Hitler with a personal message from himself. The French Ministers acquiesced and went home. Lord Halifax 'authorized the issue of a communiqué' to the press: 'If a German attack is made upon Czechoslovakia . . . France will be bound to come to her assistance, and Great Britain and Russia will certainly stand by France.'

Wilson saw Hitler on 26 September without effect. Cham-

G*

berlain then instructed him, 'We do not think it possible for
you to leave without delivering special message, in view of
what we said to French. . . . But message should be given more
in sorrow than in anger.' This special message was delivered
by Wilson shortly after noon on 27 September:

> If Germany attacked Czechoslovakia France would feel that she
> must fulfil her treaty obligations. . . . If that meant that the forces of
> France became actively engaged in hostilities against Germany the
> British Government would feel obliged to support her.

In spite of these firm words both Henderson and Wilson
continued to urge that the Czechs be forced to give way.
Henderson's final message on 28 September condemned resisting Hitler: 'This course involves far greater losses with
regard to prestige to ourselves and results in complete destruction of Czechoslovakia, which will become, like Abyssinia,
a further victim to pacifist enthusiam. The only alternative is to
compel Czechoslovakia to yield by informing her at once . . .
categorically that if she does not do so we shall not support her.'
Henderson also telegraphed, 'Is it not essential to ensure that
France should take no action without first consulting his
Majesty's Government that is not calculated to have effective
military result?' A telegram on these lines was sent to Paris
forty minutes after receipt of Henderson's prompting.

There followed Mussolini's initiative and the meeting at
Munich on 29 September. Before leaving, Chamberlain telegraphed to Prague, 'Please assure Dr. Benes that I shall have
the interests of Czechoslovakia fully in mind'. Bonnet, when
seeing Daladier off, 'begged me to urge you [Halifax] how
absolutely vital he felt it was that an arrangement should be
reached over Sudeten question at Munich at almost any price.
M. Bonnet feels that after that, and in the near future, we must
make up our minds to a peaceful modification of many existing frontiers in Europe, as the Treaty of Versailles has collapsed.'

Bonnet grew feebler when Daladier was away; Halifax
tougher in the absence of Chamberlain. On 29 September (too
late to influence the conference) he telegraphed to Chamberlain: 'Information has reached me from moderate sources in
Germany that the firm attitude taken by his Majesty's Government during the last few days . . . has had considerable effect
on German public opinion.' Halifax also saw Maisky and

explained to him that the exclusion of Russia at Munich 'in no way signified any weakening of a desire on our part, any more no doubt, than on that of the French Government, to preserve our understandings and relations with the Soviet Government'. Halifax also implied that Russia was to become a guarantor of the new Czechoslovakia. Maisky's 'general attitude seemed to me, as, indeed, it was likely to be, one of some suspicion'.

Chamberlain's mind was on different things. After partitioning Czechoslovakia he had a private discussion with Hitler on 30 September. This culminated in the signature of the Anglo-German declaration of friendship to cries of 'Ja! Ja!' from Hitler. The opening of the discussion was still more remarkable. Chamberlain said:

> he was obliged to consider the possibility that the Czech Government might be mad enough to refuse the terms and attempt resistance. In such an eventuality he wanted to ask Herr Hitler to make sure that nothing should be done which would diminish the high opinion of him which would be held throughout the world in consequence of yesterday's proceedings. In particular, he trusted that there would be no bombardment of Prague or killing of women and children by attacks from the air.

Hitler replied, 'he hated the thought of little babies being killed by gas bombs'.

XXIII

FROM MUNICH TO PRAGUE

(1) *British Version*

IN the months after Munich, British policy proceeded in a daze—confusedly aware that 'the Munich spirit' had evaporated, but at a loss for something to take its place. The third volume of Foreign Office documents[1] rambles over a variety of subjects—the execution of the Munich agreement, the revived German hostility, relations with Italy, and the beginnings of the Danzig question.

The working-out of the Munich agreement is a squalid story. The International Commission at Berlin was supposed to see fair play between Germany and Czechoslovakia. But as one British diplomatist wrote: 'Once the principle of negotiation under the threat of violence has been accepted it is difficult to find a position at which a stand is possible.' Even Sir Nevile Henderson complained. 'I never want to work with the Germans again.' Still, he stuck to his logical point—the Czechs must come within the political and economic orbit of Germany, 'there will never be any peace for Czechs or Europe till they accept that harsh fact'. Hence he supported the German case on every disputed detail.

Worse, and far more discreditable, is the affair of the guarantee to Czechoslovakia, which the British Government had promised at the height of the crisis in order to persuade the French to yield. To guarantee a helpless State when it had been impossible to defend a fully armed one was an obvious absurdity; and the British Government now tried to escape the consequences of its rash act. At the meeting with Daladier and Bonnet on 24 November Chamberlain tried to make out that the British had only intended to promise a collective guarantee of the four Munich Powers; and he was seconded by Lord

---

[1] *Documents on British Foreign Policy*, 1919–1939, edited by E. L. Woodward and Rohan Butler, assisted by Margaret Lambert, 3rd series, vol. iii, 1938–1939.

Halifax 'from a practical point of view'. 'This did not seem to
be out of conformity with the letter of the Anglo-French
declaration.' The French Ministers had been swindled and
they knew it.

The solution was more discreditable still: it was to ask the
Czechs themselves to get the British out of the difficulty. If
Czechoslovakia professed herself satisfied with a collective
guarantee the British conscience would be satisfied too. When
the Czechs failed to respond, Lord Halifax lost patience:

> His Majesty's Government cannot undertake a guarantee which
> would oblige them to go to the assistance of Czechoslovakia in cir-
> cumstances in which effective help could not be rendered.

The search for new allies was pursued with less zest than the
desertion of an old one. Russia, promised a share in the Czech
guarantee by Lord Halifax in September, was cold-shouldered
thereafter; and Chamberlain inquired anxiously whether the
Franco-Soviet pact would operate 'if Russia were to ask France
for assistance on the grounds that a separatist movement
in Ukraine was provoked by Germany'. Lord Halifax, on the
other hand, recognized the danger of renouncing Eastern
Europe altogether: 'It is one thing to allow German expansion
in Central Europe, which to my mind is a normal and natural
thing, but we must be able to resist German expansion in
Western Europe or else our whole position is undermined.'
Therefore a balance against Germany was still needed: 'Subject only to the consideration that I should hope France would
protect herself—and us—from being entangled by Russia in
war with Germany I should hesitate to advise the French
Government to denounce the Franco-Soviet pact as the future
is still far too uncertain.' In plain English: Russia should fight
for our interests, but we should not fight for hers.

The same difficulty appeared in regard to Poland. The
British Government was rightly shocked at the Polish behaviour during the Munich crisis; it had been as bad as their own.
But malicious pleasure at the mounting difficulties in Danzig
was not a policy; and by the end of the year the British were
well on the way to being entangled in the Danzig affair. One of
the permanent officials, Sir Orme Sargent, explained the dilemma after Ribbentrop's visit to Paris. If Germany were free to
pursue her aims in Eastern Europe without French interference, she might become so strong that the security of France

would be 'under imminent menace'. If, on the other hand, the French Government decided not to leave Germany with freedom of action in Eastern Europe, Great Britain might be drawn into war in order to support France.

The solution seemed to be Italy. In Lord Halifax's words: 'Although we do not expect to detach Italy from the Axis, we believe the [Anglo-Italian] Agreement will increase Mussolini's power of manœuvre and so make him less dependent on Hitler and therefore freer to resume the classic Italian role of balancing between Germany and the Western Powers.' In other words, by paying Mussolini blackmail we will encourage him to demand more. Hence the Anglo-Italian Agreement was 'brought into force', although the Italians had not fulfilled the condition of withdrawing from Spain; hence Chamberlain and Lord Halifax travelled to Rome in January 1939. Mussolini probably expected them to try to buy him with concessions at the expense of France; instead, he got a high-minded plea from Chamberlain for some assurances that Hitler was not going to war. Not surprisingly, Mussolini 'thrust out his chin' and retaliated with an attack on the British press. The visit to Rome, which should have been the triumph of Chamberlain's policy, was really the end of the Italian illusion; the price for this mistaken bet was paid by the Spanish Republic.

The British were left with France—acutely aware of French weakness yet inescapably tied to her. The only way out would have been for France to rearm on such a scale that she would need neither Great Britain nor her eastern allies—an impossibility. When Chamberlain tried to urge on French rearmament Daladier was provoked into replying with the grotesque claim that France would be producing four hundred planes a month by the spring of 1939; his more effective reply was that the British should speed up their own rearmament and not concentrate so much on the anti-aircraft defence of London. The Foreign Office and Lord Halifax, perhaps even Chamberlain, knew that the policy of Munich had failed; their hopelessness and helplessness was preparing the equally exaggerated swing the other way, which produced the wild guarantees of March 1939. As often happens, appeasement was the prelude to bellicosity.

At the beginning of 1939 British foreign policy was still pursuing its traditional course, avoiding precise commitments and seeking to balance between the Great Powers of the Continent. Three months later Britain was distributing guarantees to the States of Eastern Europe and preaching collective security against the aggressor. It was the greatest revolution in the history of our foreign policy; and the volume of Foreign Office documents, which exactly covers this decisive period, surpasses any of its predecessors in interest and importance.[1] It opens with the return of Halifax and Chamberlain from their visit to Rome—the last kick of appeasement; it closes with the announcement of the British guarantee to Poland. This great change was not the result of foresight or calculation; it sprang in an improvised way from bewilderment and anxiety. In fact, the right policy was adopted for the wrong reasons and applied by wrong methods.

In January 1939, the British Government were puzzling their heads as to Hitler's next move. They feared a German invasion of Holland and resolved to treat it as a 'casus belli'. But while they passed this on as an encouragement to their friends (France, Belgium, and the United States) they did not deliver it as a warning to their potential enemy. They were still hoping, in fact, that he would not be their enemy. Lord Halifax said to the French Ambassador on 10 February:

> The strategical importance of the Netherlands is so great that a German attack on them must be regarded as a direct threat to the security of the Western Powers . . . a German attack on Switzerland would also be clear evidence of an attempt to dominate Europe by force.

Thus Hitler would be seeking to dominate Europe only if he threatened British interests; expansion in Eastern Europe was harmless so long as it was done by respectable methods. From Berlin Nevile Henderson renewed his belief in Hitler's good intentions. Thus on 18 February:

> My definite impression is that Herr Hitler does not contemplate any adventures at the moment.

On 22 February:

> I would feel confident if it were not for the British press, or at any rate that section of it which is inspired by an intelligentsia, which hates Hitler and the Nazis so much that it sees red whatever the facts are, or by alarmists by profession and Jews.

[1] *Documents on British Foreign Policy*, 1919–1939, edited by E. L. Woodward and Rohan Butler, assisted by Margaret Lambert, 3rd series, vol. iv, 1939.

Finally, on 9 March, he argued at length that British policy should aim at switching German energies against Russia:

> The best approach to good relations with Germany is therefore along the lines of the avoidance of constant and vexatious interference in matters in which British interests are not directly or vitally involved and the prospect of British neutrality in the event of Germany being engaged in the East.

On 15 March when Hitler seized Prague, Henderson at first contented himself with sending a message to Weizsäcker 'that if this is his conception of "decency" it is not mine'. He wrote to Lord Halifax: 'What distresses me more than anything else is the handle which it will give to the critics of Munich. Not that I did not always realize that the complete subservience of the Czechs to Germany was inevitable.' As to the future: 'We cannot make war on Germany, but we can reduce relations to a minimum: at heart I am in favour of that.' Henderson at least stuck to his line: his last proposal meant in practice that the British should turn their backs while Hitler conquered Eastern Europe.

But Henderson's day was over. The Prague coup destroyed Chamberlain's faith in him, at any rate for the time being, and opened the way for Henderson's critics at the Foreign Office. It is difficult to say when Lord Halifax shook off the Munich line. On 15 March he spoke strongly to the German Ambassador:

> The immediate result was that nobody felt the assurances of the German Government to be worth very much. . . . I could well understand Herr Hitler's taste for bloodless victories, but one of these days he would find himself up against something that would not be bloodless.

But on the same day he said to the French Ambassador: 'The one compensating advantage that I saw was that it had brought to a natural end the somewhat embarrassing commitment of a guarantee, in which we and the French had both been involved.' This was a surprising prelude to a policy which ended by guaranteeing practically every State in Europe. No doubt public opinion was the main force in bringing about this great change; but there were also purely diplomatic factors. The British Government were now ready to swallow any story, however alarmist (including that of an immediate attack by Hitler on the British fleet). Hence, they at once believed the

Rumanian Minister when he appealed for assistance on 16 March. Though Mr. Tilea was disavowed by his own Government the British—and Chamberlain in particular—were convinced that a peace front must be created overnight. On 20 March Chamberlain himself drafted a declaration of collective security, which the French, Soviet, and Polish Governments were invited to sign. The French agreed at once; the Soviet Government would sign as soon as France and Poland accepted it; the Poles, however, held out—they would sign a declaration with Great Britain but not with the Soviet Union. By simple impudence, Colonel Beck and the Polish Government played themselves into the position of dictating policy to the British Government.

Men think in terms of immediate questions and of their own interests, even when they imagine that they are conducting a policy of abstract principle. The crisis had started because of Rumania; and the British continued to judge the situation from the Rumanian angle even when this proved a false alarm. Therefore aid from Poland seemed more urgent than from anyone else. Moreover, the British were conscious of their own military weakness; they needed a second front in Europe and, as a glance at the map showed, only Poland could provide it. Anxious for Rumania and ultimately for the Middle East, it never occurred to them to ask whether Poland could remain neutral in the coming war. Beck had kept them almost completely in the dark concerning German demands on Danzig; and in any case they imagined that Danzig could be somehow jettisoned without endangering Poland. The key to British policy in the decisive days between 22 March and 30 March, when Chamberlain himself drafted the guarantee to Poland, is to be found here: the British regarded Poland as the essential country and believed that her co-operation must be bought, however high the price.

Relations with the Soviet Union had to be subordinated to Polish needs and wishes. As Bonnet said, to the entire agreement of Lord Halifax, on 21 March:

> It was absolutely essential to get Poland in. Russian help would only be effective if Poland were collaborating. If Poland collaborated, Russia could give very great assistance; if not, Russia could give much less.

No doubt the British Government were influenced by reports

that Hungary, Spain, and Italy would be offended by a British
alliance with the Soviet Union (and Chamberlain was still
whining to Mussolini for sympathy on 20 March); but Poland
was undoubtedly the decisive factor. Lord Halifax remarked
to Chamberlain and Bonnet on 22 March: 'It would be unfortunate if we were now so to act as to give the Soviet Government the idea that we were pushing her to one side.' The
Ambassador in Moscow had given repeated warning that
Soviet policy was now isolationist, recognizing no distinction
between the two sides in 'the second Imperialist war'. This
did not shake Chamberlain and Halifax: they assumed that
Moscow would respond to any casual British gesture. And if it
did not, they were not perturbed: Soviet neutrality would be
almost as useful as their participation in war—in some ways
better, since it would not alarm Poland and Rumania. This is
clearly implied in a dispatch written by Lord Halifax on 27
March. The Nazi-Soviet pact was the logical outcome of the
new British policy as Munich had been the logical outcome of
the old one.

(II) *German Version*

The six months between the Munich conference and the
German occupation of Prague were the brief heyday of appeasement, when Hitler and his associates believed that they had
won the mastery of Europe without a struggle. What led Hitler
to abandon this position of vantage and to take the steps which
forced England and France into war? Though the German
Foreign Ministry was almost as much in the dark as to Hitler's
motives as we are, the new set of documents from its archives
does something to resolve the problem.[1] The answer seems to
be twofold. On the one hand the disintegration of Central
Europe was so great that Hitler could not resist the temptation
to go farther. On the other British and French policy seemed to
imply that he could advance eastwards without serious protest
from the Western Powers.

The story of Hitler's final aggression against truncated
Czechoslovakia was revealed in the Nuremberg documents and
told in a masterly essay by Sir Lewis Namier on 'The Ides of
March'. There is little to be added. At the time of the original

[1] *Documents on German Foreign Policy*, 1918–1945, series D (1937–45), vol.
iv, The Aftermath of Munich. October 1938–March 1939.

Czech crisis Hitler did not think beyond annexing the German areas. He seems to have asumed that Czechoslovakia would continue to exist, though after some loss of territory to Hungary. He became impatient when the Czechs hesitated to abandon every scrap of democracy and increasingly impatient when they continued to show interest in an international guarantee. But his final move seems to have been directed not so much against the Czechs as against Hungary. In September 1938, he had encouraged the Hungarians to arm and to invade Czechoslovakia. He was angry that they had tried to keep in with both sides and told them that they had 'missed the bus'. Moreover, the German General Staff warned against allowing a common frontier between Poland and Hungary: this would bar the way against future German expansion.

When the Slovak autonomists grew turbulent Hitler was threatened with two outcomes, either of which was unwelcome to him. Either the Slovaks would be subdued from Prague and the Czechs would recover some prestige, or Slovakia would be incorporated in Hungary, which would then become more independent than ever. The only solution for Hitler was to back an independent Slovakia. The occupation of Prague was little more than a by-product; the decisive event was the defeat of Hungarian ambitions. It would be an exaggeration to say that Hitler lost the mastery of the world for the sake of Hungary and Slovakia; but it is a fair judgement that he, like many European politicians, attached an inflated importance to these 'Balkan' trivialities. The Allied statesmen made the same mistake during the war—and perhaps do so now.

In September 1938, the British Government had been the pacemaker in appeasement and the French an unwilling second. Afterwards the position was reversed. The Germans early learnt that appeasement had been purely Chamberlain's policy and that the Foreign Office 'had striven to sabotage his plans and commit Great Britain to warlike action against Germany'. Certainly they were told by the Prime Minister's press officer that his attitude:

> had never been dictated by a consciousness of military weakness but exclusively by the religious idea that Germany must have justice, and that the injustice of Versailles must be made good;

and Sir Samuel Hoare talked of a guarantee by the four European Great Powers against Soviet Russia. But the British

Government pressed for some concrete gesture of friendship
—a further agreement on naval armaments or co-operation in
the Far East.

Hitler, however, aimed to 'split' British opinion—no doubt
an idea of Ribbentrop's; and he calculated that if the Chamberlain Government was driven to rearmament this would stir
up increasing opposition among the pro-Germans. Moreover
the directors of British economic policy, led by Sir Frederick
Leith-Ross, were constantly urging measures of economic
co-operation; and this also helped to convince the Germans that
the British were coming to them as suppliants. In fact the only
serious Anglo-German negotiations during this period were
on the coal cartel, sharing out the European export market; and
this was supposed to provide a pattern for other agreements.
The British protagonists of this policy no doubt hoped that
prosperity would make Hitler more moderate in political
methods; but the only effect was to convince him of British
weakness. Finally, the British approach to Italy in January 1939
made him suspicious that an attempt was being made to revive
'the Stresa front'. It was little consolation to know that Lord
Halifax had had discussions with 'the notorious Low' to prevent excesses in the press.

With France the situation was reversed. On Hitler's orders
the Germans ignored Bonnet's efforts at appeasement, which
culminated in the Franco-German declaration of 6 December.
These documents do not settle the controversy whether Bonnet
washed his hands of Eastern Europe during his conversations
with Ribbentrop. Clearly Bonnet did not intend to protect
Czechoslovakia; but neither of the two men mentioned Poland
—the subject did not at that time occur to them. Bonnet was
not the only advocate of appeasement. On 22 October M.
Reynaud defended himself to Abetz, Ribbentrop's representative, 'against the charge of being an enemy of Franco-German
understanding'.

> He hinted that France needed the spectre of the German danger
> in order to remain strong internally, because otherwise the willingness
> of the people to defend themselves and make sacrifices would disappear
> completely. He held the view that an agreement could not be made
> with *mous* (by which he obviously meant Flandin), but that it could
> be made with *durs* (with a plain hint at himself).

In the New Year, when the British were seeking to appease

Italy, the French took the opposite course. They talked of a war for Tunis and asked the Germans to 'excercise a conciliatory influence on Italy'. Though the Germans did not respond to this invitation, they counted on the disunity of the Western Powers and even took it out of the Italians by not revealing to them their military plans against France nor even for the occupation of Prague.

The Germans thought only of the three European Powers, still supposedly 'the Great'. They assumed that Russia was safely excluded from Europe and limited their dealings with her to trading agreements. In fact the Nazi-Soviet pact was already implicitly in operation. The United States they ignored still more confidently and rather welcomed estrangement as increasing the gulf between them.

Though the Munich conference founded Hitler's empire, it also caused his ruin. He supposed that the Munich Powers were all that mattered: if he could dictate to them, he could dictate to everybody. As well, he attributed to British policy a greater logic than it possessed: surely the British knew that when they surrendered the Sudeten areas they surrendered all east-central Europe. The occupation of Prague was a triviality in comparison. Hitler took the decisive step in his career without realizing that it was decisive or indeed noticing that he had made it.

XXIV

STALIN AND THE WEST

M. COULONDRE was the last French Ambassador to Hitler and delivered the French declaration of war. Had his account of Berlin between October 1938 and September 1939[1] appeared ten years ago it would have been useful. As it is contemporary history is now written at such a rate that M Coulondre quotes Sir Lewis Namier as an authority for his conduct instead of Sir Lewis Namier citing M. Coulondre Soon historians will dictate how events should happen.

M. Coulondre is of the school of M. Daladier, inspired by a despairing resolution. He never believed, he claims, that Germany could be appeased. But, appointed to Berlin soon after Munich, it was his duty to try; and his achievement was the Franco-German declaration of 6 December 1938. Here, unlike some other French writers, he gives an opinion favourable to Bonnet: the declaration did not imply, as Ribbentrop later made out, a French renunciation of her interests in Eastern Europe, and there is no ground for alleging that Bonnet surrendered these interests in private. This brief period of appeasement ended with the German occupation of Prague; after this there was nothing for a French Ambassador to do at Berlin except to await events. Since only a Triple Alliance could have checked Hitler, the decision had passed to Moscow.

On Moscow M. Coulondre has much more of interest indeed, he makes Soviet policy more coherent than in any previous account. M. Coulondre went to Moscow in 1936 with the intention of making the Franco-Soviet pact a reality. The obstacles came from the French side. President Lebrun, as M. Coulondre later discovered, regarded the pact as 'a swindle with no other purpose than to inoculate France with Bolshevik venom'. When M. Coulondre suggested that, in view of French deficiencies in the air, they should accept Russian aeroplanes, he received from the French Air Ministry the reply: 'Never will we agree to such a humiliation.' In May 1938, M. Coulondre went to Paris to urge the immediate opening of military

[1] Robert Coulondre, *De Staline a Hitler:* Souvenirs de Deux Ambassades 1936–9.

onversations with the Russians, in view of the approaching
Czech crisis. Both Bonnet and Daladier agreed; but, scarcely
returned to Moscow, M. Coulondre learnt that the conversations were not to proceed so as not to alarm the British Con-
ervatives. The French Government had decided that the British
and even the Polish alliances were worth more than the Franco-
Soviet pact, and it seemed impossible to its diplomacy to have
both.

M. Coulondre is emphatic: 'If the Soviets had made precise
military engagements for the defence of Czechoslovakia they
would have kept them, because it was to their interest.' The
key to Soviet policy in 1938, as in 1939, was Poland. Hence the
question which Litinov repeatedly pressed on M. Coulondre,
'What would France do as ally of Poland in case the latter,
having attacked Czechoslovakia, was herself attacked by the
U.S.S.R.?' M. Coulondre believed that France should compel
the Poles to join the 'peace front' against Hitler, with the
threat of abandoning them to the Russians if they refused. It is
true that this would have meant the end of Great Poland; but
something of the Versailles system had to be surrendered and it
is reasonable to argue that Polish domination of the Ukraine
was less essential to this system than was the integrity of
Czechoslovakia. As it was, the French Government refused to
answer the Soviet question. Since the French would neither
force Poland to be a loyal ally nor allow the Russians to attack
her, Russia was excluded from Europe; and Munich was the
inevitable consequence.

The Russians certainly drew the moral. On 30 September a
leading Soviet diplomatist said of the pact with France: 'We
nearly supported ourselves with a rotten plank. Now we are
going elsewhere.' And on 4 October Potemkin, the Assistant
Commissar, for once abandoned his reserve and said to M.
Coulondre with emotion: 'My poor friend, what have you done?
For us I see no other way out than a fourth partition of Poland.'
Writing to Paris the same day, M. Coulondre underlined the
new Russian attitude:

> The U.S.S.R. now expects nothing from France. . . . What other
> alternative has she then than to return to the policy of entente with
> Germany which she abandoned in 1931? No doubt by favouring the
> dismemberment of Poland the Soviets would expose themselves to the
> risk which they avoided in 1931 of direct contact with a country the
> energy and military power of which are superior to theirs. But to-day
> it would be the lesser evil, the only way, it seems, left to them of

diverting the Reich from the Ukraine by directing it instead into Poland in the hope that this would satisfy its greed for space.

On 16 October 1938 Litvinov himself said much the same to M. Coulondre:

> The U.S.S.R. has henceforth only to stand by, within the shelter of her frontiers, while Germany establishes her hegemony over Central and South-eastern Europe. And if by chance the Western Powers have finally the sense to want to stop her they will have to turn to us, for we shall have something to say.

Litvinov also claimed that he had said to Lord Halifax:

> Once German hegemony is established in Europe and France has been neutralised, Hitler will be able to attack either Great Britain or the U.S.S.R. He will choose the first solution because it offers him greater rewards with the chance of substituting the German Empire for the British Empire, and to carry this enterprise through successfully he will prefer to reach an understanding with the U.S.S.R.

So far the published British records do not contain an account of any such conversation between Litvinov and Lord Halifax.

All the same, M. Coulondre has probably described aright the spirit of Soviet policy, and his evidence is the more striking when it is borne in mind that Litvinov is often represented as the advocate of collective security and the Western alliance. In truth the divisions within Soviet counsels, of which so much was made then and since, had little existence, and the motive of Soviet foreign policy was self-preservation. What emerges clearly from M. Coulondre's book is that the real decisions were taken in 1938. The policy of Munich determined both that the Soviet Union would seek from Hitler a neutrality pact, based on the partition of Poland, and that Hitler would think himself strong enough to challenge Anglo-French power. What happened in 1939 was an epilogue, the working out of a tragedy on predetermined lines.

Is there a moral for the present day? In all probability the Russians are still apprehensive of German power, and they still see the same alternatives. But, since their frontier is now advanced to the Oder, it is not a partition of Poland that they have in mind. If they cannot get securities against Germany in agreement with the West they will seek to turn German power westwards, as they did in 1939. Then the West had some assets; now the Russians have already all the advantages of the Nazi-Soviet pact. A Soviet diplomatist does not even need to say to us: 'My poor friend, what have you done?'

XXV

ON THE EVE

THE FIRST WORLD WAR made a cleavage in history; and the world before 1914 seems to us now a Utopia, infinitely remote and desirable. The Second World War was a piece with what went before; and the world in 1939 can be described in terms which we can still understand. Still, it cries out for analysis; and Chatham House has done well to renew its surveys, which were interrupted by the war, with a picture of the world on the eve of Hitler's occupation of Prague.[1]

This survey differs in character from the old ones. They were written hotfoot after the events that they described. Based solely on the public record, they served partly as a work of reference, partly as acute comments by an observer with strong personal judgements. The new survey should be a work of history and research, emancipating itself from contemporary passions. As such the present volume is unsatisfactory. The imposing display of scholarship is mostly window-dressing. Though the reader is told that Anglo-French rivalry dates back to 1154, he cannot discover the terms of the Anglo-French Alliance of 1936. He would have to guess what party governed Britain, its strength in Parliament, and which newspapers supported it. We could do with less about the Attic League and more about the Anti-Comintern Pact. And the writers would do well to remember that the private jargon invented by Professor Toynbee is not yet part of the general vocabulary—nor likely to become so.

As a picture of the world the survey is out of true. The United States is dealt with in twelve pages; the Soviet Union in eighteen; Germany and Eastern Europe receive 159. This is to make Europe the centre of the world with a vengeance. There is something to be said for the view that nothing can be known about the Soviet Union, though Mr. Crankshaw does brilliantly in his limited space; and perhaps contemporary

[1] *Survey of International Affairs*, 1939–1946. *The World in March*, 1939, edited by Arnold Toynbee and Frank T. Ashton-Gwatkin.

historians should leave a blank page for the Soviet Union
marked 'Here be monsters'. But plenty is known about th
foreign policy of the United States, as Professors Langer an
Gleason have recently shown; and if the record had bee
properly studied we should have had something very differen
from the picture drawn here of Roosevelt as the starry-eye
idealist, eager to uphold collective security. In the light of ou
present knowledge there can, for instance, be no excuse fo
exaggerating Roosevelt's proposal for a conference in Januar
1938—a gesture of appeasement, not of resistance. But Pro
fessor Toynbee, who writes on America, the Commonwealth
and the Far East, treats history as a form of guesswork. H
remarks complacently at one place that his guess has actuall
been confirmed by the documents (though even this is no
correct); and he apologizes for not being able to guess sym
pathetically enough about Neville Chamberlain. Instead o
scholarship we have fine writing. Thus:

> Though the lion's head might still glower sullenly across the Nort
> Sea and the Channel at a continent once again in process of politica
> unification under the hegemony of the Third Reich, had not the lion'
> Herculean body suffered a woeful metamorphosis into the scragg
> shape of a Maltese goat, and his swinging tail into the elongate
> caudal appendage of a Chinese dragon, trailing limply round the
> indented southern coasts of Asia all the way from Suez to Hongkong

Mr. Wight, who deals with Germany and Eastern Europe, i
more sober. His background of history is solid and elaborate
but when he comes to the foreground there is Hitler and noth
ing else. According to this picture Hitler was a lunatic who
meant to turn the world upside down; and since the world wa
shaky the task was not difficult. This is to underrate Hitler'
importance. Though his character was detestable he was a
great deal more attuned to events than is often thought; and
German policy cannot be explained solely in terms of morbid
psychology.

If proof is needed we can find it in the last portion of thi
survey: the analysis of the comparative strength of the Power
by Mr. H. C. Hillman. This is genuine research, based or
figures and proceeding by hard reasoning; it alone sheds a new
light on the world in 1939. The reality of the inter-war years
concealed by the phrases of statesmen and the existence of the
League of Nations, was the eclipse of Europe. For the firs

me two non-European Powers, Russia and the United States,
warfed Europe; and by 1939 the world, and not Europe, was
rhat mattered. Everyone knows about the advance in American
conomic strength. What Mr. Hillman makes clear is the
igantic strides taken also by the Soviet Union since 1928.
Nothing could arrest it, short of the overthrow of Communism
r the dismemberment of the Union. There was a profound
ifference between the two world Powers. American resources
vere still clumsily deployed, at half-cock; the Soviet Union
vas fully strained and, because of her political system, could
emain so. None of the other Powers could keep up in the race:
taly had never ranked seriously as a Great Power; France fell
ut in the thirties; and the most that the British could ask was
modest survival, nearer to Belgium or Holland than to the
ruly great. The Germans might have been wise to ask the same.
But, unlike the British, they seemed to have a chance of revers-
ng the march of events. The British had no hope of undoing
American greatness or of supplanting it; the Germans might
till arrest Russian greatness and take it over before it was too
ate.

   This was the essence of 'Hitlerism'. Its deep underlying pur-
ose was to put Germany in control of Russia's economic
trength; far from being lunacy, this made sense—at any rate
rom the German point of view. All else, even the attack on the
Western Powers, was preliminary to the attack on Russia, as
ve now know. Hence (a bitter confession to have to make)
here was some sense in the policy of switching Germany's
ggression eastwards, though none in Stalin's policy of trying
o turn it the other way round. Where Hitler differed from his
nilitary and economic advisers (and where he was right) was in
ecognizing that Germany had not much time. He had to
ttack Russia in a hurry. Hence he started the war more or less
n a shoe-string; and Russia proved too much for him. There
s a further conclusion, valid for 1939 and equally valid for
1952. Germany had to dominate Russia if she was to be a Great
Power. Russia was (and is) a Great Power without dominating
Germany. She would be content so long as Germany left her
lone—hence Stalin's blunder of the Nazi-Soviet pact.

   In March 1939 the great question seemed to be whether
Germany would dominate Europe or perhaps the world. In
etrospect this question seems little more than an irrelevant
ntrusion, causing much misery and destruction but leaving

behind no more than a scribble in the margin of history. The
real question was already being posed: whether there should
be two Great Powers in the world or one. For, though the
Soviet Union had outpaced all others, she would be herself left
panting and exhausted if the United States were ever to develop
fully their economic resources and, still more, to display political gifts in tune with their economic strength. This great question, which will determine the future of civilization, still waits
to be resolved.

XXVI

THUS SPAKE HITLER

THOUGH Hitler finished as a charred corpse soaked in petrol, he achieved his deepest wish: he staked out his claim in history and eclipsed his rivals. The other dictators of our time—Mussolini, Stalin, even Lenin—seem commonplace in comparison; industrious politicians with a different set of tricks. Hitler had a depth and elaboration of evil all his own, as though something primitive had emerged from the bowels of the earth. At the same time, there was a superb cunning, which enabled him to exploit others. Perhaps there has never been a man who understood power better or who turned it to baser uses. It is loathsome to read of his actions, most loathsome to read his own utterances; yet, with all the disgust, it is impossible not to feel also that here was a piece of human nature on a gigantic scale. No doubt Hitler personified the ignorance, brutality, and greed of millions of his countrymen. He became more than life-size. The millions made their weight felt in all Hitler's words and acts.

Hitler lived on two planes more than most men. He was a man of action, rising to supreme power in Germany and thereafter almost a world-conqueror. He was also what for want of a better word must be called a 'thinker'. The great problem is to find a link between the two. Hitler, though evil, was great in action. He knew when to wait, when to act; his intuition simplified everything and cut to the heart of the situation. At the end of his career he made gross miscalculations which ruined him; but they were the miscalculations of a gambler who knew that he was playing for the highest stakes. But when he philosophized, he was opaque. His thought moved in a fog of his own making, a mixture of prejudices and misconceptions. The men round him were often playing a part, pretending to believe for the sake of their own advantage. Hitler had unquestioning faith in the rubbish that filled his mind. How could a man so ignorant, so enslaved by stupid dogmas, have achieved such practical success?

A new book gives a picture of Hitler at the height of h[1] power.[1] Martin Bormann, Hitler's most devoted sycophan was anxious not to lose any of his master's words; and h arranged for a shorthand writer to attend at meal-times in heac quarters. Dr. Picker performed this duty from 21 March unt 2 August 1942; and, as well, he drew on the scantier note of his predecessor who had begun his task in the previous July Hitler had overcome the difficulties of the first Russian winter Stalingrad and the entry of the United States into the war wer still before him. He imagined himself within sight of decisiv victory and could talk of his plans for making an Aryan worlc He had always been given to monologue, and success made hir pontificate more than ever. No one interrupted, hardly anyon spoke once Hitler had been launched on some theme; and th massive tedium is made worse by the fact that the shorthand writer laid down his pencil whenever Hitler ran dry. Afte all, the poor chap had somehow to eat his dinner with one hanc while scribbling with the other. These interminable meal time harangues in the bunkers, or in Hitler's special trains can be paralleled only by Coleridge table-talking, as immor talized by Sir Max Beerbohm. But at least Coleridge's hearer could nod; the participants at Hitler's headquarters had to si bolt upright and maintain an intelligent interest. It must hav been among the graver perils of high office to have to lister to this relentless bore. Yet a leading German historian ha edited Dr. Picker's notes with scholarly gravity. Each frag ment is numbered and given a title; and there is a weight introduction, combining praise and blame. Certainly Professo Ritter condemns Hitler for thinking himself a superman; bu only a great statesman would deserve to have his opinions repro duced so fully, and it is likely that more Germans will read thi book for Hitler's inspiration than for Professor Ritter's criti cism.

The table-talk is a revelation of Hitler rather as he wished t appear than as he was. He was talking before an audience o some twenty people, half of them professional soldiers, and n doubt his eye never wandered far from the shorthand-writer Though he spoke little of himself, neither he nor his listener: had any doubt that he was 'one of Germany's greatest sons' He made no attempt to hide his origins or to erase them. H[e] was the man from the gutter; and he explained on one occasior

[1] Dr. Henry Picker, *Hitlers Tischgespräche im Führerhauptquartier*, 1941–42

hat he had become a non-smoker in Vienna because he could
ot afford both cigarettes and bread. The audience was not
uited to the reminiscences of early days in the party, which he
avoured when he was with his old comrades. Once he gave a
etailed account of his coming to power, emphasizing its
egality and placing the responsibility on Hindenburg and
apen. All the same, this seizure of power was never far from
is thoughts. It was the time when he had known how to wait
nd to let his rivals destroy each other. Now he was waiting
or a similar miracle, by which the enemy coalition would some-
ow be dissolved. He hated both Russia and America, and
espised them. His dream was that the English governing
lasses would somehow come to their senses and make peace
vith him. 'If Hoare comes to power he only needs to release
he Fascists.' He had hopes even of Mr. Churchill. 'Better a
undred times Churchill than Cripps'; and he blamed the
German diplomatists for not managing to arrange a love
ffair with one of Mr. Churchill's daughters—this, he ima-
ined, would have reversed British policy.

These were mere asides. More often Hitler would philo-
ophize in the common German way. There is nothing here to
ustain the view that he was a close student of Nietzsche; it
vould be nearer the truth to say that he translated Wagner into
olitical terms. His hostility to Christianity was vulgar clap-
rap; it was a religion for women and weaklings. The Gods and
he laws of nature, which he often invoked, were merely a cloak
or his principle that the stronger were always right; this prin-
iple, though he did not know it, was soon to operate against
imself. He praised the Oberammergau passion play as a
vonderful demonstration of the Jewish danger: 'Pontius Pilate
ppears as a Roman so superior racially and intellectually that
e stands out as a rock in the midst of the Near Eastern scum
nd swarm.' Hitler was confident that he himself belonged to
Olympus, if there was one: 'the most enlightened spirits of
ll times will be found there'. And with the present period of
truggle, 'we are moving towards a sunny, really tolerant out-
ook: man shall be in the position to develop the faculties given
o him by God'.

But only one sort of men shall be in this sunny position:
Germanic men. The striking revelation of these disquisitions is
hat Hitler believed implicitly his own racial theory. This was
ot merely anti-semitism, though he held, for instance, that

a single Jewish ancestor would still reveal effects even thoug]
he was as far off as the sixteenth century. But all his judgement
were based on blood and breeding. Thus he thought that th
population of northern France had been made tougher b
the intermixture of German blood during the occupation of th
First World War; and he said of the Grand Mufti: 'He give
the impression of a man among whose ancestors there was mor
than one Aryan and who perhaps springs from the best Roma
blood.' For he held, of course, that the ancient Greeks and
Romans were of Teutonic stock; hence the true Germans wer
to be found among the monuments of antiquity, not in th
primitive forests. His illusion did not, however, extend to th
modern Italians. Mussolini was the only man among them
and even here his approval sprang from the fact that, when the
met, they were always in agreement. Only the Scandinavian
and the Dutch were to be included in the new German Empir
(the Swiss would be used as hotel-keepers); and to make thi
empire attractive to them Berlin was to change its name t
'Germania'.

This imperial theme was Hitler's favourite; he returned to i
again and again. The only human element in it was his inten
tion to develop Linz into a great city and to endow it with th
artistic plunder of Europe; this would humble Vienna and
punish the Viennese for their early neglect of him. But for th
most part his plans were far more grandiose: to turn Europ
into a German Valhalla, built of concrete instead of stage-props
Concrete fascinated him; it expressed what he imagined hi
character to be. Cities of concrete, inhabited by hard Aryar
men, and bound together by concrete roads. Such was his visior
of the future. He had already attained this ideal. These talk
were delivered in a concrete cellar, far in the Russian plains
and his dreams turned always to the empire that he had con
quered. Most empire-builders claim to benefit the 'colonial
peoples whom they have subdued; or at the very least intend t
exploit them. Hitler was concerned only with 'German soil'
It was not enough to turn the Russians into slaves; they mus
disappear. He stormed against the idiocy of denying them th
means of birth-control; at the same time they should be en
couraged in their superstition against inoculation. The Germar
conquerors were to live in their fortified towns, isolated from
the Russians and above all never interbreeding with them. Th
Russians were to become ignorant, diseased, rotten, and finall

to perish. As to the lesser Slav peoples, the process of extermination could already be begun with them. Such was the
German cultural mission, the defence of European civilization
against the barbarism of the East.

Yet, absurdly enough, Hitler had little confidence in these
Germans whose imperial greatness he was creating. He railed
against the methods of German bureaucracy and often envied
Stalin, 'a man of real genius'. Some of his hearers must have
shivered to themselves as Hitler described how he would deal
with a 'mutiny' in the Reich: 'Execute all leading men of
opposition outlook, and especially those of political Catholicism,
at once; shoot all the inmates of the concentration camps within
three days; shoot all criminal elements, whether free or in
prison, within three days.' This would involve 'some hundred
thousands of men' and would make other measures superfluous.
This, and not the sunny tolerance of moral outlook, was the
reality in Hitler's future. His 'Germania' was imaginary.
He feared and hated the actual Germans only a little less than
he hated the inferior races. The only Germans he cared for
were the men of the S.S., and they were to breed for the future
as well as to fight for it. Though he was 'one of Germany's
greatest sons', he dared not, as he confessed, drive unguarded
through the streets of any German town; it did not even occur
to him to regret that he could not walk there. Choosing terror,
he had condemned himself to a life of fear. Hitler was beyond
good and evil only in the sense that any criminal or gangster
is beyond good and evil. He believed that with power he could
do anything; and the Germans who supported him shared this
belief. Though he was wrong, they were wrong also; and most
wrong now, if they suppose they can shoulder all their faults
and crimes on to Hitler's shoulders.

XXVII

ANOTHER 'GOOD GERMAN'

ERNST VON WEIZSÄCKER was Secretary of State or, as we should say, Permanent Under-Secretary in the German Foreign Ministry from 1938 until 1943. For his activities while in this office he was sentenced as a war criminal by an American military court in 1948. His memoirs[1] are inevitably a case for the defence, not a contribution to impartial history: another illustration how these trials, with their irrelevant standards, have bedevilled the study of contemporary history. It would be equally irrelevant, as well as tedious, to repeat the case for the prosecution and to pick holes in Weizsäcker's defence; the historian must take them for what they are worth and try to find a few crumbs of information in them here and there.

A good deal of the book is far removed from politics on the grand scale. Herr von Weizsäcker was by professional training a sailor not a diplomatist; and his judgements on events before 1920 have all the simplicity of a naval officer. Thus he is confident that no one in Germany wanted the war of 1914: 'We all stumbled into war—the incompetence was more on the German, the deliberate negligence more on the Entente side.' In the routine way he blames Grey for associating with France and Russia; repeats the grievances against the treaty of Versailles; and even records the myth that the Allies had promised to disarm. His early years in the Diplomatic Service did not bring him much nearer the heart of events: he served in Berne, in Oslo, and finally on the disarmament commission. When he was recalled to Berlin, first in 1936 as the head of the political section, then in 1938 as permanent chief of the Foreign Ministry, it was exactly in the spirit in which a retired naval officer is made secretary of a golf club; he knows how to be friendly to the members and can be relied upon not to make off with the funds. Canaris, who was put in charge of the Abwehr (military intelligence), was just such another, though of a subtler character.

[1] Ernst von Weizsäcker, *Erinnerungen.*

216

Herr von Weizsäcker was tactful, presentable, and patient; his Nazi superiors (not such fools as he thinks) no doubt got exactly the man they required—someone to do the routine work of the Foreign Ministry without either turning traitor or trying to make policy on his own. Herr von Weizsäcker claims to have considered the example of Talleyrand and to have decided that in the era of total war deliberate betrayal even of a ruler who was marching to disaster was impracticable; the question of total war is, of course, irrelevant—the real difference is that Talleyrand was not a naval officer.

Why did Herr von Weizsäcker ever take the job, ever stay in it, if he knew what Hitler and Ribbentrop were up to? According to his own account, this question weighed on him deeply, and he discussed it with his friends so often that it is difficult to understand when he had time for office business. His reasons for staying were two: at first he thought that Ribbentrop could be influenced and, through Ribbentrop, Hitler. He noted in March 1938, 'The very changeableness of Ribbentrop's views seems to me to leave room to fulfil the task (certainly the only one for the sake of which I am taking this cross on myself): that of preventing a war'. Later, when Ribbentrop proved unteachable, Herr von Weizsäcker thought he might use his position to prevent war, even in spite of both Ribbentrop and Hitler.

Why then did he continue in office when he had failed in 'the only task' which had justified him? Apparently in the hope of preventing the war from spreading and in the still vaguer hope that somehow an opportunity for peace might present itself. There is a great deal about this 'fight for peace'; the fight seems mostly to have consisted in transacting the duties of Permanent Under-Secretary with a straight face. A simpler, alternative justification is put forward: that, once war had started, Herr von Weizsäcker could no more desert his post than could an ordinary seaman; it does not seem to have occurred to him that there was a difference in the two positions. Otherwise Hitler could have used the same argument—and all the major war criminals did so.

In reality Herr von Weizsäcker played a game of many deceptions. He deceived his employers by trying to thwart, or at least to weaken, their policy; he deceived foreign statesmen by trying to make them believe that German policy was more conciliatory than in fact it was: most of all he deceived himself by imagining that he was doing something important.

Some of these deceptions have left their mark in the official records and confirm the defence given here; but then they may have been put there for that purpose. Weizsäcker certainly tried to restrain Ribbentrop in the summer of 1938; and certainly tried to warn the British Government through Kordt and others. It would of course have been more effective if he could have promised the British Government a Putsch against Hitler, since according to his own account he knew of one. His spasmodic efforts were no doubt directed towards depriving Hitler of his war; but they were also directed towards attaining Hitler's objects by peaceful means. He refers repeatedly to the right of the Sudeten Germans to 'self-determination'; and he presents Munich as a victory for himself and Nevile Henderson, assisted by Mussolini, against the warmongers in both Germany and England. In March 1939, he and Henderson played the same game. They arranged by telephone that Henderson should only protest against the occupation of Prague in writing so as to avoid an unpleasant scene. Again, when the Polish crisis approached, Weizsäcker undertook the double task of 'discouraging and depressing the Poles and Hitler at the same time'. Hitler was to be deterred from war; the Poles were to be jockeyed out of the corridor without a war. His judgement on the outbreak of war is characteristic: 'It is hateful to have my name associated with this event, quite apart from the unforeseeable results for the survival of Germany and of my family.'

Once war had broken out, Herr von Weizsäcker continued to attend at the Foreign Ministry in the hope that one day peace might be offered to him out of the blue; then apparently he could have thrust Hitler and Ribbentrop aside, though this had been impossible in more favourable circumstances. He regards it as an achievement to have told the Belgian and Dutch Ministers that their countries were to be invaded, without the lame excuses used by Bethmann Hollweg in 1914.

In July 1940, there seemed a last chance of peace negotiations; at any rate Lord Lothian in Washington put out feelers through 'a Quaker'. Even when Herr von Weizsäcker resigned his post in 1943 he went as German Ambassador to the Vatican in order—so he claims—to have his ears open for the first offer of peace. The offers never came. Instead the Allied armies came to Rome; and most of his friends in Germany met their death after the attempt of 20 July. But even then Herr von Weizsäcker did not come under suspicion: he was not recalled and remained in Hitler's service to the end. To tell the truth, Herr von Weizsäcker did nothing to harm Hitler and Ribbentrop; he did nothing to harm the Allies; in fact, like the other 'good Germans', he did nothing at all.

XXVIII

FRANCE IN DEFEAT

A special chair of Vichy history will soon have to be created; nothing short of this will keep up with the flow of books on the defeat of France and the first year of Pétain's Government. Some of the participants have had to defend themselves before French tribunals; others write to satisfy their own consciences; others again—and these the most part—to display their cleverness both then and now. There are two new contributors. Weygand has published his memoirs;[1] these start with his appointment to the Near East on the outbreak of war, and end with his dismissal from the post of Delegate General in North Africa in November 1941. M. Bouthillier, appointed Minister of Finance by Reynaud in June 1940, defends the armistice and then gives his recollections of Vichy until Darlan's arrival in power in January 1941.[2]

So far as Weygand's book deals with the campaign of 1940 this is not new. Two years ago he published an account of his part in this campaign entitled *Conversations with his Son*. It now appears that Weygand has limited conversational powers: all he did was to read to his son selected passages from his memoirs and add anti-British comments. These have now disappeared. Hardly anything remains of his earlier version that Gort ruined the plan for a counter-offensive on 24 May by failing to attack at Arras; and even Churchill's refusal to throw in all the British fighter strength has now become a modest grievance.

Instead Reynaud is blamed for his obstinacy in wishing to withdraw the Government overseas. If he had asked for an armistice sooner, this would have been less severe; moreover a frank discussion with the British would have cleared away the misunderstandings about the French Fleet. There is something in this last point. It seems clear that Reynaud, in his anxiety to avoid the policy of armistice, never explained to his col-

[1] General Weygand, *Mémoires: Rappelé au Service.*

[2] Yves Bouthillier, *Le Drame de Vichy.* I—*Face à l'Ennemi, face à l'Allié.*

leagues the British insistence on the fleet being put out of reach
of the Germans. This could have been done early in June.
On 16 June it was too late; besides, the French were beyond
caring. Both Weygand and Bouthillier make out that the
British anxiety over the fleet was never communicated ade-
quately to the French Government; they would do better to
admit that in June 1940 a continued British resistance never
crossed their minds, and that they were satisfied with a theore-
tical security for French honour. Both, too, now make out that
they were taking the courageous line by staying in France.
Mandel thought differently. At the decisive Cabinet meeting
on 16 June he said, 'The Cabinet is divided. The brave men
on one side, the cowards on the other !'

The evidence of what followed the armistice is more novel.
The armistice, according to all its advocates, was 'attentism' —
a manœuvre of waiting. But waiting for what? Weygand claims
to have been waiting for a chance to renew the war against
Germany. First in his short period as Minister of National
Defence, then for rather over a year as supreme authority in
North Africa, he tried to build up French military strength on
the Prussian model of Stein and Scharnhorst after 1807. In
December 1940 Churchill, De Gaulle, and Catroux all appealed
to Weygand to bring North Africa back into the war. He insists
that he rejected their appeals as premature, not because he
was opposed to them; in fact, Weygand claims that the Allied
landings in November 1942 should be put to his credit.

In practice, waiting to re-enter the war worked out very
much like waiting for others to win it—the policy of the true
men of Vichy. M. Bouthillier is their representative. It suits
him now to say nothing of his dreams for a 'national revolution', which other accounts attribute to him in 1940; he was,
he claims, simply concerned to give France time to breathe,
and meanwhile to see what would happen. More honest than
Weygand, he writes of Pétain, 'At bottom his attitude to the
Germans was the same as towards the English'; in other
words, he waited for them to wear each other out, and imagined
an impossible outcome, when a neutral France would hold the
balance between the exhausted combatants.

Hence French policy after the armistice swung pendulum-
like, hoping never to tip over. The armistice was a swing
towards Germany. Then came Hitler's demand of 15 July for
the use of the French bases in North Africa; this was refused—

a swing towards England. Pétain and his associates had the illusion that they were recovering their independence; the height of this illusion was the defence of Dakar against De Gaulle and the British in September. But once again the pendulum threatened to swing too much in Germany's favour. Laval, though also an 'attentiste', waited for a German victory; and in October 1940 grew tired of waiting. He wished to commit France to the side of Germany before it was too late.

Thus, according to M. Bouthillier, there were two policies of 'Montoire'—Laval's policy of usurping Italy's place as the principal ally of Germany and Pétain's policy of continuing to balance. M. Bouthillier does not exaggerate Pétain's achievement; he admits that Franco's refusal to enter the war was the more decisive act. On the other hand, he exaggerates, as Weygand does too, the extent of Pétain's reconciliation with England in the London mission of Professor Rougier—an affair always absurdly inflated in Vichy writings. Throughout November 1940 Laval pushed ever harder on Germany's side. He made repeated concessions in return for fine words. Early in December Bouthillier revolted, won over his colleagues, and then persuaded Pétain to break with Laval. The details of this intrigue are the most important part of his book. Laval was dismissed on 13 December, and Pétain withstood the German storm. Flandin was called in—a swing towards England—and the Germans seemed to acquiese in his nomination. But in January 1941, Pétain characteristically swung again. He had an interview with Laval; and Flandin, in his effort to discredit Laval, published a communiqué against him which instead brought about his own fall. Once more policy swung to Germany, though under Darlan's direction. The peak of this swing was Darlan's proposal of June 1941 (described by Weygand) to allow the Axis Powers to use Dakar and Bizerta. This proposal was defeated by Weygand—the last swing towards England. In November 1941 Weygand was dismissed on German orders; in March 1942 Laval returned to power. Instead of gaining freedom of manœuvre, France was losing it, and lost it altogether in November 1942. The 'men of Vichy' were not as clever as they thought; still, in the first year after defeat France had no resource except cleverness. The great blunder of Vichy was to fail to understand when it had outlived its usefulness.

XXIX

DE GAULLE: TRIUMPH OF A LEGEND

THE career of General de Gaulle is without parallel in modern times. When he left France in 1940 he had had no political experience and only a few weeks' military experience in a minor command. Four years later this general who had never conducted a battle and politician who had never presented himself at an election returned as the undisputed master of France, ranking with Clemenceau and almost with Napoleon himself. Instead of starting as a hero and becoming a legend, General de Gaulle started as a legend and became a hero on the way. His qualities were neither tested in battle nor challenged in debate. Posterity may perhaps ponder whether any reality lay behind the legend or whether General de Gaulle was simply a creature of air, created by the only medium in which he could have contact with the people of France. Yet there is an answer to these doubts. Other Frenchmen repudiated the surrender of 1940; only de Gaulle rose to the level of the historic moment, and only de Gaulle maintained without failing a clairvoyant grasp of French feeling.

The doubts spring in part from lack of evidence or, worse, from evidence of the wrong kind. Apart from de Gaulle's own speeches, the only Gaullist testimony has been from Colonel Passy; and this was primarily concerned to tell the story of the secret service which Passy organized. On the other side, almost every supporter of Vichy, great or small, has by now told his story; and every trivial incident among Pétain's entourage has been analysed in as great detail as one of Napoleon's campaigns. The opponents of Pétain who have spoken have also been for the most part opponents of de Gaulle; indeed they have usually been keener to make a case against de Gaulle than against Vichy. General Catroux's memoirs, as one would expect, are perfectly loyal to de Gaulle; but, as one would also expect from that man of supreme tact, they are skilfully designed so as not to serve the legend. Now at last we have a full expression of the legend in historical form. M. Jacques Soustelle was for long General de Gaulle's Commissar of Information during the war;

and he is now secretary-general of the Gaullist movement. For such an experienced propagandist his two volumes betray a curious uncertainty of aim.[1] Personal reminiscence is mixed with general narrative; yet these episodes are too selective to provide a full history of the Free French movement throughout the war. Again, it is difficult to suppose that these volumes have not been written with one eye on political effect in the present; yet equally difficult to grasp what this political effect was intended to be.

If the two volumes had sub-titles, the first would be called 'The making of a Legend', and the second 'Its Victory'. When de Gaulle appealed for the continuance of the war on 18 June 1940, he established himself for good and all as the first of the resisters; this was his great historic act. But he had expected a very different response—the rallying, in fact, of all the French Empire oversea. Instead he was followed only by Equatorial Africa. This changed at once the character of the movement. If the French pro-consuls had all proclaimed their independence of Vichy, de Gaulle could never have achieved predominance. As it was, he became undisputed leader in a movement composed of junior officers and junior administrators. The successes of Fighting France in 1940 came from the personal initiative of a few adventurous men; this was the spirit of individual daring which had created the French colonial empire in the later nineteenth century. These adventurers could succeed where individual character and the single voice could still be effective. Their efforts failed where, as in Dakar, North Africa, or Syria, they ran against a solid structure of government and a hierarchy of authority. Though de Gaulle's movement in London tried to create an impression of formality, it could not rank truly as an exiled Government; it was an association of individuals, displaying to the full the individual spirit of the French revolution.

Apart from the winning of Equatorial Africa, Gaullism in its early days had one concrete achievement—the creation of a system of information from occupied France. It is this success which Colonel Passy has described at length; and it is therefore passed over in summary by M. Soustelle. In his account, the war against the Germans takes second place; the real struggle appears rather against the supporters of Vichy and almost as much against the allies of Free France. M. Soustelle's harshest

[1] Jacques Soustelle, *Envers et contre tout*. Souvenirs et documents de la France Libre (1940–4). I—*De Londres à Alger*, 1940–1942; II—*D'Alger à Paris*, 1942–1944.

words are reserved for the Attentistes, those who tried to keep
France above the battle, rather than for the collaborators, who
could be safely left to discredit themselves. This is indeed an
essential part of the story. Though de Gaulle often insisted on
the contribution of his movement to the war against Germany,
his real preoccupation was with the revival of French spirit.
As he said to Mr. Churchill on 10 June 1942, in the course of
a dispute over Madagascar: 'The only problem is to encourage
the will to resistance of the French people and to revive their
will to wage war. This aim will not be achieved by snubbing
those French who are fighting.' For de Gaulle and his followers
the greatest evil was to admit the patriotism of those who were
trying to keep France neutral or to leave a way open by which
they might return to the allied side.

This could not be the outlook of the great Powers who
were engaged in the actual war. They had to think of the
present; de Gaulle was relieved of the present by Pétain,
and could concentrate on the future. De Gaulle was accepted
by the British Government as the sole representative of
France only until the failure at Dakar; thereafter he had to
justify his claims by solid achievement and was often unable
to do so. The attitude of the American Government was even
more critical. In view of its own neutrality it could not condemn
Vichy whole-heartedly; and besides, there was in Roosevelt's
scepticism an element of almost personal jealousy not yet fully
explained. As M. Soustelle admits, Mr. Churchill was the
most sympathetic of allied statesmen; yet, to moderate American doubts, he had to press doubts of his own. In September
1942 he said to de Gaulle: 'After all, are you France? There
may be other parties in France who may be summoned, in the
course of events, to occupy a more important place than today.'
De Gaulle replied 'If I do not represent France, why discuss
with me?' This interchange summarized the essential question.
De Gaulle was not a party leader; he was not a general in command of great armies; apart from a handful of colonies without industrial resources he had no material basis. Either he
represented France or he was nothing.

In November 1942, when M. Soustelle's first volume ends,
de Gaulle seemed to be nothing. French North Africa was
liberated without his assistance, even without his being
informed; in fact, one might almost say that it was liberated
against him. De Gaulle's only contribution, described by M.
Soustelle in moving terms, was to address a crowded meeting

at the Albert Hall. M. Soustelle's second volume is less
inspiring, but more revealing. It is the story of how the man of
mythical reputation took on flesh, grasped at real power, and
prepared the way for his triumph in France. The title of the
volume, as of the first, is misleading. In November 1942, de
Gaulle was still in London, not in Algiers; and the core of the
second volume is concerned with how he got to Algiers, not
with how he left Algiers for Paris. Once de Gaulle became
chairman of a governing committee in Algiers, the legend
was officially recognized; and even those who had been most
opposed to him would seek its shelter. Yet the North African
campaign, far from being designed to benefit de Gaulle, was
expected by Roosevelt to ruin him; and Mr. Churchill said to
de Gaulle: 'I do not want to abandon you. But if I have to
choose between Roosevelt and you, I shall choose Roosevelt.'
M. Soustelle does not grasp the deep implications of that remark. He seriously argues that Mr. Churchill wanted to draw
the Americans into North Africa in order to rescue the British
army in Egypt from certain defeat at the hands of Rommel—
an argument unworthy of a man of his intelligence. His explanation of Roosevelt is even more trivial: he was a 'patrician',
excited by his unexpected elevation to the position of ruler of
the greatest empire that the world had ever known; he was set
on world-supremacy for himself and could brook no rival, only
those who were subservient. Hence he could tolerate Mr.
Churchill, but not General de Gaulle. These wild guesses reveal
the central weakness of all Gaullists: themselves the expression
of an idea, they exaggerated the importance of intellectual con-
cepts in others and failed to understand the material considerations which are usually decisive, especially in war.

M. Soustelle can explain de Gaulle's success in Algiers only
as the victory of a superior idea. And in a sense he is right.
De Gaulle triumphed not so much from his own strength as
from the insufficiency of his rivals. He had an idea without
material resources; they had not even an idea. Darlan and
Giraud represented nothing in themselves; they were merely
negation—they were not de Gaulle. Yet most of M. Soustelle's
second volume is concerned with them, rather than with his
own hero. De Gaulle simply waited in London, first for Darlan
to be assassinated, then for Giraud to discredit himself by his
political clumsiness; neither de Gaulle nor his supporters contributed anything to either event. Of course M. Soustelle has to

make out that there was a strong Gaullist movement in North Africa, only waiting to be roused into enthusiasm. This is to fly in the face of the evidence. North Africa would have been administered for the allies, and French forces would have contributed to the Tunisian and Italian campaigns just as effectively if de Gaulle had never existed. The truth lies elsewhere. De Gaulle succeeded because, in politics as in other things, nature abhors a vacuum. Both Darlan and Giraud, in their different ways, acquiesced in Roosevelt's judgement. De Gaulle alone denied it; and since even the Americans could not treat French territory as ownerless desert, they had ultimately to accept the only man who had the self-confidence to speak for France.

There is another aspect of events which M. Soustelle keeps in the background. De Gaulle was certainly carried to Algiers by his superiority as a man with an idea over the men who had none. But once he and Giraud became uneasy partners the experienced talent for political manœuvre and even for intrigue which the Gaullists had developed in London was turned to good account. Giraud was undoubtedly stupid; but he would probably not have behaved quite so stupidly if there had not been a body of clever men eager to exploit his stupidity. Indeed, this part—and it is a long part—of M. Soustelle's book suggests nothing so much as the narration by a spider of the extraordinary and unexpected accidents by which a fly fell into its web. Yet even in Algiers the political struggle was artificial. M. Soustelle refers constantly to French public opinion, as expressed in the feeling in Algiers; but the connexion was remote. Here indeed one can discover the basic flaw which was to lead to de Gaulle's failure after the war. M. Soustelle argues that all the pre-war parties had been discredited; and he complains that British and American doubts compelled de Gaulle to justify his position by accepting support from the political parties and thus resurrected what should have remained dead. The English reader is bewildered by this train of thought. He is ready to acquit de Gaulle of being a Fascist or even of having predominantly Fascist supporters; M. Soustelle himself is the proof of the contrary. De Gaulle was overwhelmingly sincere when he promised to restore French democracy and the liberties of the French people. But how can you have democracies without political parties? The contemporary answer stares us in the face: democracies without parties become 'people's democracies', and their character is now well known.

This point goes far to explain a theme which M. Soustelle constantly approaches without fully grasping: de Gaulle's relations with the French Communists. In his latter-day anxiety to present de Gaulle as the principal barrier against Communism M. Soustelle tries to claim that the Communists supported Giraud. And so, with their usual unscrupulous manœuvres for power, they did. But they also supported de Gaulle. Indeed, they might almost claim to have created him as the personification of the French resistance. It is true that, meaning to create an instrument, they created a rival. If de Gaulle had not existed, the Communists might have seized power in France in the autumn of 1944. This does not alter the fact that de Gaulle succeeded against the Communists by being like them, not by being different. He had the same readiness to dictate in the name of France; the same hostility to political parties and even to political scruples; the same fallacious promise of something untarnished with the corruptions and failures of the past. Like the Communists, he tried to make politics heroic and dramatic; as with the Communists, this often meant deliberately ignoring the material factors on which he relied. The essential difference between de Gaulle and the Communists does not appear in this book. Both talked of a temporary dictatorship; he kept his word.

De Gaulle's aim was to restore France to the position of an independent great Power. Though anti-German in the circumstances of 1940, he was equally anti-American, anti-Russian and even anti-British. He thought of France as still the greatest Power in the world, materially as well as intellectually. This flew in the face of the facts. Not merely the material facts of the dwindling French resources compared with those of others; it defied still more the spiritual fact that the French people had wearied of greatness. The despised parties, with their corruption and sectarian manœuvres, offered the French people what they desired. De Gaulle believed that the French people could be again illuminated into grandeur; he created his legend for their sake, not for his own. He was indeed narrow, unyielding, impatient of human weakness; yet with all this, more understanding than his supporters made him out. In spite of the failures and even blunders which followed the liberation of France, it is impossible to review the record of de Gaulle's achievement during the war without admitting that he earned his fame; indeed he deserved well of the Republic.

XXX

AMERICA'S WAR

To judge by the memoirs, every American in high place was
fighting a different war. Cordell Hull was concerned to restore
a vanished world of Free Trade; Harry Hopkins tried to make
the New Deal universal; Stimson wanted to renew the victory
of the First World War. Admiral Leahy was representative of
those Americans who distrusted their allies as much as they
disliked the Germans. In his own words:[1]

> Our problem in Washington would not have been difficult if we
> had not been required to distribute our men, ships, and supplies to
> support allies who, with the exception of Russia, seemed incapable of
> surviving without assistance.

His speciality was denigration, and perhaps Roosevelt
employed him as personal Chief of Staff so that his ungenerous
scepticism should balance the enthusiasm of others. He certainly fulfilled expectations. Thus, of the French Army: 'To
me, the "magnificent French Army" was only pretty fast on its
feet. It almost got away—by running.' Another example:
when Admiral Cunningham left Washington to assume command in the Mediterranean in October 1942: 'Lady Cunningham did not seem to be very happy at the prospect of her hus-
band's going back to such a dangerous spot.' He draws
repeated attention to de Gaulle's not being 'anywhere near the
battlefield' (the Admiral himself did not hear many shots fired
in anger) and describes him as suffering 'from a severe over-
supply of national pride'.

Leahy extended his scepticism to the atomic bomb. Four
days before Hiroshima Leahy said to King George VI: 'I do
not think it will be as effective as is expected. It sounds like
a professor's dream to me!' The King did not agree.

As Chief of Staff to the President, Leahy presided over the
American Joint Chiefs of Staff and also took a leading part
in the Combined Chiefs of Staff with the British. No doubt
Leahy's real function was to act as connecting link with Roose-

[1] Admiral Leahy, *I Was There.*

229

velt; still, his drops of acid must have affected the flavour of
Allied co-operation. For Leahy, in spite of his pose as a professional sailor, was a political officer, advising the most important politician in the world. His book is a selection from the
notes he made at the time for his conversations with Roosevelt;
though most of them are tedious when not unreadable, they
give a striking impression of the confused years when America
was first growing up to her responsibilities as a Great Power.

To judge by Leahy's account, American strategy was
decided by picking out objectives with the butt-end of a cigar.
So rival generals and admirals would prod at maps of the Pacific;
so too France presented itself as the obvious theatre for an
invasion of Europe. The Mediterranean and Balkan alternatives
seem never to have been weighed strategically; the American
rejection of it was political—that the British were trying to
exploit American forces 'to acquire for the Empire post-war
advantages in the Balkan States'.

Distrust of Great Britain is a constant theme. In 1942 Leahy
wrote: 'A large segment of the British Government regarded
the Mediterranean as a vital and legitimate British preserve
and were most unhappy to see the United States taking the leading role in that area.' Later Leahy thought America had been
outsmarted by the British by being drawn into the Mediterranean at all. It is not surprising that Leahy was the most fer-
vent advocate of ending Lend-Lease immediately hostilities
ceased. After a conversation with Winant Leahy noted:

> The Britons were using all of their energies to safeguard those
> things considered necessary for the preservation of the British Empire.
> We Americans were devoting our efforts exclusively to destroying the
> Germans, with not too much thought about the future.

Almost his final word on Churchill was: 'He was basically more
concerned over preserving England's position in Europe than
in preserving peace.' Though Roosevelt's attitude was less
grudging, he, too, disliked the British Empire. At Yalta he
intended to propose that Hong-Kong be returned to China
and was only deterred by the Russian demand for Dairen.
Leahy leant over to Roosevelt and said: 'Mr. President, you
are going to lose out on Hong-Kong if you agree to give the
Russians half of Dairen.' Roosevelt shook his head in resigna-
tion and said: 'Well, Bill, I can't help it.'

The policy of the Russians during and immediately after the

war becomes much clearer when it is borne in mind that they
received two constant impressions from the Americans—that
America was incurably opposed to the continuance of the
British Empire and that American forces would be withdrawn
from Europe at latest within two years of the ending of hostili-
ies. A partition of the world between 'the only two major
Powers remaining in the world', as Leahy called them, seemed
he logical conclusion, especially when the Americans were
pressing urgently for Russian help in the Far East. The Rus-
ian blunder was to suppose that the Americans were as logical
as themselves. But American policy rested on the assumption
hat Russia, like America, was fundamentally isolationist and
non-aggressive. Roosevelt wrote to Leahy on 26 June 1941:
'I do not think we need worry about any possibility of Russian
domination', and this remained his unshakeable conviction until
after Yalta.

The Russians, on their side, regarded Roosevelt's insistence
on free elections in Poland as an interference in their 'sphere'
and could explain it only as an attempt to revive the cordon
sanitaire. Neither side understood the other. If the Americans
would not divide the world with the Russians, the only alternative would have been to impose a free Eastern Europe on the
Russians in 1945 by superior force. This was also too logical
for the Americans. They hoped vaguely for a Russian change
of heart and so, as Leahy shows, drifted into the 'cold war'.
This was not an issue of power. It was a clash between two
fundamental conceptions of the world—the one logical and
ruthless, the other benevolent but muddled and undefined.

Three anecdotes from Leahy illustrate the character of the
heads of 'the only two major Powers'. At Teheran Churchill
objected to Stalin's list of 50,000 German officers who should
be brought to trial and spoke eloquently 'for maintenance of
the traditional concept of justice'. 'Roosevelt suggested that
if 50,000 German officers were too many to be tried, why not
compromise on a smaller number, such as 49,000?' At Potsdam Churchill defended the rights of the Catholics in Poland.
Stalin reflected a moment, stroking his moustache, and then
asked the Prime Minister in a hard, even tone, "How many
divisions has the Pope?"' On the way back from Potsdam news
came of the atomic bomb at Hiroshima. 'Truman was excited
over the news and said, "This is the greatest thing in history".'
On such men depend the destinies of mankind.

XXXI

CAN WE AGREE WITH THE RUSSIANS?

IF a question can be given a simple answer, it is not wort
asking. If one could say either 'yes' or 'no' to the question
Can we agree with the Russians? the matter would not b
worrying the world so much. The answer is not simple; there
fore the question persists. Of course, if the Western worl
went Communist, it could agree with the Russians—at an
rate for a short time. And if the Communist system fell t
pieces in Russia, its successor could probably agree with u
But when we ask this question we really mean, Can a Wester
world, which retains its free institutions and its independenc
agree with a Soviet Russia dominated by the Communis
party?

But we must go a stage farther in deciding what we mear
If by 'agree' we mean, Can the two systems settle down side b
side, each disarmed, each trusting each other as much as, sa
France and Italy trust each other, neither interfering in th
other's affairs?—then, any responsible writer on internation
affairs must at once say, No, that is impossible and will b
impossible so long as the two systems exist.

On the other hand, the alternative to this state of idylli
agreement is not necessarily World War III. It may be any
thing from mutual non-recognition to agreements on all kind
of limited issues, despite the suspicion on more general point
Hardly anyone in the West, except the Communists, woul
claim that full-scale agreement is possible with the Russian
here and now or even in the future. But the great majority o
people in Western Europe and, I think, a majority in th
United States, have still not made up their minds that a com
plete breach with the Soviet Union is inevitable as, say, th
majority of people in England thought it was a waste of tim
to bargain with Hitler after the occupation of Prague in Marc
1939. It is the purpose of this article to examine the no-man's
land between full agreement, which we think impossible, an
war, which we still think can be avoided.

232

In discussing any subject connected with Soviet Russia here is a preliminary warning which should be compulsory on all writers on international affairs. We know nothing about t; everything we write is guesswork, though we hope intelligent guesswork. Take the parallel case of Hitler. Though there was a good deal of secrecy connected with the Nazis, these secrets could be broken. We knew which men around Hitler had influence; we knew the general line of his ideas; we knew broadly his resources and his intentions. After all, plenty of foreigners met Hitler at close quarters, and he spoke frankly o them.

None of this is true in regard to the Soviet Union. We do not know who are the really important men in the Politburo; we do not know which of them has influence with Stalin; we do not even know whether Stalin has influence; we know little of Russian economic development since the war and nothing reliable about her military strength. No independent foreign observer has had any real meeting with Stalin since he was at Potsdam in 1945, and even then he may have been playing an elaborate part. We do not know, though we can guess, whether the rulers of Russia are Marxists or nationalists; whether they are frightened or aggressive. All our judgements have to be made from outside; none can be based on knowledge, only on information.

On a technical point, for instance, we have no means of knowing whether Soviet diplomatists abroad write honest and well-informed reports of public opinion in the countries where they are posted; just as little do we know whether Stalin reads their reports or takes any notice of them. During World War II many competent judges, from President Roosevelt and Mr. Eden downward, were confident that Russia would settle down and become a peaceful, non-aggressive state; now judges, equally competent, hold that the Soviet Union will remain a permanently disturbing element in the world. Both judgements are based on guesswork, on observation from outside; neither is based on knowledge of how the Soviet Union is governed or of how its rulers feel.

My guess, for what it is worth (and it is worth as much as anyone else's), is that the Soviet rulers are not as black as they have been painted—and not as white either. They like to think that, because they are Marxists, they are quite different from anyone else, much cleverer and much more successful. In prac-

tice, they are very like the rulers of any other country, pushed
along by events, making a good many blunders, and delighted
to keep the show going at all. They have long got rid of any
organized opposition inside their own country, and therefore
they are at a loss when they run into it elsewhere. The abuse
which they then turn on is the political method which they
learned in the days when they had opposition inside Russia;
it is simply habit like any other, though a very unpleasant
one. Of course, it would be more convenient for them if they
could 'liquidate' opposition in the outer world as they once
got rid of it inside the Soviet Union; but then it would also
be more convenient for us if the Soviet Union did not exist—
so we must not count that too much against them.

The Soviet rulers are Marxists. They genuinely think that
their system is the best in the world and that it is bound to
triumph. On the other hand, absurdly enough, they live in an
atmosphere of ceaseless fear, expecting conspiracies and wars
of intervention at any moment. In fact they are very like a
gambler who believes that he has invented an infallible 'system', yet is terrified of being robbed or even assassinated on the
way to the casino.

The Russian rulers are, in theory, revolutionary; but that
was a long time ago. A friend of mine was with the Soviet
general who was 'dropped' to Tito during the last war. The
old warrior had once been a leading guerrilla; by 1943 he
expected to move around in a staff car and then be served with
a four-course dinner every evening. In the same way the revolutionary joints of the Soviet leaders would creak a good deal if it
ever came to action. In practice, they are much like politicians
in other countries, though more ruthless in their methods; they
want to keep in office and to enjoy the very considerable rewards
which office brings. In short, though they would like to promote world revolution, they are not going to do it at the risk
of any real catastrophe to Russia, or, more especially, to themselves.

This is a very important point. Soviet Russia is a despotism,
the most complete of modern times. But this does not mean
that the rulers of Russia are not affected by the feelings of the
Russian people. On the contrary, they are in a state of continual
anxiety about the development of public opinion and constantly trim their policy in order to satisfy it. All our evidence,
such as it is, suggests that, while the Russian people are

extremely ill-informed about the outer world, they have retained a critical intelligence. Far from being made docile by ceaseless propaganda, they are more and more conditioned against it. They could not be carried into a general war unless they were convinced that Russia was the attacked and innocent party; and they would grow restless if the war was badly conducted.

There is not much purpose in trying to compete with the propaganda of the Kremlin; the competition has to come from the facts and from the good sense of the Russian people themselves. But this factor does give Western policy one tangible asset: a general war is virtually excluded from the calculations of the Russian rulers.

How then are we to try for agreement with these men, despotic, ruthless, suspicious? The answer can be found only in the world of facts, not in the world of ideals. Communist Russia and Western democracy are as separated as were Islam and Christianity in the early Middle Ages. It would have been useless to appeal to Mohammed on the grounds of common humanity and it is equally useless to appeal to Stalin.

Indeed, every appeal to ideals reminds the Russians that they are Marxists and therefore deepens the cleavage between the two communities. There is no sense in asking the Russians to cease to be Communists; and therefore no sense in demanding that they should stop Communist propaganda. For one thing, it is a mistake to suppose that Communism is caused solely by Russian propaganda. Communism is caused by resentment against economic or racial inferiority; by the appeal of a dogmatic creed to men who have lost their traditional faith; by a whole host of psychological factors which have nothing to do with Russia. In fact, Communist movements would probably be stronger and more dangerous to the democratic world than they are now if they were not under Russian influence.

But there is another and even more decisive argument. The price to be paid if the Russians ceased Communist propaganda would be too high. For it is that democratic propaganda should cease, too. But what is democratic propaganda? It is simply the truth arrived at after free discussion. If the Russians agreed to stop Communist propaganda, the Western countries would have to agree in return to silence all criticism of the way in which Russia was governed. They would have to introduce a censorship of the Press and to forbid their statesmen to make

critical speeches. This was the demand which Hitler made to
the British Government in the autumn of 1938 and which was
contemptuously refused.

After all it is hypocritical to pretend that it is only the Russians who believe in the superiority of their system and who
expect the collapse of ours. We believe just as strongly that
ours is superior; we believe that, by our preaching and demon-
strating the superiority of free institutions, Russian despotism
will one day collapse. When men demand the silencing of
Communist propaganda, they implicitly admit that Communism will be victorious in the field of open argument; no
believer in democracy should make this admission.

Thus any bargaining with the Russians must be confined
to the world of concrete interests. The first and greatest of these
interests is economic; and it is here, I have always believed
that practical agreement could most easily be reached. Communism flourishes on hardship; and it is therefore a Western
interest that Soviet Russia should become increasingly pros-
perous. Every rise in the Russian standard of life lessens the
punch of Communism as a fighting creed. It is argued against
this that increasing Russia's economic strength merely increases
her strength for war. This is a false conclusion. Russia's
strength for war does not lie in her economic resources, which
are and will long remain inferior to those of the Western
world; it lies in her resources in men and in the incredible
toughness of these men. Economic development will both use
up the manpower and soften the men.

Moreover, though this is often forgotten, economic agreements have two sides. The Russians will pay for whatever
they receive from the industrial West; and they will pay with
goods, which, if Western traders are wise, will benefit the
West as much as Western goods benefit Russia. Richard
Cobden believed that trade between two countries always
lessened the tension between them; this is a belief that has not
lost its force.

Still, we must also face the question of political agreements.
The Western world has rightly taken the line that there is
nothing to be gained by succumbing to threats and that, in
bargaining with the Russians, it must be able to show itself
strong, ready even to face a general war, if this is necessary.
But we must not fall over on the other side and make the
Russian mistake of trying, in our turn, to get our way by

reats. To guess once more about Russian policy, I would say
at the overriding Russian motive is still fear and not aggres-
on or desire to dominate the world.

This has always been true of Russian policy. Alexander I
ared the great Napoleon. The Crimean War was caused by
e Russian fear that England and France meant to control
onstantinople and to force their way into the Black Sea;
orld War I was caused, on the Russian side, by the same
ar that Germany was going to control Constantinople as
rt of her project for an empire from Berlin to Bagdad; and in
orld War II the Russians provoked Hitler's attack by refus-
g to allow him to advance on Constantinople and the Near
ast.

It is often forgotten in the West that Russia has been re-
atedly invaded from the West, but has herself never started
aggressive war into Europe. Russian troops have once occu-
ed Paris (1814) and once occupied Berlin and Vienna (1945);
t both times after a long defensive war. On the other hand,
ussia has been invaded time after time in modern history;
y Napoleon in 1812; by the English and French in the
rimea in 1854; by the Germans in 1917; by the Entente
wers during the wars of intervention in 1919 and 1920; and
y Hitler in 1941.

These things seem remote from us and particularly from
e Americans. But the Russians do not distinguish between
e Germans and the French, the British and the Americans.
or them we are all simply the men of Western civilization,
ith our higher standard of life, with our superior machines
d weapons, and with our refusal to treat the Russians as
uals. We are certainly not going to give up our standard of
fe or our superior equipment to please the Russians; all the
ore reason to treat them as equals in every question of dip-
macy.

Thus, while doing nothing to weaken Western strength, our
iplomacy should always be on the watch to lessen Russian
ars and Russian suspicions. It is a great nuisance that Russia
ould exist at all; but since she does, it is up to us who are
ot driven mad by fear and suspicion to treat her sensibly. Many
f the Russian fears are groundless; we can do nothing to meet
em. Some, however, have a basis in history and even a crazy
tionality.

This is particularly true of Germany. There can be no doubt

that the Russians fear a revived and united Germany mo~~
than anything else in the world; and so should we, if we ha~~
had the German invasion of 1941, the endless destruction an~~
seven million Russian dead. Unless we regard World War II~~
as certain, it is worth paying almost any price in order to kee~~
Germany disarmed; and the Russians will pay a price too.

We have to accept the fact that the Russians will go on bein~~
Communists, just as we shall go on being democratic; and w~~
have to accept the fact that the Russians no more believe ou~~
expressions of peacefulness and goodwill than we believe their~~
Yet even on this basis of mutual distrust, it might be possib~~
to agree on the neutralization of Germany and on the with~~
drawal of our forces to the frontiers. If this worked, it woul~~
enormously lessen Russian suspicions and perhaps even prepa~~
the way for a general lessening of tension; if it did not wor~~
the resources of the free world are still enough to defeat Russ~~
in a general war.

To put the argument on a more general plane, the way ~~
reach agreement with the Russians is to have confidence in ou~~
selves—confidence that we can conduct our political affai~~
with wisdom; confidence that human beings will not fall vi~~
tims indefinitely to the fallacies of Communism; confidence tha~~
the democratic cause can always afford to be tolerant an~~
patient. Western diplomacy in recent years has given the impre~~
sion of running away from negotiating with the Russians, ~~
though afraid that they would wear us down. Nothing is lo~~
by argument even if it goes on for ever; after all argument ~~
itself a form of agreement.

The one certain way not to reach agreement with the Ru~~
sians is the way of all or nothing: either the Russians abando~~
all their fears, disarm at once, drop their support of Communism~~
or else there is no alternative but World War III. This is n~~
the way in which any business deal is concluded. The great ai~~
of Western policy should be to estimate what the Russia~~
would like us to do and then to do the opposite. What th~~
Russians would like us to do is to decide that Communism ~~
irresistible by political methods; to spend all our resourc~~
on armaments; to tell the peoples of the world that there was ~~
escape from World War III. The alternative is to take th~~
political initiative from the Russians and to keep it: always to ~~
ready to discuss with them; always to be ready to conciliate; ~~
answer intolerance with tolerance and despotism with freedo~~

The real problem about agreeing with the Russians is within ourselves. In private life an adult knows that there are lots of ways of living besides his own; and the secret of happiness is not to interfere with the way in which other people conduct their lives. It is much more difficult to be adult in political affairs; but it is also the essential condition for a successful democracy. We shall never get an agreement with the Russians if we insist that they must look at things in the way in which we do; and we are certainly not going to start looking at things their way.

What we aim at is not so much agreement as a truce, confident that everything which lessens the tension and postpones the crisis helps our cause. This is what happened between Christendom and Islam. Neither side had any confidence in the other or accepted its point of view. But in the long periods of truce, when active warfare flagged, Christendom found ever new resources within itself and Islam did not. This will happen in every period of truce between the Western World and Soviet Russia. Democracy will show itself ever more fertile and constructive; and Communism will be shown for the barren thing it is.

XXXII

IS STALIN A STATESMAN?

THE Duke of Wellington said that the great task for a gener
was to divine what was happening 'on the other side of th
hill'. Our great task is to divine what is happening, and what
likely to happen, on the other side of the Iron Curtain.
historian is tempted to believe that if we can be clear about th
past, this will help us to foresee the pattern of the future. Me
do not learn new tricks when they are over 70: and a study o
Stalin's successes and failures in the twenty-five years he ha
ruled Russia should give us some idea at any rate of what w
can expect from Russian policy now.

A preliminary word of warning is necessary. If we ask 'I
Stalin a statesman?' we cannot use the word 'statesman' in i
Western meaning. The great statesmen whom we admir
—a Gladstone or a Lincoln—were animated by a moral sens
Though they sought power, it was to serve noble ends; the
were concerned to build a free humanity, to appease warrin
factions; to promote the peace of the world. Stalin is nc
affected by the moral principles in which we believe.

His object is power pure and simple: to keep his positio
of supreme power in Russia; to make Russia more powerfu
in the world; and, perhaps, though this is more doubtful, t
bring Communists into power elsewhere. I say this last is mor
doubtful, for it is clear that Stalin is interested in the victor
of Communists only so far as they are subservient to him. Thu
we are really asking: 'Is Stalin clever? Is he adroit in manœuvr
and far-sighted from his own point of view?' We have t
examine his record as we would that of a champion ches
player without worrying whether the chess master pays hi
taxes or beats his wife.

If we were discussing the career of a statesman in a demc
cratic country, we should not hesitate as to the answer. A poli
tician who had been continuously in high office since 1917 and
supreme ruler of his country since 1927 would be a very grea
statesman indeed. In a totalitarian country this proves little o

othing. It needed very great skill for Stalin to become dictator
n Russia; but much less skill to remain so.

Stalin has 'reigned' in Russia for twenty-four years. Plenty
f tsars and emperors reigned for far longer in the past;
et many of them were notoriously incompetent. With all the
esources of tyranny and the secret police, it is not very easy
or a dictator to be overthrown by anything short of a catas-
rophic defeat in war. Mussolini would still be ruling Italy if
e had not gone to war; and General Franco, who is certainly
ot much good at his job, is still secure in Spain. We should
herefore not give Stalin too much credit merely for the
chievement of keeping power. There is a further difficulty in
xamining Stalin's record. We have ample stories from rivals,
rom detached observers and supporters, of the ten years
etween 1917 and 1927 when Stalin was advancing to supreme
ower. The moment he attained it, darkness descended; and
ve have to judge Stalin from the outside. We see only the
ffects of his actions; we have to guess at his policy. As a per-
onality he disappeared. The curtain was lifted for the Ameri-
ans and Englishmen who saw him at Teheran, at Yalta, and—
o a lesser extent—at Potsdam. Then he vanished again into
he Russian mists; and we were left guessing once more. We
ave to build up a picture of his personality from this frag-
nentary material, then to judge the qualities which Stalin has
hown, first, as ruler of Russia, and second, in his dealings with
he rest of the world.

All the evidence that we have from the period between
917 and 1927, or again from Teheran and Yalta, goes to
how that Stalin is a political tactician of the highest order.
Ie knows how to play men off against each other and how to
eep himself in the background. In the first years of the revolu-
ion Stalin was the only one who never differed from Lenin
or challenged his leadership; yet all the time Stalin was building
p for himself a control of the party machinery which even
enin could not dispute.

Similarly, in the struggle which followed Lenin's death,
talin appeared to leave the struggle to others. He let Zinoviev
nd Bucharin oust Trotsky, then used Bucharin to destroy
Zinoviev, and himself slipped into the dictatorship imper-
eptibly. Trotsky tells that at the decisive meeting where he
vas to be drummed out of the party Stalin was the only one
vho greeted him with a handshake and a friendly word.

At the Allied meetings during the war Stalin likewise impressed the greatest figures of the Western world and made them feel that he was anxious to co-operate with them; when difficulties arose, they always seemed to come from his advisers. In fact, a myth grew up in Anglo-American circles that Stalin was a friendly and conciliatory old gentleman, who was kept on a tight rein by the remote Politburo; Trotsky fell into the same error twenty years before. Stalin certainly seems to have the political gift of translating great issues into personal terms and of getting his way by playing on the reactions of individuals. This is the essential qualification for a party manager, the job in which Stalin started his career; it is not necessarily a sign of statesmanship or even political cleverness. Stanley Baldwin had it in England to a supreme degree; yet he had no ideas, and his influence on British foreign policy was disastrous.

It may seem curious that with his great gift for handling men, even of the highest standing, Stalin should keep himself so much in the background. But that has always been his method. He prefers to let other people make the mistakes. Just as he sat quiet during the party wrangles at the time of Trotsky's struggle, so he used Teheran and Yalta in order to play off President Roosevelt against Winston Churchill; and rejected further Allied meetings when it became clear that Great Britain and the United States could not be pushed into conflict with each other.

The present situation by which Soviet diplomatists are tied to instructions from Moscow and can be disavowed if they take initiative suits him very well. The mistakes are theirs; the successes are his. This is not a system that makes for daring strokes of policy. What Stalin wants from his men is rigid obedience to orders, not criticism nor even facts that go against his policy.

It was the same during the war. Russian officers, from top to bottom, had to follow a preconceived plan without any freedom of manœuvre. It was of the Russians that Tennyson's line ought to have been written:

> Theirs not to reason why,
> Theirs but to do and die.

Strategy of this kind leads to great obstinacy in defence and to ponderousness in victory; we shall look in vain for ability to deal with unexpected difficulties or to seize the initiative quickly if some sudden chance turns up.

This is exactly what we find when we come to examine the record of Stalin's policy. After Lenin's death there was prolonged discussion of a very high order among the Bolshevik leaders as to what line of economic development they should follow. Stalin hated these clever arguments, hated—above all—the workings of Trotsky's quick mind, endlessly throwing out new ideas. For long Stalin sat silent; finally he grasped at a single idea—the industrialization of Russia by means of the Five Year Plan and, especially, the collectivization of agriculture. For this he will be remembered in history, for good or ill.

It was an attractive idea on paper, the only way indeed in which the productivity of agriculture could be so increased as to carry the weight of a great heavy industry. But it ran against the implacable resistance of the Russian peasantry. Stalin forced it through with an obstinacy as great as theirs, forced it over millions of dead bodies. Other Bolshevik leaders lost their nerve and wanted to call a halt. Stalin never wavered. He had committed himself to collectivization, and he was determined to achieve it at whatever cost in human suffering.

At the same time he always had his ear to the ground; he knew what the Russian people were thinking. He managed to give the impression that the worst hardships of collectivization were due to the blunders of subordinate officials and that he, Stalin, was trying to keep them on a more moderate line. He rebuked the Communists for being 'dizzy with success'. He himself has been often successful, but never dizzy. He gauged with calculated accuracy what the Russian people would stand; and he knew that they could stand a great deal.

He is a man of steel, ruling a people of stone, and trying to shape them; it is a painful process for both sides. Stalin is very sensitive to feeling among the officials of the Communist party; affected, though to a lesser degree, by feeling among the factory workers; and caring least for the feeling of the Russian peasants. He cares nothing at all for the feelings of foreigners, even if the foreigners are Communists.

Thus, when we come to foreign policy during the long period of Stalin's power, we see that it has a single aim: Russian security. He wants to keep Russia remote from the rest of the world and to prevent any kind of foreign influence or interference. Foreign Communists are exploited to serve the needs of this policy.

This was shown from the beginning. In 1923, when Stalin

was only mounting to power, the German Communists wer
ordered into rebellion in Hamburg, not in order to win
victory in Germany but solely to make things easier for Russi.
Similarly, the Chinese Communists were ordered to work wit
Chiang Kai-shek so as to make Russia more secure in the Fa
East; and this brought them almost to destruction in 192.
Both these were great blunders; since Stalin was not ye
supreme, one cannot ascribe them to Stalin alone.

His first undoubted initiative was in 1933 when he switche
international Communism over to the Popular Front an
Russian policy over to collective security. Here his purpose wa
clear. He feared the strength of Germany and wanted to ensur
that Hitler should not lead a crusade of united Europe agains
the Soviet Union. His aim was to keep Germany divided fror
the Western Powers; and since the split was already there, h
had an easy time of it.

It is sometimes said that he welcomed the Spanish civil wa
in the hope of setting up a Communist state in Spain. Thi
is to exaggerate his enthusiasm for Communism. Rather, h
hoped that the civil war would increase the tension betwee
England and France on the one side, and Germany and Ital
on the other, and that thus Russia would be left in peace at th
other end of Europe.

As to the crisis of Czechoslovakia in 1938, historians ar
still debating whether Stalin ever had any serious intentio
of going to the help of the Czechs. He certainly never reveale
his intentions to the Western Powers; but then he was neve
given any encouragement to do so. Perhaps we can detect her
an example of Stalin's usual method: hanging back himsel
shifting the responsibility on to others.

There can, however, be no doubt of his initiative in the nex
crisis, the conflict over Poland which started World War II
The Nazi-Soviet pact was as much Stalin's decision as Hitler'
—in fact, more so, in that Stalin had an alternative and Hitle
had none. It is easy in retrospect to see what led Stalin to hi
decision. Alliance with the Western Powers would hav
involved Russia in difficult events: she might even have had t
bear the brunt of the war from the outset. The Nazi-Soviet pac
enabled her to stand aside and to watch the troubles of others
it was a choice for neutrality and for isolation.

All the same it was the most gigantic blunder in Stalin'
career. It allowed Hitler to conquer all Europe and then t

urn with tremendous force against an isolated Soviet Union. Two things led Stalin to this mistake.

First, he was out of date in his information. He thought that England and France were stronger than they were and that therefore he had achieved a balance in Europe; and he thought this simply because England and France had been strong years before.

Second, and more decisively, he did not understand the difference between democracies and dictatorships; he lumped them all together as states pursuing solely a cynical policy of power (as he was); he never allowed for the influence of public opinion in democratic countries, or realized that there are many strokes of Machiavellian policy which are impossible for them.

We can go even further. Though he regarded all foreign governments with suspicion, he believed that it would be easier to get on with a totalitarian country than with a democratic one. If there has ever been a period in which Stalin was sincere in his attempts at collaboration, it was between August 1939 and June 1941, when he was working in friendly neutrality with Nazi Germany. It might even be said that, so far as Stalin got on with Churchill and President Roosevelt, it was because he saw them as 'war dictators', not as the freely elected leaders of democratic communities.

The Grand Alliance of World War II was not the outcome of Stalin's policy; it was forced on him by Hitler, and he would never have entered it except for the German attack. During the war Stalin showed great qualities as a military leader. He had the capacity to hold out against staggering blows; to wait patiently for his opportunity, and then to pursue his victory relentlessly.

In his dealings with his allies the same qualities appeared as faults. Certainly he made great gains for Russia; but he could have made them by conciliation and friendship instead of by disputing with his allies and finally estranging them. Allied policy also made mistakes: sometimes they gave concessions where they should have been firm; sometimes they resisted where they might have been generous. Still, it seems very unlikely that genuine co-operation in peacetime with the Soviet Union was ever possible.

Stalin suspected others of having the same motives as himself, and therefore distrusted them. At the same time, he underrated the courage and capacity of democratic statesmen. He

thought that he had only to stand aside for the Western world
to dissolve in political and economic anarchy.

In 1947 the Marshall Plan forced him to a decision; he made
the wrong one, even from his own point of view. If America
had the evil design of dominating all the world that he attri
buted to her, the effective way of opposing this would have
been inside the Marshall Plan organization; instead he thought
he could halt it by threats. Ever since, he has been making
tactical gains at the expense of strategical losses.

The Communist seizure of Czechoslovakia in 1948 is a
striking illustration. It made Czechoslovakia perhaps a more
secure outpost of Soviet power; but only at the price of stirring
up alarm and resistance in the whole free world.

More recently the war in Korea has reinforced the same
lesson. It started because Stalin thought that America and the
United Nations would retreat before a show of force. When
they did not, his only course was to keep doggedly on; though
he could have built up a capital of goodwill in the West by
settling the Korean war on terms of reasonable compromise.
There is his greatest weakness. He knows how to wait, but
not how to conciliate; and since he does not understand com
promise, his policy always leads in the long run to a head-on
collision.

Looking back over the whole record, we can agree that
Stalin has some high qualities of statesmanship. He has infinite
patience and obstinacy. No difficulties will ever wear him down
or make him relax. He is a master of defence, whether in
politics or war. On the other hand, he is barren of constructive
ideas; fear is the only argument he uses and perhaps under
stands.

He lacks the greatest quality of the statesman: he does not
know how to co-operate with other men of equal political
stature and to trust them. When dealing with others, his only
tactic is to divide them; if this fails, he has no resource except
to wait. Whenever he overcomes his natural reluctance and
takes an initiative, he does this rigidly and with the same
dogmatic obstinacy as in defence. Once committed to a policy
he clings to it despite all difficulties and failures.

The great mistake we make in the West is to suppose that
Russian policy is 'clever'. Quite the reverse: it is without
flexibility or imagination, incapable of a sudden initiative.

It may be objected that this estimate of Stalin is based prin cipally on an already distant past and that the picture of him lumbering cautiously along does not correspond with the vast gains which the Soviet Union has made in 1945 and the following years.

Though these gains were made, they showed little subtlety or cleverness in their making. Eastern Europe fell into Stalin's hands at the end of World War II simply because of the vacuum which followed the collapse of German armed strength: the Russians moved on until they ran against the lines of the Western allies. As to China—certainly the biggest Soviet success since 1917—no one was more surprised than Stalin when it went Communist.

We know that at the end of the war he was expecting to do business with Chiang Kai-shek, and the harsh bargain that he drove with respect to Manchuria was evidence of this. Of course, the defeat of Germany and Japan changed the picture of the world for everyone—including the Russians. But they took longer to adapt themselves to these changes than did anyone else; and to some extent have not made the adaptation even yet.

No doubt their attacks on rearming Germany and Japan are in part a political manœuvre to weaken the forces of the West; but partly, too, they are simply old tunes in which the Russians, Stalin included, still believe. Any interpretation of Russian policy is bound to be highly speculative, but it is at any rate an arguable proposition that its greatest defect is to be out of date.

Stalin has continued to see Russia as weak when she has shown herself as strong; he sees her as still encircled and isolated when in fact she is secure and with all great powers willing to be her friends. Far from being clever, Soviet policy since 1945 has been heavy-handed.

With more skill and understanding the Soviet Union could have made practically all its present gains and yet possessed a real security in co-operating with the other great Powers. Like all men, Stalin judges the present in terms of the past, and it is a handicap that his memory is longer than that of others. He is always thinking of the wars of intervention which ended in 1921, of the way in which he was cold-shouldered by the Western Powers at Munich in 1938 or betrayed by his close associate Hitler in 1941, instead of judging the situation in terms adapted to the second half of the twentieth century.

I

His outlook and policy are so old-fashioned as to be almost prehistoric, and it is difficult to analyse his career without thinking of those ponderous, slow-moving monsters from a dim antiquity.

What should be our line of policy in answer to a man with Stalin's past? Pretty clearly, it is no good appealing to him on grounds simply of goodwill; no good even suggesting what is best for the Russian people. Stalin will leave others alone only as long as they are stronger than he is. Moreover he will always be trying to divide his opponents, and if he does more against them, it will be through others, his satellites, not by risking himself.

The last thing to expect—if history is any guide—is direct Russian aggression. Stalin will not fight a world war unless it is forced upon him. What is more, once he recognizes that the democratic front against him will not crumble, he will be ready to strike a bargain and—so long as the balance of forces remains the same—he will keep his bargain as he did with Hitler between 1939 and 1941.

Western policy cannot hope that Russia will change her course. Changes can only come among the satellites, as they have already come with Yugoslavia. Our great object should be to make the satellites feel that if they move away from Russia they will not be changing one master for another, but will gain real independence. More broadly, the answer to Stalin can be summed up in three maxims: Be strong; be united, and then be friendly.

XXXIII

MR. 'X' RIDES AGAIN

Mr. George F. Kennan is an important member of the American State Department—indeed, if ideas are what matter, perhaps its most important member. In 1947 he published, as 'X', an article on 'The Sources of Soviet Conduct', which has been the intellectual basis for American foreign policy ever since. He has just been nominated Ambassador to Moscow; and in the meantime has had a year off to think about the principles of foreign policy. The results of his thoughts are presented in a slim volume of comments on the history of the last fifty years.[1] At the beginning of the century, he says, Americans 'had a sense of security such as I suppose no people had ever had since the days of the Roman Empire'. Now the position is 'almost reversed':

> Our national consciousness is dominated by a sense of insecurity greater even than that of many of the peoples of Western Europe who stand closer to, and in a position far more vulnerable to those things that are the main source of our concern.

What went wrong? Why did America lose her security? It could be argued that the Americans simply miscalculated, as we did also in this country. They supposed, as we did, that this country and France could hold Germany in check and thus maintain a Balance of Power in Europe without assistance, and more recently they, like us, underrated the increase of strength which had come to Soviet Russia as the result of the Bolshevik revolution.

Mr. Kennan is not interested in such humdrum explanations. He insists that American foreign policy was wrong at its very foundation; it thought in terms of morality and international law instead of in those of 'power realities'. Wilson was wrong when he indulged 'in the colossal conceit of thinking that you could suddenly make international life over into what you believed to be your own image'. Roosevelt was wrong when he demanded 'unconditional surrender' and when he

[1] George F. Kennan, *American Diplomacy*, 1900–1950 (Secker and Warburg).

failed to realize that war 'cannot in itself make a positive contribution to any democratic purpose'. All Americans were wrong when they tried to maintain the Open Door in China instead of following 'a policy carefully and realistically aimed at the avoidance of a war with Japan'. The Fourteen Points, the League of Nations, the Atlantic Charter—all nonsense. 'When you tally up the total score of the two wars in terms of their ostensible objective, you find that if there has been any gain at all, it is pretty hard to discern.' The appeasers were right after all ! The Americans, and all the rest of us, ought to have recognized changing conditions and done a deal in good time with Japan and with Germany—preferably with Weimar Germany. During the First World War the Americans ought to have 'kept open their lines of negotiation to the enemy, declined to break up his empire and overthrow his political system'—in other words, they ought to have preserved Imperial Germany and Austria-Hungary. In both wars they ought to have thought about the Balance of Power and not about liberating peoples or 'making the world safe for democracy'. For, 'our national interest is all that we are really capable of knowing and understanding'.

These ideas are presented with deceptive modesty and charm. They are not new ideas. They were the ideas of Metternich: ignore the feelings of the peoples, preserve a Balance among the Great Powers, and so maintain the peace of Europe. They were the ideas of Bismarck, though he pandered to popular sentiment by calling his system of alliances a 'League of Peace'. More recently Mr. E. H. Carr used these ideas to preach appeasement of Hitler in his brilliant book *The Twenty Years' Crisis*, and later, when Russia had taken the place of Germany, to preach appeasement of Stalin in the columns of *The Times*. For that matter, they are ideas which come inevitably into the mind of every student of diplomatic history. Mr. Kennan is indubitably right when he maintains that any policy must fail if it ignores 'power realities'.

But, even assuming that he has brought every factor into account, he has done the sum wrong. His book is implicitly an argument in favour of alliance with Germany and Japan against Soviet Russia; and he includes in an appendix two articles urging that the United States should follow a policy of 'containment' until Communist rule in Russia comes somehow or other to an end. But if, in fact, 'power realities' are all that matter the arguments in favour of appeasing Soviet

Russia are much stronger than were those for appeasing Germany or Japan. 'Horse-trading' never had a chance with Hitler; Stalin has always been ready to practise it, and there is every probability that it would ensure some sort of peace for quite a number of years.

Yet everyone knows that a simple power-bargain, such as, say, Metternich struck with Napoleon, is impossible for a democracy, whether American or British. Mr. Kennan has not only done his sum wrong; he has done the wrong sum. He admits this himself when he suggests that the kind of policy he advocates would only be possible with a basic change in the American Constitution, and then adds: 'I am afraid the chances of change in the direction I have indicated are so slight that we must dismiss the possibility.' Why then begin a speculation, one of the assumptions of which is admitted at the outset to be impossible? Metternich and Bismarck could hoodwink their Emperors (though less often than they wanted to) and could persuade these slow-witted autocrats that they were serving the cause of conservatism or the interest of their family when they were, in fact, sustaining the Balance of Power.

Democracy is less easily deceived. It is no good telling a democratic community that things will always be the same— that there will always be rival States and, at best, a Balance of Power. Every community in the modern world is committed to the proposition that things are capable of improvement. Men everywhere are determined to have a better world; and if they cannot get it from the free democracies they will turn—as in many countries they have already turned—to the Communists. The Communist programme, from world peace to the Five-year Plan, is a grim parody of the noblest aspirations of mankind. Should we therefore jettison these aspirations and leave Moscow as the only home for idealism in the world?

Mr. Kennan claims to be a realist; and presumably the test of realism is success. In that case, Mazzini and Garibaldi were more realistic than Metternich, Wilson more realistic than Bismarck, Roosevelt more realistic than Hitler. Can it be that those who had the higher ideals and tried to apply them won solely by accident? I do not believe it. If Communist practice conformed to their ideals, they would win and would deserve to win. As it is, the way to defeat the Communists is not to have no ideals but to have better ideals and to take them seriously. It is the idealist, not the so-called realist, who has in the last resort the true sense of 'the national interest'.

XXXIV

THE TURN OF THE HALF-CENTURY

THE nineteenth century has been called the age of Hope; the twentieth century has been the age of Hope Fulfilled. In the first half of the century Western man has achieved every ambition which he set before himself since the time of the Renaissance. He has conquered space, disease, poverty. The scientific method which he has perfected guarantees that he can do anything that he wishes. Atomic energy will give him infinite power; and, if he survives long enough, he will conquer death itself. He has mastered all nature, including his own; for it is only in the last fifty years that families and therewith populations have become 'planned'.

In the social world, too, Western man has shaken himself free from the chains of ignorance and tradition which Rousseau denounced. In 1901 Habsburg, Hohenzollern, and Romanov still towered in Europe; now, every royal dynasty, great or small, has gone, except for the few that have long had only decorative uses. Hereditary right, whether of monarch or noble, now counts for nothing anywhere in the Western world; the House of Lords is too trivial to be an exception. Every Government throughout the world claims to represent the majority of inhabitants in its country; and nearly all make at any rate a show of universal suffrage. Most of all, mankind has been prised up from its roots of custom and traditional belief. Apart from a few surviving sentiments of humanistic morality, reason and self-interest have become the sole motives of man's conduct; the exception is his readiness to sacrifice himself for the nation-State—and even this seems to be dying in most of the Western world.

Every dream of the eighteenth-century philosopher, every theory of the nineteenth-century radical has been fulfilled. If an Englishman could have learnt on the last day of 1850 what his descendants would accomplish in the next hundred years he would have been incredulous with admiration and delight; but it would have amazed him still more to learn that at the end of these hundred years we look forward to the next half-century with harsh anxiety, if not with despair. The first half of the twentieth century has had its share of bitter experiences for the West: two world wars, two Russian famines, the planned slaughter of millions in the Nazi gas-chambers. Yet after all these the most optimistic of us would only dare to say, ' If the next half-century is no worse than the last we shan't do so badly !' A gloom hangs over the future such as the Western world has not known since the first renascence in the twelfth century. It is perhaps a mitigation to bear in mind that this gloom is confined to the world of Renaissance Europe which has now grown into the Atlantic community. Most of mankind outside Europe has still achieved little or nothing; and is therefore still in the age of Hope. From this point of view Asiatic Communism is the last version of nineteenth-century rationalism; like its precursor, it holds out the illusion of infinite possibilities.

Europe has ceased to be the centre of the world. Though it is always unsafe to guess how the present will appear to the eyes of the future, this is a generalization which is likely to stand the test of time; it is the greatest shift in the world balance since the upheavals of the fifteenth century. From the time of Columbus until the time of Gandhi, Stalin, and Mao Tse-tung, European man—and especially the educated classes of Europe—lived on the plunder of the rest of the world. The process has been running down in the last half-century; and its end is now in sight. If that were all, if our gloom was merely the gloom of a French aristocrat on the fall of the Bastille, knowing that his privileges were ending, we could find some consolation: loss of privilege for a few means greater freedom for many. No doubt the game is up for the inhabitants of this island; in the long perspective of history this would be a small price to pay if the inhabitants of Asia were to achieve in the next half-century something like the freedom from want that we have known.

But is this all? Is our gloom confined to a small area which is losing its geographical and historical privileges? Is it merely, as the Communists maintain, a symptom of the decline of capitalism? Or is it not more fundamental—a realization that the values of Western civilization, and not merely the privileges of Western Europe, are perishing before our eyes? The Russians and the Chinese can master our machines; will they ever have our respect for individual lives, our recognition of the human spirit in every man? The Western world called in America to save it in two world wars; and is now looking to it for salvation in a third. Yet the Americans show none of the confidence that goes with success. On the contrary, the United States is racked far more savagely than we are in Europe by anxiety for the future. This anxiety is disguised as a hysteria against Communism; it springs more deeply from the consciousness of infinite power which man has gained and dare not use. After all, the American ideal is the refrigerator in every home; this is the Russian ideal too. The only difference is that in America the refrigerator has arrived.

Yet there is something else which should be placed on record for the benefit of the future. Although apprehensive and perhaps despairing, we are not decadent. Claudian, writing in the fourth century A.D., was sharply aware that he was an inferior poet to Virgil. The philosophers and scientists of Western Europe are not inferior to their predecessors; even the politicians of the last half-century make a creditable showing. Nowhere in Western Europe can you point to the signs which show that a civilization is in decline. Hitlerism was the nearest thing to it; and this was a disease which Western Europe seems successfully to have overcome. Gibbon said of his history: 'I have depicted the triumph of barbarism and religion.' Western man can still hold his own against both. In fact, he is more sensible, more critical, more tolerant, more intelligent than he has ever been; he has even survived the shock of discovering that when Utopian dreams are translated into real life the perfect world is still far away.

On the whole Western man has justified the hopes of eighteenth-century democrats: the people, it has turned out, can be trusted. It may well be that, just as Greece ceased to be the centre of the ancient world, Western Europe—or even the white nations generally—have ceased to dominate the world of modern times. In that case, the greatest historic success of the Greeks is still before us: to take our conquerors prisoner. The world outside Europe has learnt to handle our machines; it has still to be won for our ideas. At the very least, this task will provide some interest and occupation for the next fifty years. Better that than emulate mediæval man, waiting for the end of the world in A.D. 1000, and sit in helpless contemplation of the universal catastrophe that may well have come before A.D. 2001.

XXXV

UP FROM UTOPIA: HOW TWO GENERATIONS SURVIVED THEIR WARS

IN 1923 everyone was conscious of being 'post-war'; this war was the Great War, the World War. Once it had been the War to End War; and even after five years no one supposed that it would have a rival. In 1950 men were conscious of being more pre-war than post-war. The war they lived through had not even been dignified with a name of its own; it was merely World War II, a repeat performance, and interest was already focused on World War III. After the first war, memorials to the dead were put up in every town and village—in England, in France, in Germany, in the United States, though not, I suppose, in Russia. Millions of names were inscribed on these memorials: for King and Country, for God and the Fatherland, for Peace and Freedom. After the second war there were no new memorials. The names of the dead were added to any blank space that could be found on the existing memorials. The dead, if commemorated at all, were honoured in some practical way —a village playing-field, a new heater for the local library. King and Country, Peace and Freedom—these made no fresh appearance. After World War I men went on celebrating Armistice Day for twenty years—and it was abandoned in 1939 only because the sirens would cause confusion. After World War II there was no armistice; and by 1950 men had forgotten which day they ought to celebrate. The Declaration of Independence, the fall of the Bastille, Shakespeare's birthday, are more alive in our memories.

World War I seemed unique, a cosmic catastrophe. England had not been involved in a Continental war for a hundred years, the United States never. Even France and Germany, Italy and Austria-Hungary had been at peace for more than a generation. Only Russia had had recent experience of war—hence perhaps the different path which Russia followed at the end. Before 1914 there had been a universal conviction that war was at last impossible, a confident assumption that human affairs would

improve indefinitely. When it came again, war seemed incredible, unnatural, and men therefore tried to saddle individual statesmen with 'war guilt'. The Allies blamed Kaiser
Wilhelm; the Germans blamed 'the Entente criminals',
Poincaré and Izvolski. By 1923 the more enlightened had
changed their tune and were blaming their own statesmen.
English liberals turned on Sir Edward Grey; American on
President Wilson; only the Germans continued to find themselves guiltless. But before long, the search for individual
criminals began to flag. Instead, men sought the 'causes of
war' as though war were the most unusual, instead of the most
regular, of human activities. Not every civilization has Christianity; not every civilization has machinery; not every civilization has monogamy: they all have war.

World War II startled men less. They were dejected at
having to go through it again; but they were not surprised.
Everyone over thirty could remember World War I. So far as
men sought for causes, they sought them for this particular war,
not for war in general. And the causes this time were easy to
find—almost too easy. Hitler and Mussolini had planned war
as Wilhelm II, or Poincaré and Izvolski, had not. Even the
Germans acquiesced in this conclusion—they showed themselves eager to repudiate Hitler in a way that a previous generation had not been prepared to repudiate, say, Bethmann
Hollweg. Indeed the conclusion is so obvious as to be tame;
besides, it does not lead to any 'constructive' outcome. With
Hitler and Mussolini dead, the causes of World War II were
certainly removed; but how could war be prevented in future?
By 1950, minds had moved forward—had discovered, instead
of war criminals, those who really should be blamed for World
War II. They were not Hitler and Mussolini, or even their
supporters, but those who failed to oppose them.

The statesmen of the pre-1914 era had been condemned for
not negotiating with Germany enough; the statesmen of the
pre-1939 era were condemned for negotiating with Germany
at all. 'Appeasement'—that is, the attempt at conciliation and
agreement—was discovered to have caused World War II;
and so, in a sense, it had. From this it was easy to jump to the
general conclusion: 'Appeasement' was the cause not only
of World War II, but of all wars. Certainly American policy
by 1950 was designed to show that American statesmen had
learned from the mistakes of the first 'post-war'. Whether

standing on your head is the reverse of falling down may, however, be debated.

To consider the cause of a single war instead of the cause of war in general shows, at any rate, a practical spirit; and the second 'post-war' seems more practical, more realistic than the first. Being incredible, World War I could not be justified merely as a war, a struggle for survival or even for conquest. Therefore it had to be justified by reference to high ideals— the War to End War, the War to Make the World Safe for Democracy. Wilson's Fourteen Points dominated the last two years of World War I, and no man in modern history so focused the ideal hopes of mankind as Wilson did for a few brief months at the opening of 1919. The contrast between these hopes and the reality of the following years produced the disillusionment characteristic of the first 'post-war'. Indeed, 'post-war' became a synonym for embitterment, a political hangover on a gigantic scale. Men had died in millions, endured the mud and filth of the trenches—for what? To return to a world very like the old one. Those who had remained at home writing tracts on wartime ideals were even more disillusioned than those who had fought. 'War achieves nothing' became the common remark. In reality, World War I achieved a great deal: it would have been worth waging simply to turn the Germans out of the countries which they had invaded. But in addition, it liberated from alien rule peoples who had had no expectation of liberation when the war began. All this was brushed aside by the dogma, 'war achieves nothing'. Therefore the things the war had achieved—national freedom for hitherto unknown peoples, even the liberation of Belgium—were nothing; by definition worthless. The men of 1923 reached disillusionment as much by what had been done as by what had not.

The peoples who fought World War II were determined not to be deceived a second time. They fought for survival, not for ideals. And quite rightly: apart from the United States, survival as independent states was the immediate issue. In 1923 men were still lamenting that the Fourteen Points had not been applied; in 1950 few recollected the existence, and none the terms, of the Atlantic Charter. After World War II men's aspirations were lower and their achievements higher than after World War I. The Germans were denounced more fiercely in World War II and treated better afterwards. Economic recovery in every country was more rapid and yet accompanied

by fewer promises. In 1950 no one was surprised that Utopia
had not been reached. Their error was perhaps the opposite:
they were content with too little, not ashamed to find that things
were turning out much as they had expected. In 1923 men
everywhere felt that they had been deceived, merely because
Utopia was not in sight. If they had been asked to fight a new
war there would have been a universal explosion—indeed,
danger of a very minor war drove Lloyd George out of power
for life in 1922. Now men go off obediently to what may be the
opening of World War III, and no one complains that Western
statesmen have thrown away their victory, as men complained
against Wilson and Clemenceau. Men in the West were not
asked a second time to fight the War to End War; they were
asked to fight the Germans and they did so successfully.

There is another side to this acquiescence in the hardships of
the present and the future. Though there was more talk of
ideals in World War I, more serious ideals were at stake in
World War II and were taken more seriously. The Kaiser's
Germany was branded a military despotism, a tyranny; as a
matter of fact it was a constitutional monarchy and could have
qualified as a founding member of the United Nations. The
Tommy, *poilu* or doughboy of World War I thought that he
was being exploited; believed, rightly, that there was little
difference between himself and the German soldier in the
opposite trench. Hitler's Germany really was a bestial tyranny;
the concentration camps, the extermination of the Jews, the
Gestapo, were all real. No Allied soldier who saw Buchenwald
or Dachau could doubt that the war had been worth while.
And not only Allied countries were liberated. Italy was genuinely liberated from Mussolini; and, whereas the Germans had
not thanked the Allies for ridding them of Wilhelm II, this time
they at least had to pretend gratitude for being relieved of Hitler.
After World War II the peoples of the Western world were a
good deal more doubtful that their ideals could be universally
exported; on the other hand, they were much more confident
that those ideals were genuine and worth defending.

The difference of spirit in the times had another cause.
World War I was, on the whole, a bourgeois war: the masses
fought for their masters, not for their own convictions. The
Right fought enthusiastically, without reserve; the Left fought
regretfully or not at all. The fifth column, a phrase in World
War II, had been a reality in World War I. Every nation had

a pacifist or anti-war group, led by men of noble character—
MacDonald, Debs, Liebknecht, Adler, Lenin. By 1923
MacDonald was on the point of becoming Prime Minister;
Lenin had ruled Russia for six years; even the French pacifists
around Caillaux had been restored to favour and Clemenceau
discredited. In World War II it was the Left that fought with
conviction, the Right with regret. Winston Churchill has
described how, in his first months as Prime Minister, he was
received with cheers from the Labour, and silence from the
Conservative, benches; many of those who cheered him (including even Herbert Morrison, the Home Secretary) had
been imprisoned as war-resisters in World War I. Similarly in
the United States, World War I had been backed by the richer
and more educated classes, by the legendary figures of Wall
Street; and Wilson had won the votes of the masses in 1916
by keeping out of war. The opposition to Roosevelt, on the
other hand, came from conservative Republicans; and support
from the men of the New Deal. The labour movement in
England and America supported World War II without
reserve; it was the capitalists who found themselves involved
in a struggle against collective bargaining, social security, and
equal opportunity between rich and poor. Bourgeois ideals are
abstract, fine phrases for a peroration. Working-class ideals are
concrete, drab in a speech, but more telling when it comes to
vital statistics. After 1918 young English people were promised
Homes Fit for Heroes; after 1945 English children got orange
juice and free milk. Years ago an American writer deprecated
political democracy with the phrase: 'The rich want liberty; the
poor want ham and eggs.' In 1950 the 'poor' of the Anglo-
Saxon world wanted both and were in a fair way to get them.

The year 1923 was 'post-war' in feeling as well as in time.
'Post-war' excused every evil. Unemployment was 'post-war';
sexual immorality was 'post-war'; discontent in Asia was 'post-
war'. For, though the age imagined itself to be progressive,
Utopian, looking to the future, in reality the 'normalcy' that it
demanded was a romantic version of the days before 1914, when
capitalist economics and Christian morals had supposedly
worked without a flaw. Harding, Bonar Law, Poincaré, Strese-
mann—the representative statesman of 1923—were all concerned to restore a vanished past. For that matter even Wilson's
ideal of self-determination was a dying echo of Gladstonian
doctrine, not a vision of the future. The statesmen of 1950—

Truman or Attlee—looked forward. Maybe their vision did
not extend very far; but at least they had escaped from the illusion that it was possible to retrace their steps. In this they were
representative. No Englishman imagined that it was possible
to restore the British Empire as it was in the nineteenth century;
no American imagined that the United States could ever again
lead a life of irresponsible isolation. Or rather, though a few
imagined these things, public opinion rejected their dreams.

It is a temptation to make this the conclusion. The English-
speaking world of the second 'post-war' was more mature,
more level-headed, more adult, than that of 1923; incredible,
indeed, that it should have improved so much in less than a
generation. In 1923 a conclusion based on the English-speak-
ing world and that of Western Europe could have passed a
verdict on the world as a whole. Western capitalism was still
master. The statesmen who met at Paris in 1919 had called
themselves the Supreme Council; and they truly supposed that
they were supreme in the world. Even when the United States
withdrew, the destinies of the world seemed to depend on the
decisions of England, France, and Italy. Add a reconciled
Germany, rank the Japanese as honorary Europeans, and the
world would be complete. Much of the disappointment of that
post-war world sprang from the illusion that the Big Three,
squeezed away in the western extremity of Eurasia, controlled
events. Here lies the greatest contrast with 1950. Once upon a
time, Western Europe issued orders to all the world; now it
could not even defend itself. Though there were endless meetings of Western European statesmen, no one supposed that
these could dictate events elsewhere; hitherto they have produced only paper projects for co-ordinating European defence
before it is too late. Even the United States, despite its preponderance of material resources, stood on the defensive; it
allowed things to happen, instead of determining the agenda
of history. The Western world of 1950 improved socially and
politically on the world of 1923; but now it existed on suffer-
ance, not of its own right.

The Atlantic community ceased to be the centre of the world
culturally as well as politically. In 1923 it seemed certain that
Western values and beliefs would soon encircle the globe.
All other civilizations—Mohammedan, Chinese, Hindu—
were dead or dying. Soon everyone would wear a collar and tie;
keep office hours; exercise vote by ballot; practise birth control;

drive an automobile; pay an income tax; enjoy freedom from arbitrary arrest. By 1950 it had become clear that Western man exported his mechanical powers without exporting his ideas. His economic, military, cultural weapons were being turned against him by those who lacked his virtues—though perhaps they had virtues of their own. The first post-war knew Communism; but it seemed then a disease of Western civilization, not a challenge to it. The first Bolshevik leaders were men of European mind, concerned to draw Russia more into Europe; their isolation was imposed upon them by the blunders of Western statesmen. The Communist movements of Germany, France, and Italy grew out of earlier Socialist movements; they were not created or, at first, directed from without. Communist Russia was certainly idealized by millions of workers in Western Europe; but it was an ideal because it was supposed to be accomplishing the Western principles of Socialist democracy, not because it repudiated Western values. Moreover, Communism was still regarded as a European problem. No one noticed the Congress of Eastern Peoples which met in Turkestan in 1921.

By 1950 liberal civilization, supreme and universal after World War I, had lost much of Asia and now seemed in danger of losing the continent of Europe as well. European statesmen talked more sensibly, perhaps even acted more sensibly, than after World War I; but their spur was a new fear, not a new wisdom. In 1923 men's minds were taken up with the French occupation of the Ruhr; if only German reparations could be settled, the world—it was believed—would be secure and at peace. In 1950 who cared about reparations? Not even the Russians, now that they had carried home their loot. Who cared about 'the German problem'? The only German problem was when and how to arm the Germans against the Russians; it seemed beyond the bounds of credibility that the Germans themselves might again menace the world. Thus it was not only better sense that made the men of 1950 resist the excuse of labelling everything evil 'post-war'; they had found a larger label, one that could stretch even farther. Both labels served the same purpose: they enabled men to evade their problems or to give out that they were insoluble. When men said unemployment was 'post-war', they meant that nothing could be done about it except to lament that World War I had taken place. And when men say that

Communism is sweeping Asia, they are halfway to implying that nothing can be done about *it*.

As a matter of fact, many 'post-war' problems of the twenties found a solution in the thirties; but these solutions did not depend on merely waiting until the effects of World War I should wear off. Thus Keynesian economics (a very different matter from Keynes's ill-founded attack on reparations) broke the problem of mass unemployment. In the same way, 'Communism' would lose its hypnotic, paralysing sound if there were a serious attempt to answer the question: 'What causes men to become Communists?' The mortal error of the Western world is to imagine that Communism is caused by terror—by the secret police and the concentration camp. These are part of Communism, not its cause. Communism is caused by the sense of economic and social injustice; by unquestioning belief; by the longing for Utopia. The Western world will get Communism only if it is false to its own standards and tries to fight Communism in kind. The answer to intolerance is tolerance; the answer to intransigeance is compromise; the answer to unquestioning enthusiasm is scepticism; the answer to grievances is to redress them. The men of 1923 erred when they looked back regretfully to the past and lamented that the Great War had taken place, instead of facing their problems as they came. The men of 1950 made the same mistake when they regretted the growth of Communism and lamented the days when Russia was not a Great Power. The appeal of Communism was real; and so was the strength of Soviet Russia. To suppose that either of them could be made to disappear was the last of the Utopian illusions which the men of 1950 had inherited from a previous generation.

In 1923 men thought that the only alternative to Utopia was to be disillusioned and embittered. But men will not live for ever in cynicism and despair. Fascism and Communism, new Utopias, were called in to take the place of the liberal Utopia that had failed. But the men of 1923 were wrong: there is a third way between Utopianism and despair. That is to take the world as it is and to improve it; to have faith without a creed, hope without illusions, love without God. The Western world is committed to the proposition that rational man will in the end prove stronger and more successful than irrational man. If the Western world abandons this proposition, it may conquer Communism but it will destroy itself.